PROFITABLE IDEAS

Studies in Critical Social Sciences Book Series

Haymarket Books is proud to be working with Brill Academic Publishers (http://www.brill.nl) to republish the Studies in Critical Social Sciences book series, edited by David Fasenfest, in paperback editions. Other titles in this series include:

The Apprentice's Sorcerer: Liberal Tradition and Fascism
Ishay Landa

Crisis, Politics, and Critical Sociology
edited by Graham Cassano and Richard A. Dello Buono

Dialectic of Solidarity: Labor, Antisemitism, and the Frankfurt School
Mark P. Worrell

The Destiny of Modern Societies: The Calvinist Predestination of a New Society
Milan Zafirovski

Engaging Social Justice: Critical Studies of 21st Century Social Transformation
edited by David Fasenfest

The Future of Religion: Toward a Reconciled Society
edited by Michael R. Ott

Globalization and the Environment
edited by Andrew Jorgenson and Edward Kick

Hybrid Identities: Theoretical and Empirical Examinations
edited by Keri E. Iyall Smith and Patricia Leavy

Imperialism, Neoliberalism and Social Struggles in Latin America
edited by Richard A. Dello Buono and José Bell Lara

Liberal Modernity and Its Adversaries: Freedom, Liberalism
and Anti-Liberalism in the Twenty-First Century
Milan Zafirovski

Marx, Critical Theory, and Religion: A Critique of Rational Choice
edited by Warren S. Goldstein

Marx's Scientific Dialectics: A Methodological Treatise for a New Century
Paul Paolucci

Race and Ethnicity: Across Time, Space, and Discipline
Rodney D. Coates

Transforming Globalization: Challenges and Opportunities in the Post 9/11 Era
edited by Bruce Podobnik and Thomas Reifer

Western Europe, Eastern Europe and World Development 13th-18th Centuries
edited by Jean Batou and Henryk Szlajfer

PROFITABLE IDEAS
THE IDEOLOGY OF THE INDIVIDUAL IN CAPITALIST DEVELOPMENT

BY MICHEAL O'FLYNN

Haymarket Books
Chicago, Illinois

First published in 2010 by Brill Academic Publishers, The Netherlands
© 2010 Koninklijke Brill NV, Leiden, The Netherlands

Published in paperback in 2012 by
Haymarket Books
P.O. Box 180165
Chicago, IL 60618
773-583-7884
www.haymarketbooks.org

ISBN: 978-1-60846-199-8

Trade distribution:
In the US, through Consortium Book Sales, www.cbsd.com
In the UK, Turnaround Publisher Services, www.turnaround-psl.com
In Australia, Palgrave Macmillan, www.palgravemacmillan.com.au
In all other countries, Publishers Group Worldwide, www.pgw.com

Cover design by Ragina Johnson.

This book was published with the generous support of Lannan Foundation and
the Wallace Global Fund.

Printed in the United States.

10 9 8 7 6 5 4 3 2 1

Library of Congress Cataloging-in-Publication Data is available.

CONTENTS

ACKNOWLEDGEMENTS

The various ideas and arguments of this book were worked out intermittently between 2003 and early 2009. During this time I have received a great deal of support at the University of Limerick, particularly from faculty members and students at the Department of Sociology and the Department of Politics and Public Administration. In particular I would like to thank Dr. Lucian Ashworth whose various suggestions helped with the development of key themes running through the book. I must also thank Dr. Owen Worth, who has consistently provided much needed encouragement along with valuable criticisms and suggested improvements. The same is true of associate lecturers and staff tutors that I had the good fortune to work with at the Open University. Other than this I wish to express gratitude to Professor Terrell Carver who pointed out problems with an earlier draught, to Professor David Fasenfest who has helped in the later stages and to Lesley Kenny for performing the unenviable task of proofreading and correction. Last but not least I would like to thank Jackie O'Flynn for her continued interest and encouragement, without which the final stages of preparation would have been a lonesome affair. Those that have helped make this book possible can in no way be held responsible for whatever errors remain. That responsibility is mine alone.

INTRODUCTION

Over the course of its development, the capitalist system has been defended according to a set of assumptions, principles and theories based on the perceived interests of the individual. This focus on the individual is bound up with the development of capitalist social relations in a complex yet distinct way. The individual was given primacy as the capitalist system struggled against the restrictions of the pre-capitalist feudal order. The development of the new system involved the promotion and defense of free, voluntary exchange relations under the rule of law. This was justified in terms of the perceived interests of the individual. The demand for minimal government interference or participation in economic life intensified accordingly. The early devotees of the individual believed that they stood for freedom from government and other sources of collective power. With the consolidation of capitalist relations the demands for limited government, unrestricted exchange relations and individual freedom came to be viewed as synonymous. The principles that eventually gave coherence to the modern liberal individualist tradition were underpinned by this association.

The tendency to posit the centrality of the individual has been continuous throughout the history of modern capitalist accumulation. The desire to maximize individual freedom and the desire to minimize obstacles to capital accumulation have long been expressed in the same breath. This has been very useful with regard to the legitimization of the system as a whole.

The ideology of the individual is best understood when examined against its historical social function. To this end it is necessary to set the theories and arguments offered by individualists over time against the varied historical conditions in which they have arisen. The assumptions and principles underpinning individualist arguments and theories cannot be taken as given. As such, the following chapters address all of the above in the context of the interests generated under the capitalist system over time.

The primary focus of the following pages is on modern individualist doctrine, which from its earliest expression has involved some variation of the idea that the role of the state should be limited to that of protecting life, liberty and property. This demand (habitually justified on grounds of efficiency) is bound up with the presumption that individual freedom can only be realized through the protection of private contracts.

Though demands for the protection of private contracts and for unrestricted trade and accumulation have been repeated for hundreds of years, the classical liberal tradition was not really recognizable as a coherent political tendency in Europe until the 19th century. Much of the agenda and many of the assumptions, principles and arguments that eventually came to characterize that tradition were developed when capitalism was in its embryonic stage. Therefore, the focus on the individual and on individual freedom cannot be considered a product of the classical liberal tradition. The primacy of the individual was insisted upon as soon as property-owners and their representatives came to regard capitalist relations as the basis of their freedoms. That such a view would emerge was perhaps inevitable. In pre-capitalist Europe, when capitalist relations had not yet come to dominate economic life, the control of private property helped owner-entrepreneurs realize levels of independence that were previously unheard of.

The kind of individual independence and power made possible by unhindered individual control over productive assets underpins the individualist notion of the individual. When individualists claim to stand for the individual they stand for the individual's unhindered control over what is individually possessed and all the benefit that this brings. When they refer to individual freedom, they refer to the freedom of individual economic agents to go about their business unhindered by government or other sources of collective power. The idea of individual freedom is understood within the terms and confines of the capitalist market system. Freedom means free, unrestricted, private control over personal capacities and properties under the rule of law.

Exclusive control over productive assets requires government protection, along with guarantees that government interference in the trading world be minimized. For early individualists, this function of government became synonymous with liberty. The ideal that emerged simultaneously was that of a social system in which individual freedom is maximized, that is to say, the individual is left with no master other than the law.

Since individual freedom was thought to require liberal government (i.e., one that limited its own powers and activities for the sake of perceived individual rights), a regime that interfered with the rights of private property, or the process of capital accumulation, was generally considered to be tyrannical. The demands for an end to tyranny, for non-interference in private contracts, intensified as capitalist relations developed. The notion that freedom depends on the protection of private property was held with the greatest conviction among those in control of productive assets in the emerging capitalist market.

There is not one key text or event that can be taken as the point signalling the emergence of political individualism. Its development spans several centuries, and key principles have been drawn together into a coherent whole relatively recently. The early expression of individualist ideas must be dealt with in the context of the emergence of indivisible property and contract relations under feudalism. To this end, the first chapter sets the early propagation of individualist ideas against the development of contract relations and related political antagonisms as they surfaced under feudalism. It then becomes necessary to link the related transformation of social, political and economic conditions to the development of scientific knowledge, and to the rapid development of the forces and relations of production. Following this, the second chapter pays attention to the writings of key individualist thinkers of the 17th century, such as Thomas Hobbes and John Locke. The point is to highlight the individualist outlook of these authors and outline the logic of their doctrines while considering the circumstances in which they were produced. The third chapter deals with the expression of individualist ideas through religion, as among the Puritans, but also against religion, as during the enlightenment period. It begins by considering the role of religious asceticism, paying some attention to the relationship between Protestantism and the rise of capitalism. It thereafter shows how individualism found expression through the struggles against the influence of religion, which marked a growing consciousness of the obstacles standing in the way of individual property rights and accumulation. In order to focus on particular intellectual responses to observable human conditions accompanying capitalist development in the early 19th century, the fourth chapter focuses on the writings of Thomas Malthus. The chapter highlights the interests underpinning his famous doctrine on population pressure. Though sympathetic to the landed aristocracy, his doctrines are entirely consistent with individualist demands for the maximization of private control over productive resources and the removal of regulations hindering accumulation. The fifth chapter begins by linking Malthusianism to the social-evolutionary doctrines developed by Herbert Spencer and others. The chapter considers the extent to which social Darwinism was constructed around individualist assumptions and moral precepts, and thereafter relates them to the sharpening class antagonisms of the 19th century. Chapter six, which considers the relationship between individualist thought and democratization, focuses on the individualist conception of democracy. Attention is given to the response of individualists to the form of democratization pursued by working populations in industrialized nations up to the 20th century. In order to illustrate the development of related doctrines in the 20th century, the seventh chapter focuses on the ideas of one key economist, F.A. Hayek, with particular attention paid to his explanation of fascism, socialism and social democracy. Chapter eight considers how the free market ideas of Hayek, Milton Friedman and others began to hold sway in the last quarter of the 20th century. The success of their doctrines is first of all explained in terms of the imperatives of capital accumulation under changed historical circumstances. It shows that from the mid-1970s to the first decade of the 21st century there was a great impetus to remove existing obstacles to capital accumulation, particularly after the collapse of the USSR. The chapter highlights the role of free market ideology with regard to the implementation of neoliberal policies in various countries and explains how much of the world came to assume that there would be no significant challenges to the free market system in the future. Chapter nine deals with the current (2009) abandonment of neoliberal policies and the decline in enthusiasm for free market principles in the face of the global economic downturn. The chapter focuses primarily on events taking place in the United States from 2007–08 onwards. The reason for this is that the symptoms of the global economic slump are being revealed daily. They are presenting themselves more rapidly and more dramatically in the United States than in other industrialized nations. Another reason has to do with the fact that the United States is the leading capitalist power, which means that changes in policy and ideology in the United States regularly find expression across the world in short order.

In short, the following chapters offer a historical analysis of individualist ideas as they relate to the continued maintenance of relations and conditions necessary for capitalistic accumulation. Liberal individualism, including present-day free market doctrine, is analyzed in terms of concurrent economic and political conditions and corresponding social relations. The various doctrines are examined in the context of their complex development, with necessary connections made between theories, moral precepts, arguments and policy agendas arising from the needs and consequences of capital accumulation up to the early 21st century.

CHAPTER ONE

THE DECLINE OF FEUDAL IDEAS

Individualism first emerged as a set of demands advanced by opponents of the feudal system of relations that was widespread in Medieval Europe from the 11th century onwards. In order to appreciate exactly what early individualists stood for, it is worth briefly examining this system of relations to which they stood opposed. One of the most obvious aspects of feudalism was that land was not owned by those occupying it, or freely bought and sold by private owners, but was usually held in return for military service (Critchly 1978:11). Individual property rights did not count for much, where individual freedoms, rights and responsibilities were of lesser importance than status and duty. The system was served by a set of enabling myths, including the notion that the feudal ruling class had inherent qualities of the sort suited to political, social and spiritual leadership. The economic relations were based upon divided or shared ownership, as opposed to the capitalist system, which presumes property indivisible. The basic economic unit was the manor. Prevailing social, political and economic relations revolved around the manor and the people attached to it were usually isolated from wider communities even if well integrated in their own immediate communities. Except in large towns, there were few markets, that is, few permanent centres for exchange (Dugger and Sherman 2000:84). The laws standing over the feudal system were appropriate to agricultural production at a low technological level. Laws of tenure ensured social order and the efficient application of existing technology in production. The property-less classes, who provided services in return for military protection, were in no position to decline the arrangements under which they lived their lives (Collins 1982:21).

In order to benefit from the exploitation inherent in the feudal system, the ruling classes needed to ensure that those producing goods remained tied to the land. As such, feudal society was one of great class distinction. There was a ruling class, consisting of lords and higher clergy, and lower classes, consisting of artisans, vassals and land-less laborers. The Lord of the Manor was not free to dispose of land. It was under his control, but not actually owned by him as private property.

The laws controlling tenure of land were not consistent with the use of property as a capital asset. It was not to be bought and sold freely (Collins 1982:21). For the sake of the system it was important to ensure that those performing the labor, which was necessary for society to function, remained bound to the land and obliged to perform services. That they performed services meant that they were prevented from enjoying all of the wealth that their labor created.

Under feudalism, status was largely determined by birth (Marx and Engels 1992:5). Feudal religious authorities created the impression that the resulting relations and conditions were in accordance with the will of God.[1] They promoted beliefs and values that helped the productive classes to accept their subordinate position and to understand their obedience as duty. The values and beliefs presented the prevailing system of exploitation in terms of reciprocal relations between the upper and lower classes. This was achieved through a combination of religious doctrine and analogy to feudal experience. In Europe, Christianity was made compatible with feudal power relations and attendant prejudices. The established virtues of the period, such as duty, loyalty and charity, were bound up with the acceptance of paternalist rule. Under feudal ideology the Lords (both secular and religious) were thought to perform an essential service, watching over and caring for the people just as parents do with their children (Hunt 1995:5). God was thought to watch over his flock (the world) as the feudal lords watched over their flock (the common people).

A great part of the maintenance of the feudal order was directed toward the realization of internal peace, which depended on both the higher and lower strata recognizing duties and obligations toward one another. To this end, the inequalities inherent in the status system were explained according to a paternalist world-view, which created the impression that everything was ordered perfectly and all things would run smoothly so long as peasants did not "encroach on those above them". Since all had a specific role and function in society, it was just as important that Lords did not "despoil peasants". As such, the untrammelled acquisitiveness that became more evident with the growth of the free cities offended the supporters of the feudal system, who insisted

---

[1] In addition to this they supplied a code of moral behavior (usually under the guise of spiritual aid) that was consistent with existing exploitative relations (Hunt 1995:4).

that craftsmen and merchants must receive what will maintain them in their calling and no more (Tawney 1948:23).

That the feudal ruling class was made up of both secular and religious lords was no accident. This arrangement helped all classes to live their lives in accordance with the 'custom of the manor', which was a contract of sorts, reflecting the necessary reciprocal relationship between the upper and lower classes. In that the lords were said to oversee things, they had to provide protection for the people and to administer justice wherever it was needed. Their rule was legitimated with the help of a paternalist ethic, which fostered an acceptance of duties and obligations to the lord, as well as a fundamental respect for existing arrangements. Though the system was extremely unequal and exploitative it depended on widespread recognition of obligations on the part of society to provide for the poor (Hunt 1995:4–9).

The Christian assumption that the rich had obligations towards the poor was a great obstacle to early capital accumulation. The lords could not dispute these obligations if they wished to operate under the guise of paternalism. In order to legitimate the roles in which their privileges were involved, the lords had to accept such obligations. But in order for the owners of moveable capital to legitimate the privileges produced through private contract relations, it was necessary to reject obligations relating to status and explain all socio-economic phenomena in terms of the choices, actions, capacities, prejudices and efforts of individual actors (Lukes 1973:73–84).

The feudal lords accepted that the existing economic system was imperfect and that poverty emerged in a haphazard fashion. Those reduced to poverty when times were hard were considered 'deserving poor'. Since it was recognized that such misfortune could befall anyone, the setting aside of a portion of produce for poor relief was seldom questioned (Hunt 1995:28). In any case where provisions needed to be made available, it was realized off the backs of the commoners. It benefited the lords since it created the impression that they had a great love for the people (which is possible). It provided further justification of their role and position in the social order. Moreover, the provision of relief meant that the conditions were less likely to deteriorate to levels that provoked unrest (though this still happened from time to time).

It was by way of spiritual direction that the vassal, artisan and serf were encouraged to understand the benefits of the existing system. That system was inconsistent with the existence of a market in land. It was inconsistent with the development of a labor market. Feudalism depended on the performance of labor under allotted functions. It was to be carried out according to duty and not to be sold as a capital asset. Peasants were bound by duty and were not free to offer their labor in the market at its going price (MacPherson 1962:49). The development of accumulative behavior and individualist doctrines caused great upset, as will be explained below. The tendency towards continuous and unlimited increase was treated as evidence of sinfulness and was condemned by the medieval doctrinaires. The Church's treatment of avarice as sin, and its prohibition of usury, was entirely in keeping with the times; but for the most part the church was preaching to the converted (Tawney 1948:35–36). It was the early bourgeois class that was out of place with respect to the prevailing morality. The capitalist mode of production (in which bourgeois interests and corresponding ideology were involved) had to develop within the confines of this older economic system and in spite of the economic restrictions placed upon it.

The feudal aristocracy could maintain its place in the sun without private ownership over the means of production because the relation between ruling and laboring classes did not depend on simple contracts. Before the spread of capitalist relations, the ruling class maintained its position by means of legal privilege and hereditary rule. It was exactly this 'customary' or 'status' society, along with the laws underpinning related privileges that were necessarily challenged by the rising bourgeois class. The task of undermining the ideas and values relating to nobility and paternalism meant substituting them with the idea that all individuals are equal. The advocates of the contract society were determined to see individualist values replace those built up around the customary society. Once it became apparent that the status system was an inefficient means of appropriating the labor and produce of others it was considered necessary (by the bourgeoisie at least) that all persons enjoy equal freedom and equal rights under set rules. These early individualists saw no need to mix class relations with legal definitions of status (Collins 1982:131). All that they demanded was the protection of the person and the enforcement of contracts. The development of humanist philosophies during the renaissance period and from the 15th century would help in this regard, undermining as they did the myths serving feudalism. Claims relating to the possibilities for the development of the human mind and personality undermined claims of uniqueness on the part of the nobility, which depended upon society's recognition of the significance of blood and noble birth (Struve 1973:26). Rejecting the notion that noble traits could not be acquired, the humanist ideologues of the early bourgeois class eventually considered that ordinary people (initially those with property) were capable of governing. With greater and greater conviction, prevailing notions of inherent characteristics were replaced with notions that all persons are of equal worth to begin with. This view was totally inconsistent with the ideological maintenance of the feudal system of relations.

The Role of Scientific and Technological Knowledge

In order to explain the rise of bourgeois styles of thought and behavior it is necessary to highlight the social, technological, political and economic changes that took place concurrently. The growing importance of the individual had a great deal to do with the growing importance of moveable capital, particularly its capacity to give individual persons great power over particular sections of the community. This power was an indication of changes in relations of production, which were greatly effected by changes in forces of production, which had reached a higher level of sophistication partly in consequence of the development of modern scientific method.

The emergence of modern science had an enormous effect on social, political, economic and moral thinking. Where the 16th century humanists had developed modern humanities, 17th century natural philosophers founded modern science (Toulmin 1990:43). The works produced by thinkers such as Newton and Descartes, brought with them the promise that scientific methods could be employed in efforts to uncover all that was still unknown to humankind. Newton's discoveries were treated as evidence that his method of enquiry was superior to anything that had existed before. The belief that the nature of human societies could be revealed through the application of his method generated great optimism, which was well expressed by Alexander Pope, who wrote: Nature and natures' laws lay hid in the night. God said 'Let Newton be!' and all was light" (Bullock 1985:52).

If Newton's discoveries left question marks about accepted wisdom, the great scientist René Descartes (1968) set out to do so purposefully. Descartes insisted that all existing beliefs should be subject to the most intense scrutiny. He wished to undermine all existing perceptions of the world and thereby separate truth from falsehood. He insisted that all knowledge required scientific validation and wished to establish a method of enquiry by which things could be known for certain.

Though Descartes did not value the beliefs prevailing among the lower classes, he did believe that almost every individual, no matter their position in the social system, was capable of arriving at certainty. He claimed that "there is almost none so gross or so slow as to be incapable of acquiring correct opinions and even of reaching the highest knowledge, if they are guided correctly" (Descartes 1968:182). It must be said however, that Descartes was conservative in political outlook; one of the first tasks assigned to his method involved attempts at proving the existence of God. Insofar as scientific certainty could be used to this end, and insofar as it could be used to create the impression that the prevailing social order was as it should be, it would not necessarily conflict with the interests of the church. The impression of certainty, realized by means of scientific methods, was just as readily used to support long-standing dogmas as undermine them (Toulmin 1990:x).

According to Stephen Toulmin it was Descartes, along with the few early modern thinkers mentioned above, who persuaded people to think about the world around them in a scientific manner. It was suggested that these few scientists convinced humankind to use rational methods to deal with problems facing human societies (Toulmin 1990:9). Descartes was certainly influential, and he did much to convince his fellow scientists that the only way to understand the world was to divide it into its constituent problems. He thought it necessary to divide up each problem at hand into its elements, examine each one separately, and thereafter build knowledge gradually, by degrees.

With the aid of Descartes' methodological individualism, some thinkers arrived at the conclusion that society could only be understood in terms of its constituent parts. As such, it was presumed nothing more than the aggregate of individuals. The most obvious example among the theoreticians to build upon this approach was Thomas Hobbes (1968), who published his famous work, *Leviathan*, in 1651. Hobbes' individualist outlook was one that was developed among the advocates of the emerging market system, which required, for purposes of legitimacy, that events be explained independently of the observable relations and conditions that restrict and guide human action. To understand society required understanding its individual units. But though social systems form a complex web of social, political and economic relations, it was individuals, rather than the *relations between* individuals, that were presumed to comprise society.

Modern scientific thought took hold as more and more thinkers were persuaded to conduct their thoughts in this orderly way. Thereafter, a rational habit of thinking took root, particularly among the trading classes. It is safe to say that along with the development of long distance trade, the putting-out system, the enclosure movement and the slave trade, scientific rationality must be regarded as the fundamental precondition underpinning not only capitalistic accumulation, but the individualist principles and economic outlook attached to it. Not only did modern science set in motion an accumulative cycle with regard to material production, it produced a similar effect in the sphere of mental production. The cycle of experiment-knowledge-experiment brought with it a power of prediction that was later to transform the world technologically, economically, politically, socially and spiritually. Science gave rise to more efficient methods of production which were favorable for the promotion of individualistic doctrines, which in turn aided capitalistic accumulation and more innovation in science and technology. Once the cycle was underway, science, religion and political thought were meshed together. The interrelated rationality, asceticism and capitalistic vision of the good life were soaked up in economic life and action.

Technological Development and Social Change

Armed with scientific methods of reasoning, the propertied classes of Europe set about breaking up traditional ties and customs wherever they most hindered them. It is probably worth noting that at the period when modern science was developed, Europeans were no more technologically advanced than were the Chinese. Europe may even have been more primitive in terms of sanitation, urban planning and labor saving technologies. Modern science gave the Europeans an edge over other cultures of the world; it enabled them to surpass all technological advances that were achieved elsewhere. No one knows why it was the Europeans that developed these methods first, only that they did, and that along with human activity, modern science helped to produce the habits of mind necessary for the emerging economic system of relations.

The art of experimentation led to an increase in scientific and technological innovations which helped to facilitate and abridge labor (Smith 1976:11). The abridgement of labor led to an explosion of surplus value and an increased capacity to reinvest. In order to create more and more wealth for reinvestment, more innovations were constantly required. Continuous improvements in the forces of production, along with improved procedures of scientific management, had the effect of drawing all sections of society into the same type of economic relation, and setting all individuals in competition with one another (Marx and Engels 1992:7).

The development of scientific habits of thinking made possible the special kind of acquisitive behavior and the distinctive mindset associated with a capitalist market society. Where science provided the means, religious asceticism gave the propertied classes of Europe a rationale for endless accumulation (Tawney 1948:85). The emergence of religious asceticism, of course, was not an independent development. Religion was affected by the new scientific methods as it adapted to new social and economic circumstances. Theoreticians began to conceptualize human nature in a manner more suited to new scientific categories of the mind. This helped to bind technology and religion, along with economic and political theory together to form the rationale underpinning capitalist society. It was all of these that led to the set habits and values which Max Weber referred to as the "spirit of capitalism" (Weber 1976:183).

In Weber's explanation of the rise of capitalism, the reformation (the religious revolution fuelled by objections to the doctrines and practices of the medieval church) was thought to have played a major role. Of course, this was not the cause of the acquisitive behavior that had taken hold of European societies from the 16th century. The objections underpinning the reformation were made because a large section of the community, which was compelled through economic necessity to behave in a particular way, did not wish to view that behavior as sinful. As Christopher Hill explained,

> it was very much nicer for a business man, finding himself under strong economic pressure to indulge in actions traditionally held to be sinful, to be told that those actions are in fact in accordance with the will of God. It is convenient to have these views expressed not only to the victims of your actions but also to third parties who might well sympathise with the victims, and to have them expressed from the pulpit with all the authority of a theologian.[2]

----

[2] Puritanism was advanced in 16th century England as Calvinist theologians preached on social issues. The first to do so in an organized way was William Perkins, a preacher who lived in England from the mid 1500s until 1602 (Hill 1958:212–222).

The reason why the reformation is sometimes thought to have provided the impetus for the development of capitalist relations is that these relations did not develop in the East, where there was nothing similar to the European reformation of the 16th century. Of course, it is perhaps more significant that the East experienced no similar changes in the structure of social economy. This had much to do with the failure in Eastern countries to apply scientific methods to production, even though a great deal of scientific knowledge used by Europeans had been developed there. The problem was that the peoples of the East had not developed methods for putting it to practical use. As such, they never realized the same advances in production and commerce as the Europeans. Without the same strict rationality, scientific knowledge was produced in a haphazard fashion in the Orient. Modern science demanded a systematic recording of facts. The scientific and rational methods of thinking developed by the Europeans brought them immense wealth and power which they eventually used to subjugate a significant portion of humanity (Toulmin 1990:x).

Modern science had a great effect on the conduct of trade, on the advancement of labor saving technology and even on ethics and religion. The scientific advancement on which the modern era prides itself became self-perpetuating when its applicability to economic life was fully appreciated (Toulmin 1990:ix). As soon as it was, the actors operating the European markets began to adopt rational habits of thinking and acting. Modern commercial society was advanced with the above developments, which made possible the necessary book keeping practices, the calculation of capital in terms of money, and rational calculation of probable profitableness of various business ventures (Weber 1976:18). Soon this rational approach to business was extended all across society and effected the political and economic arrangements that governed people's lives.

From the Putting-Out Stage to the Contract Society

As capitalist relations took shape, the conflict of interests between the feudal and bourgeois classes became sharper. The transition to capitalism was a slow process not only due to hostility on the part of the representatives of aristocratic feudalism, but because the mass of ordinary people were wary about leaping out of well-worn feudal institutions into an as yet uncertain bourgeois system.

The capitalist spirit finally took hold because new potentialities of production had become evident. Increasingly, people saw that progress was fettered by existing political, economic and moral confines. As Harold Laski (1936:23) explained it:

> Little by little, the new men, and their new methods, pointed the way to a volume of wealth unattainable by the older society. The attraction of this wealth aroused expectations, which that society, given its premises, could not fulfil. Men therefore begin to doubt the legitimacy of those premises. The attitude to usury, the acceptance of the guilds as a rational way of controlling production, the notion of the church as the fit source of ethical criteria, all begin to appear as inadequate because they stand in the way of the potentialities revealed by the new spirit.

The development of scientific methods of production and long distance trade, urbanization, the emergence of a proletariat and the growth in power and influence of the property-owning classes all emerged around the same time. It was only insofar as the owners of moveable capital developed interests that were opposed to the interests of the aristocratic power and of the property-less, that they could become fully conscious of them.

In order to safeguard their interests, the owners of capital needed to defend contract relations which had become widespread when merchant capitalists began leaving raw materials with workers in their homes. This period in the development of contract relations from the 14th century onwards is sometimes referred to as the 'putting-out' stage (merchants paid workers for their labor and returned to collect the finished product). What was novel about the putting-out system was that nothing was purchased from the laborer besides labor power.

The factory system developed from this basic set of relations. Under the factory system the capitalist owned the workshop, tools and raw materials. Workers were necessarily concentrated in one place. Labor was divided up and all workers had to perform their respective tasks under the tutelage of the capitalist-overseer. Some commentators like to depict this as an evolutionary transformation.[3] The most important development of course was that the early capitalists had managed to get workers to enter wage-contracts. Once they had done so, laborers no

---

[3] Dugger and Sherman have suggested that the handicraft system 'evolved into the putting-out system and the putting-out system evolved into the factory system' (Dugger and Sherman 2000:124).

longer had anything to do with the design, use or sale of the finished product.

Any independent crafts-persons that remained (save those that had found a special niche for themselves) would find it hard to make a living once the far more efficient factory system took root in society. Once the premises, the necessary raw materials and manufacturing equipment were appropriated, owners of capital were positioned to accumulate, transform it into labor and capital once more, and so on, in a cyclical fashion. During the putting-out stage, this system was in its infancy, but it did threaten the economic, social and political power of the aristocratic classes, who wished to see it restricted in accordance with the Christian ethic (Hunt 1995:26).

The early bourgeois individualists thought of themselves as the foes of privilege. They opposed prevailing privileges as they organized productive labor around their own private stores of capital, positioning themselves between the producers and consumers in order to accumulate at every stage in the labor process. The bourgeois class only grew in power and influence to the extent that it gained control over labor power, thereby building exploitation into the labor process itself. This contrasted sharply with the feudal system. Since the feudal aristocracy had little to do with directing production, they were not so disposed to do something about the inefficient manner in which labor was performed.

The workers organized by the bourgeois class began to produce in a far more efficient manner than had been achieved previously. Modern scientific method, when coupled with human ingenuity in an environment of free enterprise, led to an explosion of scientific and technological discovery. New knowledge about mechanics, engineering, thermodynamics, chemicals and so on, led to an evermore efficient exploitation of human labor power and the world's natural resources (Collins 1982:20). The more bourgeois relations held sway the more they ate away at the fabric of feudal life and corresponding world-view. The emergence of new economic and social relations made necessary new legal relationships. The rising class required indivisible property ownership, free labor and a political system wherein there was a distinction made between personal and economic relations and, to use Marx's words, 'the political institutions which govern, and sanction, these relations' (Marx and Engels 1992:5). This was necessary so as to safeguard individual property rights and the social relations necessary to facilitate capitalistic accumulation. The power wielded by the emerging bourgeois class was not, unlike the feudal ruling class, intended to be fixed and hereditary. So long as money could be inherited by the following generation it did not need to be. The new ruling class would reproduce itself solely through legal inheritance of property under the protection of a centralized state.

The capitalist market system developed on a gradual basis when new technologies were put to continuous use from the 15th century onwards (Parry 1961:16–21). Technological advances assisted the development of a continuous and rationalized system of long distance trade. An 'Age of Exploration' was set in motion in consequence of a few key inventions, such as variations of the telescope and the compass, which enabled adventurers and traders to navigate much more accurately and for far greater distances (Hunt 1995:15–20). This led to a concentration of wealth and power in the cities and among merchants trading there. The favorable position in which the merchants found themselves allowed them to put the wealth they had accumulated to work. Once raw materials and tools could be bought in bulk on the commodity market, the capitalist was in a position to control not only the selling of produce, but labor power and the entire productive process. Capitalists, once in control of entire operations, could distribute the wealth created as they saw fit. The many skilled crafts persons that had lost control of production were soon put to work for a wage. The capitalist simply purchased their labor power as any other commodity. The subsequent concentration of wealth allowed those with the capacity to invest to further entrench themselves in between crafts persons and their crafts (Hunt 1995:15–16).

Competition for work among the growing laboring class made them willing to undercut each other and accept wages that failed to reflect the wealth that they created. Those running capitalistic enterprises knew that their workers would work for even lower wages if the security offered under Christian paternalist arrangements was removed altogether. This is partly why the early bourgeois theoreticians did all in their power to undermine the presumption that individuals have obligations toward one another. This eventually led to the establishment of new churches and a new morality (Tawney 1948:8). The establishment of state churches, along with centres of confinement, helped to centralize control and to establish the monarch as moral arbiter (Foucault 1967:42–48).

For the most part, the early bourgeois class conducted their day-to-day business far away from the manor system. The business interests of the merchants were concentrated in the towns. They distanced themselves from the wider feudal arrangements and created a mini society of their own, within which they were free to develop a new way of life, independently of the duties and obligations associated with the manor.

As more and more economic and social power was vested in the hands of the owners of capital, bourgeois ideas increasingly held sway. Since paternalism was antithetical to the acquisitive behavior necessary for the development of capitalism, the arguments forwarded by representatives of capital were often opposed to the conventional viewpoint. Of course, bourgeois intellectuals understood that the philosophical assumptions propping up paternalist arrangements needed to be discredited if their system was to advance. As such, they offered alternative ideas, which were designed to destroy paternalism from the ground up. With the help of a bourgeois secular intelligentsia, operating independently of the traditional authorities, these ideas managed to work their way into society through the moral sphere.

It was well understood that, if not restrained, acquisitive behavior and its attendant value system would quickly unravel the whole fabric of feudal society. The aristocracy condemned acquisitive behavior and resisted capitalist development. It was in their interests to do so since it was undermining all of the status relationships that were really the life-blood of that society (Hunt 1995:8). They realized that the accumulation of wealth in society would mean that an enormous social power would be concentrated in the hands of one group.

The need to preserve status relations was only one reason to oppose further development of the new system. Accumulative behavior inevitably led to the creation of a massive laboring class with nothing to sell but its labor power. This group would become increasingly discontented and unpredictable as the consequences of capitalist accumulation presented in society. Where the feudal system had managed to keep such discontent under wraps (relatively speaking), the emerging capitalist order was bringing it to the fore. The subsequent demise of feudal relations was slow only because the intransigence of the feudal lords was great. The loss in control over economic life would yield a loss in power, influence and their status in society generally.

With the feudal lords struggling against the capitalists for supremacy, and each class producing knowledge that was consistent with their respective political designs, there could not but be division and conflict. As such, very different styles of thinking were being fostered at the same time. That which was consistent with the emerging contract society found its first coherent expression in the works of early individualist thinkers, such as Thomas Hobbes and John Locke. The individualist doctrines expressed by Hobbes were formulated at a time when individualist concepts were beginning to hold sway. The sphere of jurisdiction given to individual persons through continued accumulation of productive capital gave rise to the demand for individual independence from collective demands. As the structure of social economy developed further, the owners of moveable capital became more conscious of their interests and formulated definite political demands which were oftentimes presented in the form of universal principles. The writings of Hobbes are perhaps the most noteworthy in this respect. The principles championed were consistent with the demand for maximum bourgeois control over society, under strong government. Hobbes advocated rights and freedoms necessary for bourgeois dominance, but believed that monarchical absolutism was necessary to secure them.

CHAPTER TWO

THE INDIVIDUALISM OF HOBBES AND LOCKE

As I have explained above, the doctrines produced by early individual-ists revolved around property rights. The property of individuals was regarded as their private business and nothing to do with the wider community (MacPherson 1962:19). Supporters of the emerging system of capitalist property relations stood in opposition to trade restrictions frustrating its extension. Any attempt to curtail the actions and societal effects of capitalism was condemned as an affront to the freedom of the individual. The desire to undermine those predominant customs and assumptions that were inconvenient to the emerging economic system influenced the thinking of the earliest individualist theoreticians. This was aided, of course, by Cartesian science.

With the aid of Cartesian methods, Hobbes developed an explanation of how human societies operated and how they should be organized. He believed that he had identified the main features of human nature and that such knowledge could be used in the development of the kind of social arrangements most conducive to human happiness. The problem, as Hobbes saw it, was that human beings were acting contrary to their true nature (MacPherson 1962:101–105). Societies comprised human beings that were by nature selfish and aggressive. For Hobbes, any understanding of the social system required knowledge of the natural drives and desires (considered inherent) motivating the individuals of which it was comprised. Hobbes' unflattering interpretation of human nature rationalized the existence of a centralized absolutist state. Hobbes supported monarchy because he believed the effects to be beneficial for all concerned, but especially to those with property. He thought that human nature was such that the absence of strong government would lead to absolute chaos. He did not entertain any romantic notions about this form of government. The notion of divine right was not given any credence by Hobbes. Absolute monarchy was the "best of all conditions for a commonwealth" because of its success as a means of keeping order and securing property (Hobbes 1998:126).

Hobbes' prescriptions for human happiness were presented alongside speculation about man in a 'state of nature', which was intended to impress upon people what life would be like if there were no common power able to overawe selfish and aggressive individuals. Hobbes set aside the law standing over the society in which he lived and treated the socially acquired behavior and desires produced therein as though they stemmed from human nature. As such, the behavior of individuals was presumed the result of natural drives. Hobbes assumed that individuals would behave the same in the 'state of nature' as they did in the social system with which he was familiar and supported (MacPherson 1962:22).

Hobbes knew that in order for his individualist conception of human nature and society to take hold it would be necessary to eliminate particular assumptions. In the first place, the poor could no longer be thought of as a by-product of the economic system. It was important to atomize society, to think of the poor as being made up of abstract beings, to think of each individual apart from society and each as responsible for his/her own circumstances and morality. The conception put forward by Hobbes and his followers was a more sophisticated version of that which already existed throughout the mercantilist period. The views expressed in Hobbes' *Leviathan* were by no means original. As E.K. Hunt pointed out, the intellectual wing of the bourgeois class already believed that all human motives stem from a desire for whatever promotes the "vital motion" of the human organism (Hunt 1995:29).

Hobbes' speculations relating to human nature were of no use at all to those attempting to justify paternalist relations. Hobbes, having justified monarchy and having discredited paternalism on the basis of scientific principles, had brought a certain degree of coherence to early individualist ideas. He had enabled those with the capacity to invest to ridicule the ideas of Royalists, which were inadequate since they ignored the drive for self-preservation and other supposedly natural attributes of human individuals (Hayes 1998:53–64). Hobbes wished to justify monarchy according to the idea that all phenomena, be they billiard balls, human beings or forms of government, follow the same basic scientific principles (Berman 1651–1738).

Rather than depending on religion as a guide to behavior, Hobbes thought that political rights and obligations could be deduced from the interest and will of individuals (MacPherson 1962:1). Hobbes was so convinced that he had uncovered man's true nature that he felt confident enough to claim that he knew exactly what laws should be set down by government. If the nature and needs of humankind were known, the proper function of government could also be known.

Hobbes was sure that the only purpose of government should be that of providing the best environment to facilitate individuals to compete against one another in the trading world. He presupposed the relations necessary for a complex market society, conceiving of labor as a simple commodity "exchangeable for benefit, as well as for any other thing" (MacPherson 1962:62).

Insofar as labor was treated as a commodity and human beings were considered to be basically selfish and aggressive by nature, Hobbes suggested that government should only concern itself with the protection of persons from arbitrary violence and the protection of property, so that individuals could be free to pursue their selfish interests. The owners of capital were bound to seize upon Hobbes' unflattering conception of the person since they sought to create an economic system wherein individuals would recognize obligations to no one but themselves.

However scientific Hobbes' doctrines may have been they were colored by a particular class prejudice. In his writings, the laboring classes were often depicted as lazy, but motivated to work by the goad of necessity. In contrast to this, the "higher ranks" were often depicted as individuals motivated by ambition. This differentiation of people into ranks betrays, according to Hunt, an implicit elitism (Hunt 1995:28–39). The emerging bourgeois individualists were appreciative of this. Hobbes had built for them a model of human nature and human society that justified the coercive institutions required for the development of the market system. Hobbes' postulates on human nature, which he considered to be absolutely certain, were bound up with a set of assumptions and beliefs that were already taking hold among the rising bourgeois class. These ideas first emerged and spread when, as Laski explained, "the banker, the trader, the manufacturer, began to replace the landowner, the ecclesiastic, and the warrior" (Laski 1936:11).

Insofar as individual industry, self-reliance, responsibility and thrift were character forms necessary for the proper functioning of the emerging system, these forms were encouraged as alternatives to those traits supposedly proceeding from existing paternalist arrangements. Notions that individuals (property owners) had any duty to the society of which they were part, were rejected outright. The existing world-view and morality was abandoned for the sake of what R.H. Tawney (1948:267) referred to as the "naïve psychology of the businessman". In other words, it gave way to the belief that the riches accumulated by individuals were due to their own unaided efforts. This individualist philosophy enabled the investor to proceed, as Tawney (1948:267) put it, "in blind unconsciousness of a social order without whose continuous support and vigilant protection he would be as a lamb bleating in the desert".

Individualists, from Hobbes to the Puritans, to the English political Economists, insisted that no one should depend on or presume that they owe anything to the wider community. Though voluntary charity was not ruled out, the notion that the wealthy should have any *obligation* or duty to care for the poor was rejected. Individual self-reliance on the part of the propertied classes and the property-less was promoted above everything else. Individualists thought that paternalism of any kind encouraged laziness and imprudence. Particular thinkers, such as Malthus, and later economists such as Joseph Townsend, believed that "only the experience of hunger would goad them [laborers] to labor" (Hunt 1995:38–39). It was held that any commitment to economic equality, or any similar ideal, would involve unnecessary burdens on those of superior industry and encourage idleness on the part of the lower classes.[1] Hobbes' scorn for distributive justice was underpinned by these class-based assumptions. The doctrines that he produced anticipated the replacement of the customary concept of justice with a more convenient individualist conception (MacPherson 1962:63–64). His brand of individualism foreshadowed the 'night-watchman' state of liberal political economy. It anticipated the development of the free contract society, which was expected to consist of 'free individuals' with no master other than the law (Bird 1999:11).

Hobbes' Materialism

Hobbes was the first political thinker to have seen the possibility of deducing obligation directly from, as C.B. MacPherson (1962:88) put it, "the mundane facts of men's actual relations with each other". Insofar as his analysis was built around observable behavior within human societies, his analysis may be regarded as 'materialist'. But it must be pointed out that Hobbes' analysis was a-historical. In Hobbes' work, the behavior of individuals within the confines of the emerging capitalist market order was simply attributed to 'human nature' (MacPherson

---

[1] This was a long-standing view, but was most famously forwarded by Thomas Robert Malthus at the end of the 18th and in the beginning of the 19th centuries (Malthus 1973a).

1962:22). There was no sense that human nature might have a historical component. Hobbes followed in the tradition of Descartes, who had left no room for the idea of a changing human nature, which had been part of 15th and 16th century humanism (Toulmin 1990:27–46). He began by considering the real conditions in which people lived, but he employed a mechanistic materialist approach, which was tied to the reductionism of Descartes as well as to Galilean mechanics (Tuck 1989:104). Hobbes had bought into the promise of comprehending everything 'by reference to the laws of mechanical motion'. He sought to explain phenomena by 'resolving' them down to their parts. This method was briefly outlined in his preface to *De Cive*, in which the investigation of the authority of the state and the duties of citizens was compared to examining the workings of a watch by dismantling it (Tuck 1989:105). Hobbes was not willing to acknowledge, as Marx did two centuries later, that the 'laws' governing human behavior are entirely different to those of physics. The laws of physical science remain constant over time. They exist independently of relations between people and conditions experienced by them (Machan 1990:5).

Insofar as Hobbes ignored the difference between the regularities observable in human behavior and the laws revealed in the physical sciences, the results proceeding from his speculative analysis were presented as irrefutable scientific fact. Hobbes (1968:6) thought that his observation of human behavior had led him to 'absolutely certain' postulates about human nature. Having established these he considered the most important to be "the postulate of human greed by which each man insists upon his own private use of common property [and] the postulate of natural reason, by which each man strives to avoid violent death as the supreme evil in nature". The tendency on the part of individuals to invade and destroy each other was thereafter considered to proceed from natural drives.

The notion that 'human nature' determined human behavior offered opportunities for those wishing to proscribe for society according to particular political agendas. It was precisely the notion that the desires, faculties, needs and instincts of individuals are given and that they are more or less independent of the social context that provided the foundation upon which Hobbes constructed all of his political arguments (Lukes 1973:73).

Hobbes favored absolutist rule because he thought that, given the nature of human beings, it was the only reliable means of realizing peace and prosperity. As far as Hobbes was concerned, only an absolute authority could safeguard individual freedom. Of course, this is not sufficient reason to distinguish Hobbes from later individualists. The social order promoted by Hobbes was basically the same as F.A. Hayek's 'Great Society'.[2] Perhaps the *means* by which the necessary relations therein were to be safeguarded set Hobbes apart from later individualists, but his aims were much the same. His intention was to see the creation of a social system wherein the 'intelligent' and 'industrious' (those with the capacity to invest) could live their lives to their own best advantage.

Hobbes understood the role of government to be that of creating favorable conditions for the accumulation of wealth on the part of those with property. He considered Monarchy more effective than bourgeois democracy with regard to maintaining the necessary relations. It was considered the only certain means of maintaining the internal stability necessary for the proper functioning of the capitalist market system. He reasoned that, without internal peace, there would be no opportunity to accumulate for anyone. As such, strong government was considered the best of all possible alternatives.

Insofar as Hobbes did not promote democratic principles, contemporary individualists, such as Annabel Patterson, prefer to trace the 'intellectual roots' of 'the liberal tradition' back to John Locke and no further. Patterson (1997:16) claims that in the political circumstances of their time, Hobbes and Locke represented polar opposition. It remains the case however, that the ideas in question had already found expression in Hobbes' works. Though some modern protagonists refuse to recognize this, others, such as John Gray (1986:8), are prepared to admit Hobbes' "uncompromising individualism", his "egalitarian affirmation of the equal liberty of all men" and his emphasis on "rights as distinguished from duties".

It is important to remember that Hobbes favored the economic domination of society by the propertied classes. Though he insisted that those with property had to entrust someone with absolute authority, this was because he believed that without the absolute power of a single man, "people would still be saddled with the constant need to watch, distrust,

---

[2] Though these thinkers may have differed in many respects, they both advocated the type of social system in which individuals would control what is individually possessed. There are also similarities in this respect between Hayek's 'Great Society' and Popper's 'Open Society' (Popper, 1966; Hayek, 1978; Hobbes, 1998).

anticipate and get the better of others" (Hobbes 1968:11). He was certain that individuals would enjoy peace only so long as there existed "some one assembly or one man who has the right to arm, muster and unite, on each occasion of danger or opportunity, as many citizens as the common defence shall require" (Hobbes 1968:78). The implication of this is that the leviathan could refer to bourgeois democracy as well as to absolute monarchy. Of course Hobbes did not believe that the former was feasible. There was no question but that government needed to have absolute authority over its subjects.

Hobbes' doctrines would need to be built upon, failing as they did to provide the propertied classes with the right to revolt if their interests were threatened. The bourgeois class had to wait for John Locke to promote a system of government more fitting with the social and technological changes taking place. Locke thought it possible to establish government by consent. Of course consent was to be understood in a manner consistent with the maintenance of private power over and above that of government or collectives. The same theory of social contract used by Hobbes to condemn rebellion was thereafter used by Locke to justify it in certain circumstances (Taylor 1992:260). This does not mean that they were poles apart; it only means that Locke thought that the right of revolution was necessary and Hobbes did not.

Hobbes Versus Locke

As I have pointed out, some contemporary individualists create distance between the ideas of Hobbes and Locke. The latter is considered a liberal due to the 'optimism' that pervades his thought and also because, as John Gray (1986:13) explained, he saw "no inherent obstacle to the permanent establishment of a free society". As such, Locke's works are widely regarded as the first expression of genuine liberal principles and are sometimes held up as a standard for measuring all other styles of liberal thought.

Locke's writings offer a view of the conflict of interests that arose in consequence of the rapid development of capitalist relations toward the end of the 17th century. His works remain influential today because they are underpinned by a political commitment to the continued maintenance of the market order and are also consistent with the development and maintenance of contemporary bourgeois democratic institutions. As such, Patterson and Gray find it easy to read their own liberalism into Locke's political thought. To them, Locke's works appear to contain everything that could be desired by the modern liberal democrat (MacPherson 1962:194).

Among the novelties of Locke's political thought was his insistence that the ruling body should not have the authority to betray the trust of 'the people'. He thought it necessary to establish a right on the part of the people to rebellion under certain circumstances. According to Locke (1980:124), the people could justly rebel "against any government that betrayed their trust". Of course a government was only thought to betray the people's trust where the accumulation of wealth and property was obstructed. The view that government should represent the owners of moveable capital over and above the productive classes is clearly expressed in Locke's writings.

Though certain authors such as Alan Ryan (1984:48) have suggested that "to see Locke as no more than an apologist for capitalism is ludicrous" it cannot be denied that his works contain such a defense. Though no thinker is simply an apologist it must be acknowledged that Locke's setting down of property rights anterior to the state, along with the right of revolution, were supplied for the class that was trying to realize its title to a full share in the control of the state (Laski 1936:11). This did not mark the beginning of a new style of thinking. As R.H. Tawney (1948:258) explained, Locke merely poured into a philosophical mould, ideas that had been "hammered out in the stress of political struggles". As with Hobbes, Locke speculated about human nature and deduced rights from what he considered to be the needs and will of individuals. Unlike Hobbes however, Locke and the individualist theoreticians following his lead, were more inclined to emphasize the principle of government by consent within the confines of the emerging capitalist market order.

The Second Treatise on Government

One of the main tasks that Locke set for himself was that of removing the inconveniences inherent in Hobbes' doctrines. For the most part he agreed with Hobbes analysis of, and proscriptions for, the society that was emerging. Like Hobbes, Locke's conception of freedom was consistent with the buying and selling of labor power as a commodity, which was supposed to ensure the freedom of individuals from dependence on the wills of others. He was determined to show that human nature works in a particular way and that the only sensible form of government is that which suits it. Locke began with his desired political/economic system and thereafter decided what "man's" natural rights should be.

As is usually the case, Locke's view of human nature was created to fit his own particular ends. The great achievement of 'human nature' theoreticians was that they managed to create the impression that things had been worked out the other way around. But Locke's method was particularly clever. He forwarded his arguments in full cognizance of the religious doctrines that were most familiar and acceptable to people. The initial explanation of the relationships between individuals in a *state of nature* was provided alongside regular citations from the Bible. In order to gain credibility, Locke employed Hobbes' 'scientific' postulates on human nature, but presented them in a manner consistent with the existing religious world-view. Religious thought was also undergoing change as the advocates of the new economic system tried to spiritualize the processes involved. They eventually came to believe that God instituted the market and exchange, which was a view that helped guide, not only religious, but also social, political and economic activity (Hunt 1995:31).

In his *Second Treatise on Government*, Locke attempted to square his political individualism with the inconvenient Christian belief that "God...hath given the world to men in common". Having convinced himself and others that it was not his intention to go against the will of God, he insisted that though the world was originally given to all persons in common, God "hath also given them reason to make use of it to the best advantage of life, and convenience". In order to facilitate this, God had given all individuals property in their persons and property in their labor. Locke considered the individual to be "proprietor of his own person and capacities, owing nothing to society for them" (MacPherson 1962:3). As such, for Locke, respecting the will of God meant respecting people's God-given rights over their properties. This meant recognizing that the labor of people's bodies, along with the goods produced, were private property. Locke (1980:19) explained that whatever an individual "removes out of the state that nature hath provided, and left in, he hath mixed his labor with, and joined to it something that is his own, and thereby makes it his property". This was a roundabout way of saying that whatever people find in nature, make useful and make use of, becomes their property. This was not a justification of the modern institution of private property, only that of personal property. The field that was worked, the fish that was caught and the house that was built, were all considered the property of those that had performed the necessary labor. What Locke was saying was that though the earth had been given to humankind in common, it could rightfully be appropriated by individual persons since it had through their labor "something annexed to it that excludes the common right of other men" (Locke 1980:19).

Insofar as Locke treated labor power as a commodity (wholly alienable from the individual), individuals were considered 'free' to sell their labor power to others outright, the same as any other commodity. Once a person had sold their labor power to another they could have no say as regards its use thereafter. For example, the labor power of servants did not belong to them but to their employer. This conception of labor power as a commodity was essential for the purposes of justifying the extension of property rights over all the forces of production. It enabled Locke to assume that both the "turfs my servant has cut; and the one I have digged... become my property" (Locke 1980:19–20).

The claim that the labor power of servants could be appropriated by another did not square with the idea that whatever people mix their labor power with must become their property. If servants had property in their labor power then the turfs cut by them should naturally belong to them. But the fact that Locke denied this does not mean that he had completely broken with his previous arguments. He reasoned that since some of God's creatures appeared to be less industrious than others, He must have intended that they sell their labor power to others in order to survive. Insofar as God intended persons to use their talents, He must have intended labor power to be treated as a commodity and to be purchased by those possessing capital. Even though each individual born into the world possessed property in their labor power, it did not follow that they would always be the proprietors of it. There was no great leap of logic. Locke's possessive assumptions set him on a particular path of reasoning and his God was inevitably transformed into a rampant capitalist.

Locke (1980:45) regarded labor power as something wholly alienable from the individual. In Locke's own words "a freeman makes himself a servant to another, by selling him, for a certain time, the service he undertakes to do, in exchange for wages". He presumed the existence of a labor market, and clearly approved of it.

With regard to the accumulation of land, Locke (1980:21) claimed that it could not be supposed that "[God] meant it should always remain common and uncultivated. He gave it to the use of the industrious and rational". It was suggested that although God had given the world to men in common, He couldn't really have meant it. What He really intended was for the 'industrious' to put it to use.

In the flow of his arguments Locke (1980:20) admitted that the appropriation of property by an individual had to be limited to "as much as any one can make use of to any advantage of life before it spoils". He was well aware that this limitation did not hold for wealth held in the form of gold or silver. This one limitation recognized by Locke (1980:23) turned out to be irrelevant. A person could accumulate gold and silver without fear of it ever spoiling. Money ensured that acceptance of the spoilage limitation did not conflict with his advocacy of liberal property ownership or the process of accumulation.

Money and Social Power

John Locke depicted the free use of money as an expression of consent on the part of the entire community to the inequality made possible through its use (MacPherson 1962:203). He understood money as a simple device invented to facilitate exchange between persons operating freely in the market. Since he treated money simply as a lubricant in the process of exchange between the buyers and sellers of commodities and labor power, he did much to obscure the social power it afforded to particular actors. It was as though money was nothing other than a veil, which covered over the same exchange relations as could be found in a barter economy (Sherman 1995:160). Since this human invention facilitated trade it was therefore beneficial to all concerned. And insofar as people used money they were thought to tacitly agree to the emerging system of relations and its inequalities. Locke claimed that individuals could be said to have agreed to an unequal possession of the Earth since they had "found out a way, how a man may fairly possess more land than he himself can use the product of" (MacPherson 1962:208).

As with other individualists, Locke considered it essential that the 'industrious' took charge of the land, cultivate it and produce goods. He thought that unless productive property remained under the control of such individuals there would be no production and people would starve. Locke did not dispute the fact that the appropriation of land by some individuals left none for the rest. However, he denied that there was any injury on their part. Insofar as they had tacitly agreed to the use of money, they had consented to the rules of the game (Locke 1980:30). It was because the property-less had realized their various inadequacies that they had come to accept that the resulting inequality was necessary. As Locke saw it, the property-less benefited from the superior industry of others.

The above arguments depended upon the internalization of one of the greatest myths of the capitalist order, namely, that the proprietor is responsible for creating the goods and the wealth in society. As such, he thought that rather than causing injury to others through appropriation of land, the proprietor "may truly be said to give ninety acres to mankind", since more is produced from ten acres of managed land than "a hundred left to nature" (Locke 1980:24). Locke could make such claims only insofar as he ignored the exploitative nature of the class system. Where there was an increase in wealth it was attributed to the personal efforts of those that accumulated it. The institution of private property, which allowed for the appropriation of labor power, and upon which power and privilege was built, was taken for granted. This was also the case with regard to the policeman and the law court thereafter (Hobhouse 1911:51).

It was precisely because labor power was treated as a commodity that individualists, such as Locke, could consider personal wealth as proceeding from the efforts of the owners of capital. Insofar as labor power was appropriated, it was spent not by the laborer but by the individual that had purchased it from the laborer. Labor power was purchased and put to use by individuals and wealth was created afterwards. This is why Locke's turf-digging servant could not mix his labor with anything. The labor power of servants was not theirs to spend. As such, there was no need to give any credit to the servants, whose labor power had been used to provide 'ninety acres to mankind'. The proprietor deserved all credit for the resulting use-value. It was the appropriation and reinvestment of capital by individuals that ensured the common stock of humankind would continue to increase (MacPherson 1962:211).

Government by Consent

One of Locke's greatest concerns was that government still had the potential to impinge on the perceived rights of the individual. Absolutist government brought uncertainty, which was why Locke sought to establish, on top of property rights, the right of the people to rebel if circumstances required them to do so. He argued that resourceful individuals had created government in order to protect their property and enjoy peace at the same time. People had agreed to give up their 'natural rights' to civil society on the condition that particular ends would be met. Fear had driven practical individuals into society and under governments for protection. Those that depended on their superior industry had to follow them. Though individuals had agreed to give over much of their natural power to a central authority, Locke insisted that they "could not conceivably have delegated absolute arbitrary power to any government, but must be understood to have retained the right to alter the frame of government" (MacPherson 1980:xiv). Locke insisted that if any government failed to respect the institution of private property then that government was no longer performing the role for which it was created. Given such conditions, 'the people' would have to have the right to rebel. To this end, Locke argued that if not for the protection of 'the person' and property, individuals would never have agreed to hand over their 'natural power', as possessed in a state of nature, to a governing authority in the first place. In Locke's view a government that did not protect property rights could not be considered legitimate. A governing authority that was ultimately beyond the control of the propertied classes was unacceptable (MacPherson 1980:xv).

Locke (1980:73) insisted that "no government can ever have any right to take any part of any man's property without his own consent". In order to prevent such attempts it was necessary to ensure that the right to vote in elections was confined to the propertied classes. The property qualification was considered essential since there could be no guarantee that universal suffrage would coexist with the perceived rights of the individual. The masses might deny those with great wealth the right to unlimited private property. Without formal recognition of such rights bourgeois society could not exist at all.

It was considered important to insist, as Locke (1980:78) famously did, that "the community perpetually retains a supreme power of saving themselves from the attempts and designs of any body, even of their legislators, whenever they shall be so foolish, or so wicked, as to lay and carry on designs against the liberties and properties of the subject". Of course by 'the community' Locke could only mean the propertied classes, since the lower classes and women were excluded from his vision of civil society. He thought that interference from government, or the property-less, in matters that did not to concern them should be resisted strenuously. In effect, Locke's government by consent had to involve the subjugation of an entire society to the collective will of one class (Locke 1980:55). This may appear inconsistent with Locke's (1980:17) earlier insistence that the "natural liberty of man is to be free from any superior power on earth... [and] under no legislative power, but that established by consent". But it was only the liberty and consent of those individuals to whom Locke was allied that mattered. The main problem that Locke (1980:17) had with absolute rule was that the accumulation of capital could not be guaranteed in an environment where the individual is "subject to the inconsistent, uncertain, unknown, arbitrary will of another man".

Locke's class-based conception of freedom was such that once a person had sold their labor power to others they were considered to have chosen to give up their liberty for convenience sake. The property-less could not exercise their freedoms in the capitalist market order because they were in no position to act independently of the will of others. The property-less classes were not deprived of their freedoms by anyone else. They had simply chosen to depend on the will of an employer; they had abandoned their own freedom and independence.

Since the freedom required by Locke was a function of property, it could not be realized by wage laborers, beggars or women. The liberty so perceived was necessarily limited to a small segment of society. The rest would be free in principle only. This limited liberty was all that was desired and tolerated by Locke.

Rule of Law

Locke believed that without a fixed law there could be no such thing as individual freedom. He also believed that the set of rules that made up the law should proceed from the will of the majority. In saying as much, Locke suggested that individual freedom began only when the individual was subjected to the will of the majority.

Though it may seem contradictory, Locke's (1980:67) individualism was actually collectivist. It was a bourgeois collectivism. When Locke said 'majority' he really meant the majority of the propertied classes. When the individual was subjected to the collective will of this majority, freedom was said to reign. Freedom was thought to be under threat only when the collective will that individuals were forced to obey also included the will of the property-less classes.

Locke was chiefly concerned with the freedom of individuals to control production and to accumulate wealth. He knew that they could only do so insofar as they could rely upon the "united strength of the whole society to secure and defend their properties" (Locke 1980:23). The problem with the absolutist system of government that prevailed during Locke's lifetime was that it provided no (1980:48) guarantee of the right to accumulate to the heart's desire. This was why Locke considered this system of control to be arbitrary, and why he insisted that "arbitrary government" was "inconsistent with civil society". The fear always present in Locke's writings was that of abuses of power by governments. He thought it best to limit the power of government and prevent the lower classes from participating in politics. The main reason for the existence of government in the first place was to protect those with property from those that had none. If given the opportunity to have a say in matters of government, the property-less might use it mischievously. As I have explained above, this was the main reason why Hobbes had favored monarchy above democratic governance.

Locke (1980:73) insisted that the supreme power should never be allowed to "take from any man any part of his property without his own consent: for the preservation of property being the end of government, and that for which men enter society". Universal suffrage was unthinkable because it offered such a threat. It would certainly impinge upon the liberties championed by individualists. As far as Locke was concerned "the great and chief end...of men's uniting into commonwealths, and putting themselves under government, is the preservation of their property". What had been absent in the state of nature was "an established, settled known law" (Locke 1980:66).

Locke thought that the lower classes had no business in matters of government, but he did not state his feelings explicitly for fear of contradicting the notion of 'government by consent'. At the same time, Locke felt that property rights were too important to jeopardize, and protecting property meant the necessary exclusion of all but those with property from having any say in matters of government. Locke (1980:78) insisted that 'the people' must always have the right to "rid themselves of those, who invade this fundamental, sacred, and unalterable law of self-preservation, for which they entered into society". References to 'the people' enabled Locke to present the interests of his class as the interests of society generally. He managed to portray the inconveniences of his class as threats to the entire community, which to his mind, were everywhere. But in order to win people over to the individualist cause, he needed to be as inoffensive as possible. He also needed to avoid contradicting himself, which required a great deal of vagueness and political obscurantism.

Though Hobbes and Locke were different thinkers in many respects, the doctrines that they produced were underpinned by similar assumptions. Both helped create the individualist conception of society as a big market place in which "individuals related to each other as proprietors of their own capacities" (MacPherson 1962:3). Both depicted society as though it consisted simply of relations of exchange between proprietors, some of whom had only labor power to use in exchange. To them, society had no reality beyond the individuals that constituted it. They both considered that the proper role of government was that of creating an environment in which the individual was free to pursue individual interests without fear. It was thought best that all business remain free from state interference, such that healthy competition between individuals would continue. This was expected to produce greater freedom and happiness for all.

Though these thinkers did have different opinions with regard to what style of government would best facilitate peace, freedom and prosperity, their doctrines were deigned in accordance with the rule of capital in civil society. The individual freedom demanded by both Hobbes and Locke presupposed an environment in which those doing the actual productive work would be forced to alienate both their labor power and their liberty. They compromised all liberties that could be enjoyed universally for the sake of the exclusive freedoms bound up with ownership of property and the social power attached to it.

It is fair to say that Locke did not disagree with Hobbes' core political views. Both insisted that it is not the business of government to do more than endorse "laws which promote the skills which improve returns [and] laws by which idleness is prohibited [and] industry is stimulated" (Hobbes 1968:151). Locke treated the paternalist notion of distributive justice with as much contempt as Hobbes (1968:147), who had argued that "it is logical that those who equally enjoy the peace should pay equal shares".

It would be a mistake to treat Locke's individualism as though it represented a significant departure from that of Hobbes. The main difference between these thinkers was that, unlike Hobbes, Locke did not consider absolutist rule consistent with the long-term interests of the owners of moveable capital. He believed that a limited constitutional state would better facilitate peace, freedom and prosperity (MacPherson 1980:vii). Nevertheless, Hobbes and Locke advocated systems of social organization, along with attendant principles, that were almost identical. Their conception of freedom was built around the set of rules and institutions forcing people to alienate their own capacities to labor. Though it may not have been by conscious design the doctrines proffered by Hobbes and Locke were part of a wider effort to augment the economic control of the bourgeois class over the wider community. Their individualism was not advocacy of a social system in which all individuals would be free to realize their full potential. In fact the opposite is the case.

The relations and conditions characterizing early capitalism necessitated the formulation of individualist presuppositions, theories, arguments and values. In order for the market system to function, people needed to behave in a particular way, and that behavior needed to be rationalized. As such, an individualist morality developed concurrently with theories and doctrines. As I will explain in the following chapter, the degree of enthusiasm with which this morality was promoted depended on the conditions produced within the system.

In explaining individualist morality expressed in terms of responsibility, thrift, self-reliance, industry and so on, the following chapter identifies their promotion through Puritan religious doctrines, but also through the secularism promoted during the Enlightenment period. Though this morality is evident throughout Locke's works, it is necessary to set aside an entire chapter to explain the relationship between interests and the morality that comprise individualism. As such, the following pages will show how certain values serve to legitimate the policies designed to safeguard the wealth, power and prestige of the investing classes.

CHAPTER THREE

INDIVIDUALISM, RELIGION AND SCIENCE

The power relations underpinning capitalist market societies helped give rise to styles of moral thinking consistent with practices essential to capitalist accumulation. At a particular stage in the development of capitalist relations, people embraced the religious beliefs appropriate to these relations.[1] It is certainly the case that some of the religious ethics that emerged after the reformation were fitting with the interests of the owners of moveable capital. There are definite links between *later Calvinism*, for example, and the acquisitive behavior of capitalists, and to the set of values attendant to such behavior.

To acknowledge the existence of links between religious doctrine and acquisitive behavior does not mean accepting the argument that the latter was the offspring of the former, as Max Weber (1976) suggested in his famous work *The Protestant Ethic and the Spirit of Capitalism*. This conclusion was drawn from the Calvinist disapproval of instant gratification and their glorification of hard work. Weber thought that these principles created an environment in which wealth was no longer produced for immediate enjoyment but for the sake of reinvestment. Insofar as this was the case Weber (1976:53) thought that religious practice and doctrine had given shape to the 'capitalist spirit', and, by extension, the system of relations referred to as capitalism.

Though the explanation appears to make sense, the notion that Calvinism was the parent of capitalism cannot be taken for granted (Tawney 1948:212). Since the capitalist spirit involved little other than acquisitive behavior, an individualist morality and rationally planned accumulation, it was certainly older than any of the Puritan expressions. It was towards the end of the medieval period, that is to say, from the 15th century onwards, when it became apparent that new technologies and new relations of production could not be exploited in full under the

---

[1] Individualists do not deny that the perceived legitimacy of market system depends as much on values as it does on scientific arguments in its favor. Authors such as John Gray freely admit that the 'liberal' order has at times sought the support of religion (Gray 1986:x).

legal and moral restrictions of the old order, that such a spirit took hold. By the beginning of the 16th century, the body of moral rules limiting acquisitive behavior slowly began to unravel. With further development of bourgeois relations came a sophisticated bourgeois morality and a growing perception that prevailing church dogmas required refutation. The early reformers found that the best way to challenge church doctrine and authority was to suggest that all individuals were capable of interpreting the Bible for themselves.

The interpretation of God's will provided by established religious authorities was treated with greater and greater scepticism as the decades of the 16th century passed. This interpretation was no longer unanimously accepted as a guide on morality and immorality. By the second half of the 16th century, Calvinist thinkers, such as John Robinson, made sure of this by insisting that the evils of the church had in the past sprung from the governors, not the people. Robinson claimed that nothing "hath more in former days advanced, nor doth at this day uphold the throne of the Antichrist, than the people's discharging themselves of the care of public affairs in the church, on the one side: and the priests, and prelates arrogating all to themselves on the other side" (Ashton 1851:213).

The shift to Protestantism and the rise of capitalism were connected, according to Max Weber (1976:56), but not in the order that 'naive historical materialism' suggested. Weber insisted that the "origin and history of such ideas is much more complex than the theorists of the superstructure suppose". The approach offered by Weber, which was offered as an alternative to Marxism, presented particular religious ideas as the root of the modern spirit of capitalism. However, Weber's 'spiritual' reductionism served to obscure the simple fact that religion and society are interconnected. Instead, religion (Calvinism in particular) was treated as something that was almost independent of society, influencing people and altering their values, desires and behavior.

The idea that Puritanism produced the changes in thought and behavior that led to the emergence of the capitalist system has little foundation. There is more reason to believe that Puritanism was something fashioned by the existing social system. In the first place, Puritans were very diverse in their teachings. They were not all so concerned with religious democracy. They did not all hold to the notion of predestined salvation. Not all of them were completely preoccupied with hard work and frugality. But even if Puritans were as coherent and consistent as they appear in Weber's work, there is still no reason to believe that arguments relating to religious democracy, tolerance of different faiths, the glorification of hard work and frugal living, or attitudes toward the idle sections of the community, had their origin in the articles of faith advanced by Calvin, Robinson, Knox, Cartwright or Milton. The religious professions of belief singled out by Weber may have affected society to some extent, but they did so because they mutated over time. The doctrines thought to proceed from religion were shaped according to circumstances. Puritan ideas spread quickly in particular countries at particular times, and tended to correspond with the development of individualist thought and commercial behavior. This was very much the case in 17th and 18th century England, as Montesquieu noticed when he famously pointed out that the English "had progressed furthest of all peoples in three important things, piety, commerce and freedom" (Tawney 1948:xv). This progress did not necessarily follow in that sequence.

The thoroughness of the cycle of capitalist accumulation that was set in motion in England had more to do with the fact that it was isolated from its rivals by the sea than with religion. In England it was possible to create a safe environment in which people were free to associate with, or do business with, whomever they wished. This relative freedom facilitated the cross-fertilization of ideas, which was necessary for further scientific and technological development. It also made possible the application of modern scientific methods to production, which generated profit, and thereafter inserted a profit motive into behavior and thought. This was aided of course by Puritanism. But early commerce and the freedom underpinning modern scientific enquiry offered a spark much brighter than that of any religious conviction. But even so, to assume the modern capitalist accumulative cycle has a cause will always require an overstatement of the importance of one of the conditions underpinning it. To suggest a cause is simply to choose, in an arbitrary manner, some factor presenting at a certain point in history, and to claim that it represents the beginning. Weber's thesis rested upon such an arbitrary point. He implied that the modern capitalist system began with Puritanism and ignored the fact that the system advanced by puritan ethics existed already and on a significant scale in Medieval Italy and Flanders (Tawney 1948:84).

The accumulative cycle was advanced greatly with the employment of rational methods of doing business. The system needed a code of morality that would sanction a rational approach to acquisitive behavior. As such, the religious beliefs that evolved with the free cities were such that usury and avarice were no longer regarded as sinful. The Calvinists of course, being the creed of early urban people, knowing no other way of life than the commercial, could not help but view credit and capital as indispensable. So, unlike the medieval clergy, they did not regard financiers as evil. Such people could not be considered sinners because they were indispensable for the proper functioning of the society in which Calvin and later Calvinism emerged. The acceptance of the realities of commercial practice as a starting-point was of great importance. The values arising from the religious teachings of a belief system that had begun with an acceptance of basic capitalist relations could not but aid the development of bourgeois values (Tawney 1948:108).

Puritan values took hold at a time when the advances in methods of production had the effect of clearing large numbers of people from the land and of concentrating people in urban areas. The Calvinists formed their opinions in an environment where people were detached from the land and where those with no capital had to sell their labor power to those that had. The *later* Calvinists dealt with by Weber, had found the capitalist spirit already in existence. Since they had established a tradition of free enquiry into religious matters, they were in a position to organize their religious doctrines and practices around the individualist ethos that was emerging. These doctrines grew up precisely in locations where the accumulative cycle was in full swing. Those already possessed with the capitalist (individualist) spirit found in Calvinism, as R.H. Tawney (1948:226–227) put it, "a tonic, which braced its energies and fortified its already vigorous temper".

It is certainly the case that the particular religious convictions identified by Weber did help to develop the attitudes and habits necessary for the development of bourgeois society. Most would agree that since the Protestant beliefs encouraged reinvestment and helped produce a sober and subservient laboring class, they facilitated accumulation. But while it may be true that Puritanism helped shape the social order, it was also itself colored by the social relations characterizing that order (Tawney 1948:xix). There was a reciprocal relationship between Calvinism and the values conducive to capital accumulation. Taking the example of England, it is clear that Puritan values did not just emerge across the country in a random manner, but took hold precisely in areas where textile and other industries were developing (i.e., in the clothing towns). As Tawney (1948:204) pointed out, the industrial towns rose up like "Puritan islands from the surrounding sea of Roman Catholicism".

That Puritanism emerged in the 16th century was no coincidence. In previous centuries there was not a great source of labor power cut free from the duties and obligations of feudal society. It had not always been possible to treat labor as a simple commodity. The development of a rational means to organize that labor, made it possible for the owners of productive enterprises to profit on a rational and continuous basis through the exploitation of those who had nothing to sell but their labor power. The ability to organize formally free labor into a productive force was an important factor in itself. If not for the presence of a laboring class there could be no bourgeois class, no sale of labor as a commodity, and therefore no modern capitalist system (Weber 1976:21–22).

As the bulk of the independent crafts people and those employed in cottage industries were eliminated, production and trading became large-scale. It was when production and trade became continuous and well organized that the manufacturers and merchants began, as Weber explained, "to acquire an inner cohesion" and began to form branch organizations (Weber 1976:19).

As productive enterprises became larger, they were organized on a rational scientific basis, with the division of labor most likely to maximize profits. The investors' adherence, both to good scientific practice and to their own Puritan values, was entirely consistent with the necessary "rational utilisation of capital in a permanent enterprise and the rational capitalistic organisation of labor" (Weber 1976:58). As business became continuous, sales and reinvestment were planned rationally. Everything became a matter of checks and balances, and rational book keeping became an intrinsic part of productive enterprises thereafter (Weber 1976:22).

While Weber recognized the importance of science and technology as well as that of prevailing economic conditions and/or class relations, these were considered less important than were the enabling properties of Puritanism and the Protestant ethic generally. He recognized this while occasionally acknowledging that religion in itself appears to be the result of economic conditions. But for the most part he emphasized the impact of religion on thought and behavior, while paying little attention to the context in which religious life takes shape. In his attempts to avoid 'economic determinism', Weber (1976:36) ended up treating religion as a force that contributed significantly to the emancipation of the bourgeois class from economic traditionalism. He did not think it was sufficient to simply say that Puritan ideas were consistent with capitalistic enterprise; he was sure that they had caused it. He dismissed the 'theorists of the superstructure' only to construct a base/super-structure model of his own. Weber's base was the Protestant ethic and his superstructure was capitalism. Against his anti-determinist claims, Weber thought it possible to reduce social being to religious roots. He was convinced that asceticism and industry were turned into virtues through religious practice. Insofar as these were particularly strong in Calvinism, Weber thought that Calvinism had caused acquisitive behavior and the subsequent accumulative cycle.

Weber was rightly criticized by Tawney for treating Calvinism as more unique than it was, and for exaggerating its stability and consistency. A great deal of Weber's evidence was taken from a late phase in the history of the movement, and little attention was paid to the profound changes through which Calvinism passed in the century following the death of Calvin (Tawney 1948:xvi). Weber did not like to admit that these changes might have been in response to new methods of attaining wealth, or that religious doctrines might be shaped according to new expectations. The political doctrines advanced by the bourgeois class in the 17th century certainly had little to do with the body of ideas promoted by Calvin. Calvin had denied toleration of non-conformists. He repudiated the doctrine of separation of church and state. He rejected democracy in church organization, along with the notion that the people had the right to revolt against unjust rulers (Wolfe 1941:11).

The positions and principles advanced by those following Calvin's example were abandoned as the circumstances required. Puritans such as John Knox, for example, insisted on the right of the people in the interest of their religion to overthrow the existing government. When Queen Mary asked Knox's opinion on the matter of subjects resisting their princes, he replied: "If Princes do exceed their bounds, Madame, and do against that wherefore they should be obeyed, there is no doubt that they may be resisted, even by power… [T]o take the sword from them, to binde their hands, and to cast them into prison, till that they be brought to a more sober minde, is no disobedience against Princes, but just obedience, because it agreeth with the Word of God".[2]

---

[2] This quote is taken from D.M. Wolfe's *Milton in the Puritan Revolution* (Wolfe 1941:11).

Since the religious ideas of the older social order were inconsistent with the new level of expectation, it became convenient for individualistic minded people to revise their religious belief system. So, as the capitalist market system took root, attitudes to usury underwent change. Attitudes toward acquisitive behavior changed. Attitudes toward the poor changed. They changed as quickly as the rising class became conscious of its interests as a class. Thereafter, the established Christian values could no longer be relied upon as a guide to ethical practice in economic life, especially if a negative attitude toward capitalistic accumulation was expressed. Insofar as it stood in the way of 'the potentialities revealed by the new spirit', the existing religious world-view needed to be replaced with another. The owners of capital abandoned the established church and embraced those religious beliefs that were consistent with the capitalist spirit. Thereafter, they began the necessary task of transforming the whole culture to suit the new potentialities and demands (Laski 1936:23).

Puritan ideas held sway at a time when it was considered more important to present the kind of activity related to continuous acquisition and reinvestment of wealth as pleasing to God. In order to create this impression, representatives of bourgeois interests began the task of transforming God from a philanthropic feudal aristocrat into an advocate of unbridled acquisition. They did this through the religious denominations to which they belonged. The propertied classes may not have been aware that God was changing his politics to suit them since their God was a product of their politics. As Bertrand Russell (2001:84–85) once explained, "the man whose muscles are taut believes in a God of action, while the man whose muscles are relaxed believes in a God of thought and contemplation".

Spiritual and Materialist Explanations

According to Weber it was Calvinism that generated the inner loneliness, which drove individuals out of communities. It was the Calvinist creed that left it up to each individual to interpret God's will and understand the word of God by looking into his own heart (Weber 1976:104). Catholics had priests interpreting the Bible for them, but Protestants were simply given a Bible and told to read and interpret it alone. It may be argued that that this was the method promoted by Protestants rather than Protestantism per se. It suited the bourgeois individualists to look deep into their own capitalist hearts in order to find the will of God. This allowed for the interests of the individual to determine God's will. It was adapted to whatever the faithful individual regarded to be a pious life, which, for the investing classes meant industry and frugality.

It was not Protestantism that pushed individuals outside of community life and freed them from the values of the wider community, but the individualist ethic that the value system was constructed around. As the capitalist market economy developed, particularly in the decades after the bourgeois revolution in England, it required a philosophy that would justify self-seeking and acquisitive behavior. This demand gave rise to the new theories about human nature which came to characterize classical liberalism, along with related values. These values, with which emerging religious beliefs were imbued, eventually eclipsed the prevailing paternalist ethic (Hunt 1995:26–30). Those that valued self-reliance managed to extend their morality into the consciousness of the wider community through Protestantism. It was in consequence of the prevailing individualism that Protestants were not provided with priests to save them from themselves. All that remained for them to do was to organize their whole lives according to what they understood to be pious principles (Weber 1976:109). Of course they found it much easier to organize their principles around the way in which they conducted their lives. But this was the whole point.

Weber (1976:121) focused on Calvinism in particular because it seemed to be all about "proving one's faith in worldly activity". Those that did not appear to engage themselves fully in work of some kind were thereafter treated as sinners. This was the case with the wealthy as well as the poor. Those that worked hard pleased God. Each individual was encouraged to pursue whatever it was that they understood to be their 'calling' and to plan their lives rationally in accordance with God's will. Within the Protestant creed generally, there was room for major reorganization of values. That which became virtue and that which became sin would all depend on the sectional interests underpinning restless industry. As such, hard work and frugality were thought to please God and idleness was displeasing to Him. Though the wealthy could easily avoid working hard in order to live, the Calvinist ethic discouraged them from wasting time in idleness and from indulging in vulgar displays of wealth. They were obliged to organize their lives according to God's wishes also. They decided that the best way to serve God was to follow their own particular 'calling', which involved the reinvestment of their profit in labor power, in improved means of production and the pursuit of increased profits thereafter.

All of the faithful were encouraged to be industrious, but not in order to enjoy the benefits that came their way as a result. The Calvinists did not accumulate great wealth in order to live like lords. That would be sinful. But accumulation was in no way sinful where the intention was to reinvest wealth rather than squander it foolishly. Since God had intended everything to be made use of, the owners of property were thought to have a duty to their possessions. The greater the possessions the greater became the responsibility to put them into circulation, increase them, and repeat the process again. The capitalist system found its ethical foundation in the ethic of ascetic Protestantism, but did not grow out of this ethical foundation in the manner that Weber (1976:171) suggested.

Puritanism did not produce aestheticism or the work ethic associated with it. It did not create the impression that idleness displeased God or that hard work pleased Him. It did not give rise to the notion that poverty was the result of immorality. Some of the early Puritans were little concerned with the features ascribed to Puritanism by Weber. Leonard Busher, for example, was mostly concerned to put an end to religious persecution. He hoped that some day it would be lawful "for every person or persons, yea, Jews and papists, to write, dispute, confer and reason, print and publish any matter touching religion, either for or against whomsoever". Not only would such freedom put a stop to burning and hanging for the sake of religious differences, in Busher's view, it would also put an end to the need for executions for theft, or oppression of the poor "by usury and little wages... Then shall the poor, lame, sick, and weak ones, be stocked and whipped; neither shall the poor, stranger, fatherless, and widows be driven to beg from place to place".[3]

The idea of wealth for its own sake was not a Puritan invention; it was something that was adopted by them. As Laski (1936:21) has pointed out "the capitalist spirit was present in men like St. Godric or Jacques Coeur or the Florentine bankers long before the end of the fifteenth century". Though Weber denied that it was his intention, his thesis rested on a spiritual determinism. He spoke of asceticism as though it was a product of, rather than something adopted by, particular religious

---

[3] Quoted in Wolfe's *Milton in the Puritan Revolution* (Wolfe 1941:27–28).

practices. It did not occur to him that the propertied classes might have introduced the values relating to abstinence and self-discipline into their particular set of religious beliefs. Weber did not draw sufficient attention to the cross contamination between religious, social, political and economic developments. As was the case with law, he treated religion as though it was free-floating and autonomous, as though it was something apart from society. He drew little attention to religion as a means of bringing morality into line with capitalistic behavior. Weber believed that religion came into being in an independent manner. He didn't wish to explain how or why it took particular forms in particular political, economic and social circumstances, or why particular forms correspond with particular levels of technological development. What he did was create the impression that religion was the source of asceticism, which he claimed, "was in turn influenced in its development and its character by the totality of social conditions, especially economic" (Weber 1976:183).

Religious asceticism had as much to do with the interests of bourgeois individualists, as it had to do with the various religious creeds adopted and developed by them. The Calvinist ethic benefited the owners of capital in two ways. It allowed them to engage themselves in the pursuit of ever-increasing profit without being overly burdened with any crises of conscience. And, as Weber (1976:177) pointed out, it provided those that invested their money with "sober, conscientious, and usually industrious workmen".

Once frugality and industry were promoted as the highest of virtues, more people began to live their lives in accordance with them. Those with wealth consumed far less than they had the means to. The subsequent reduction in personal consumption served to facilitate reinvestment. Of course this virtue of frugality, along with the virtues associated with hard work and industry, were entirely in keeping with the long term interests of the propertied classes.

Once accumulative behavior was coupled with the ethical compulsion to save, a relentless accumulative cycle came into being and profits began to self-perpetuate (Weber 1976:172–176). When industriousness and frugality are successfully promoted at the same time, this must be the result, but this does not mean that the 'spirit of capitalism' sparked off the accumulative tendencies in the first place. It is more likely that later Calvinism took the features of a commercial civilization for granted. The delayed gratification necessary for any start-up business found its rationale in the creed that was shaped by the petit-bourgeois entrepreneur.

Insofar as Weber considered religion to be of central importance, his explanation of the emergence of the capitalist system was welcomed as an alternative to Marx's explanation. Though Weber may have highlighted factors neglected by many Marxists, these factors were not avoided for the sake of Marxist analysis, which in this case does not simply require attention to class antagonisms, the development of technological knowledge, the subsequent development of the forces of production and its effect on economic life. It also requires attention to developments in the realm of culture, such as the advancement of religious asceticism and related values (Sherman 1995).

The body of ideas constituting Weber's 'spirit of capitalism' did not emerge in a vacuum. The spirit of capitalism was not the product of some force outside of society moulding individual thought and action. It was a product of society, which remade society in turn and was itself refashioned. Puritanism provided the scope for individualists to legitimate the behavior necessary for the capitalist market order to develop, while at the same time moulding individual characters to suit. The moral precepts involved were such that the victims produced by the market could be blamed for the conditions in which they found themselves. Puritans helped create the impression that vice was the cause rather than the result of poverty. However, the spirit of capitalism cannot be attributed to the influence of Calvin, who had no intention of relaxing the moral dogmas governing economic transactions and social relations (Tawney 1948:85). Instead, the fact that later Calvinists justified acquisitive behavior is evidence only that the capitalist spirit was spreading across society. There is no reason to presume that Puritanism was the cause of the major social transformation that followed. Puritanism is far better understood if it is recognized as being rooted in capital accumulation, as a moral expression of individualist thought. It involves ways of thinking that provide a rationale for the conduct of business within the confines of a modern capitalist system.

Individualism and the Enlightenment Tradition

The above discussion concerns the development of individualism within expressions of religious belief. It must be remembered, however, that individualist ideas were also developed by people struggling against the influence of religion. In some cases these ideas emerged from the continued conflict between religious and scientific thinking. To explain such development it is worth examining some of the Scottish and French

Enlightenment thinkers of the 18th century. As with the bourgeois
Puritans, many Enlightenment thinkers recognized the potentialities of
the new system that was emerging. They realized that further development required more than an appropriate morality. The development of
the free contract society required the right to free speech, association,
property and an end to arbitrary rule. Realizing such goals would involve
a relentless attack on the intellectual and moral basis of the prevailing
institutions, beginning in the 17th century, through most of the 18th.
The intellectual movement commonly referred to as the Enlightenment
was bound up with (though not limited to) such concerns. The reason
why it is usually spoken of in the same breath as the French revolution
of 1789 is that both emerged alongside popular opposition, in the 18th
century, to the cruelty of 'unenlightened' rulers. Both the revolutionaries
and the Enlightenment theoreticians that came to prominence during
this period were concerned with the consequences of arbitrary rule and
religious intolerance. Enlightenment thinkers were driven by the desire
to put certain freedoms in their stead.

Science and Freedom

The various thinkers agitating for social and intellectual revolution
in the late 17th and 18th centuries were in no way bound together
according to one ideal or vision of how society should be organized.
They had different ideas with regard to the best form of government
and what role government should play beyond the task of maintaining
order. However, there was broad agreement on the issue of religious
intolerance and intolerance towards minorities.

There were different reasons why greater tolerance was demanded. It
was not always simply for the sake of common humanitarian concerns.
Thinkers such as Voltaire believed internal peace and stability to be
essential for the economic development of nations. He was sure that the
main effect of religious and political persecution was that of enriching
neighboring countries at the expense of one's own (Laski 1936:175).

The Enlightenment was as much about science as it was about freedom. From the 17th century onwards, a fundamental distinction was
made between modern and traditional, rational and irrational, scientific and superstitious styles of thought. The former in each case was
thought to fall into the broad body of 'enlightened' thought, while the
latter was considered 'unenlightened'. Though the resulting distinctions

may not always be fair or accurate, it is this dichotomy into which styles of thinking and world-views have been categorized ever since. 20th century thinkers, such as Bertrand Russell (2001:52) for example, have advocated clear demarcations between scientific ideas (based on evidence) and unscientific ideas (those depending on hopes, desires and/or unquestioned authority).

The shift away from religion and religious doctrines during this period was unsettling for the church. The calls for an end to tyranny and for human emancipation were often accompanied by attacks on paternalism, which was considered inconsistent with independence and even individual reason. Locke, for example, thought that all men "except lunatics and idiots" should be free of parental authority. Individuals did not need to be subject to paternal or parental power. He thought that the existence of a paternal power discouraged individuals from employing their own reason in the conduct of their own affairs. As far as Locke was concerned, paternal power was the same as the power that parents have over their children. Parents govern children for their own good until such time as they come to the age of reason (MacPherson 1962:244).

Locke's conception of Enlightenment is best understood in light of this opposition to paternalism. He agreed fully with Immanuel Kant's (1963:3) suggestion that:

> Enlightenment is man's release from self-incurred tutelage. Tutelage is man's inability to make use of his understanding without direction from another. Self-incurred is this tutelage when its cause lies not in lack of reason but in the lack of resolution and courage to use it without direction from another. Sapare aude! Have courage to use your own reason!—That is the motto of Enlightenment.

The Enlightenment thinkers discovered that when science, reason and the idea of freedom were combined, the result was a critique that could serve to pull apart the old system of ideas. The authority of religion, along with the status relations to which it gave ideological support, was damaged further with every insight produced by the secular intelligentsia accompanying capitalist development.

Once modern science had developed to a certain level it could no longer be contained in accordance with the interests of the established church. It was eventually employed in the production of revolutionary ideas, which unsettled the religious authorities. Though there were certain exceptions (e.g., among the Jesuits), the established church generally supported absolutist rule and maintained a reactionary attitude to the ideas that emerged independently of the prevailing power structures. The Enlightenment thinkers knew this and did everything in their power to increase the pressure. This body of thinkers wished to create the space for a different world-view to prevail. They did this by, as Laski (1936:164) put it, "breaking into pieces the old self-confidence of its opponents".

Unlike the moderns before them, a significant number of Enlightenment thinkers engaged themselves in a conscious and relentless attack against existing sources of knowledge. They believed that progress would come once humankind understood that reason leads to truth and truth leads to freedom. They were not content to find alternatives to existing superstition and convention. They were determined to destroy all unenlightened thinking (existing interpretations), which they considered detrimental not only to human freedom but to the common good.

If the Enlightenment thinkers believed that man's intellectual capacities were the key to human emancipation, the individualists among them, such as Voltaire, wished only the propertied classes to use such capacities. Voltaire did not trust the laboring classes, since they were considered the source of all fanaticism and superstition (Laski 1936:214–215). He thought that if the laboring classes had the opportunity to do so they would destroy all freedom. But in spite of his mistrust and scarcely veiled contempt for the common people, he did everything he could to promote the idea that universal progress in knowledge, freedom and conditions of life was on the way.

The last thing that the investing classes wanted was an educated laboring class demanding a share of control over resources, or one that saw the necessity of engaging itself in theoretically informed action in order to realize collective goals. It is well known that Voltaire had favored the prohibition of educational studies for working men. "On my land", he wrote, "I want laborers and not tonsured clerics" (Laski 1936:215). The reproduction of ignorance among the property-less would always be necessary. If the laboring classes were to realize that they had minds of their own they might be less inclined to perform the labor necessary for the private gain of investors. Voltaire was sure that workers would not exert themselves sufficiently unless they were maintained at subsistence level. He thought that popular Enlightenment would interfere with the interests of the rising class and that all hopes for the development of a social system attendant to those interests would be lost if ordinary people were permitted to meddle in argument (Laski 1936:215).

Theory, Reason and Practice

During the Enlightenment period, theoretical and practical agitation for freedom became one and the same (Blair-Bolles 1997:250). Thinkers such as Voltaire linked science and freedom together, believing that the former offered the means of developing theoretically informed action. Towards the end of the 18th century, there was a relentless demand for freedom of speech, the press and assembly. In England, bourgeois control was realized through putting power in the hands of elected representatives. The electorate consisted of men with property and the government was made responsive to their choices. To make their choices effective, it was necessary to grant broader liberties, which, as MacPherson (1966:8) pointed out, "had to be demanded in principle for everyone".

The development of Enlightenment thought had much to do with the historical context and related conditions experienced by each theoretician involved. Many were only too aware that they were reacting to the environment in which they found themselves. They began to think that if there was to be progress of any sort, existing doctrines based on myth and superstition would need to be discredited. The Enlightenment figures were sure that freedom, tolerance, security of life and property, were the conditions that would lead to a better and brighter future. The production of new knowledge that challenged prevailing dogmas was celebrated by Immanuel Kant, who considered the Enlightenment to be "man's final coming of age". It amounted to the "emancipation of the human consciousness from an immature state of ignorance and error".[4]

It must be remembered that the Enlightenment became a possibility only because those involved had been armed with the methods of reasoning previously developed by modern scientists such as Newton and Descartes. According to Toulmin (1990:9), it was these thinkers that committed the modern world to thinking about nature in a "scientific" way, and to use more "rational" methods to deal with the problems of human life and society. What was new and unique about the Enlightenment period was the link forged therein between science and freedom (Blair-Bolles 1997:250). Scientific theories of man were

---

[4] This quote is taken from Roy Porter's *Studies in European History: The Enlightenment* (Porter 1990:1).

offered in the place of 'unenlightened ideas', which were regarded as the source of all oppression and misery in the world.

Popular Enlightenment and Political Satire

The development of Enlightenment thought was related to the emergence of new material conditions of life, which gave rise to new economic, social and political relationships, all of which required a legitimating ideology. Insofar as religion failed to provide enough justification for the new system of relations that was developing, science became the means of doing so. It also provided a yardstick with which the bourgeois could measure other styles of thinking. It enabled critics such as Voltaire to show that the philosophical and religious ideas of 18th century France were completely groundless. Of course, Voltaire did not attack the existing belief system only in his political writings. He also did this in his plays and novels, perhaps most famously in his satirical work *Candide*. In this particular work the church was also subject to an intense criticism. Like many thinkers of the day, Voltaire (1818:397) believed that behind the misfortunes and calamities of the day, one would always find religious zealots or a passionate religious commitment of some sort. It followed from this reasoning that in order to escape such misfortune humankind would need to undermine the power of the church. In order to explain the consequences of superstition and intolerance Voltaire had *Candide* (the main character in his novel of the same name) travel through lands where church authority was either present or absent. While travelling through South America, Candide ended up in what seemed to be a perfect community, situated in a place called Eldorado. He wondered why there were no priests to be found in this unusual place, but later found out that in Eldorado *all* were priests. It only seemed that there were no priests because there was none performing the role of priest by social function. The people did not pray because they had nothing to pray for. Candide was so astonished by this that he went to find answers from the oldest and wisest man he could find. As he conversed with the wise old man he was bewildered even further. "Do you mean to say" asked Candide, "that you have no monks teaching and disputing, governing and intriguing, and having people burned if they don't subscribe to their opinions?" The man replied "We should be stupid if we had" (Voltaire 1947:80).

This satire was in part directed against intolerant religious authorities and religious fanaticism. Ridicule and criticism were as much a part of the Enlightenment project as was science. The French *philosophes* reasoned that if existing ideas and existing institutions were sufficiently ridiculed and discredited, the authority enjoyed by them would eventually be undermined.

The specific targeting of the religious establishment was understandable, especially given that the legal injustices of the day depended on the moral authority of the established church. Voltaire and others understood this well and put much of their energies into attacking what they saw as the main causes of humankind's misfortunes.

Voltaire had a particular distaste for arbitrary government and religious intolerance, but he did not wish to put an end to class domination and corresponding state repression. He did not favor broad democratic participation and generally opposed attempts to create a more egalitarian kind of society. Voltaire thought that it was important to ensure that the property-less remained governed by religious sentiment. Religion would always be necessary, he insisted, "if the rich are not to be murdered in their beds" (Laski 1936:213). The replacement of religious interpretation with scientific analysis was necessary for the purposes of good government, but the laboring classes would still need to be guided by superiors. Voltaire wished to secure the intellectual dominance of the rising class. This meant destroying the credibility of those that stood in their way. It did not mean popular Enlightenment.

The bourgeois class was opposed to certain aspects of religious authority, but not religious authority generally. They could not allow religion to interfere with opportunities to accumulate, but as the fear expressed above by Voltaire suggests, religion would still be necessary to keep the working classes in their place. Religion offered hope of future salvation to the property-less, as Laski explained, "on condition that they were orderly, hard-working, and well-behaved". For the owners of capital "religion became a private matter between the citizen and his God or church; for the poor, it became an institution with the social context of necessity for public order" (Laski 1936:171). The Enlightenment thinkers were sure that a better order was about to emerge and did everything in their power to speed up the process. Voltaire saw that the way to do this was to argue against intolerance, to ridicule superstitious thinking, which provided a rationale for related practices, and to introduce British empiricism into French intellectual life (Laski 1936:251–257).

Visions of the Good Society

Although Voltaire may have challenged many of the established ideas of his day, he accepted many others. Unlike other Enlightenment thinkers, such as Rousseau, he bought into the general assumption that inequality was both natural and inevitable. Though he thought it possible for society to be less cruel and intolerant than it was, Voltaire (1818:363–364) believed that 'natural inequality' could never be avoided, and so it had to be accepted.

During the Enlightenment period, conceptions of freedom and liberty differed according to the interests of different parties across society, just as they do today. The rising class conceived of freedom in a manner consistent with their loathing of the trade restrictions that directly affected them. In the run up to the French revolution this discontent was translated into harsh criticisms of the existing system. However, it was not only bourgeois revolutionaries and their ideological wing that rallied against the inefficiencies and against the injustices that were characteristic of the old system. Excepting those that benefited, most people wanted change, even if their motives varied. People were united only in the conviction that things had to change. There was no one vision as to what form the new society should take.

Through the promotion of scientific speculation, Enlightenment theoreticians generated new hope that true understanding of people and society was possible. It was assumed that upon such understanding the foundations for a better world would be laid (Porter 1990:3). It was held that humankind was heading for better things. It was thought theoretically possible to remake society in such a manner that would guarantee the greatest happiness and freedom for all. Enlightenment thinkers forwarded doctrines of human perfectibility; some of the key thinkers, such as Marquis de Condorcet, proposed plans as to how the lot of humankind could be ameliorated in the immediate term. Like many other thinkers of the day, Condorcet did not believe that 'human nature' would prevent the achievement of a society in which the problems faced by humanity would be solved. The abolition of war, tyranny, and intolerance was considered entirely possible. Likewise, the English thinker William Godwin entertained the idea that conditions of life could be continuously improved purely through the exercise of reason (Gray 1986:18).

The French revolution was of course a *bourgeois* revolution. However, it must be said that the bourgeois revolutionaries were at this time a group existing among, and only partly in control of, the oppressed layers of French society. While it cannot be denied that the bourgeois revolutionaries played a leading role in both movements, it is necessary to recognize that these were not the only agents involved. They were, however, predominant in terms of propaganda, which is partly the reason why Marxists thinkers have tended to depict the Enlightenment as the manifesto of the "bourgeois struggle against aristocratic feudalism" (Porter 1990:42). They knew that this struggle constituted a wider effort within which the expression of bourgeois class interests was only a part. The lower classes despised the inhumanity of the old regime just as the bourgeois class did. In order for the revolution itself to succeed it was necessary to have peasants and laborers on side. To this end, it was necessary to create the impression that the propertied classes, in pursuing their own interests, were also pursuing the interests of the nation and freedom for all persons (Laski 1936:208). Of course when the propertied classes said the words 'freedom' or 'liberty' it was always in reference to a liberal regime of property ownership operating under the protection of the state.

Insofar as the church had failed to offer new values to suit the new set of power relations, the owners of moveable capital gave their support to a new generation of philosophers and religious leaders, especially those with a respectful attitude toward individual property. Voltaire was especially prized because he promoted necessary bourgeois virtues such as thrift, prudence and enterprise. Likewise, the freedom championed by Voltaire appealed to the propertied classes because it was a freedom designed to facilitate the above qualities (Laski 1936:170).

Enlightenment critique was forwarded in such a way as to have the broadest appeal possible. The bourgeois criticisms emerged amid a much greater wave of opinion and bourgeois opposition to trade restrictions existed amid wider discontent with the existing social, political and economic circumstances.

The Intervention of Rousseau

While the development of bourgeois society was unrestricted after the revolution, to view the Enlightenment as a bourgeois project is to downplay the diversity that existed. The agitation that enabled the bourgeois class to take control of the state was not in every case agitation *for* a bourgeois society. The well-known Enlightenment thinker,

Jean-Jacques Rousseau, promoted a set of freedoms that were totally inconsistent with bourgeois control over the wider community. Rousseau contested all those freedoms that infringed upon the freedom of the majority of people.

Unlike Voltaire, Rousseau did not think that the problems faced by humanity were caused by religious fanaticism and intolerance. He was certain that the happiness of humankind depended on the realization of a more egalitarian distribution of wealth. Human misery stemmed from the social order and not from wickedness or fanaticism. Rousseau famously claimed that:

> if men are wicked it is because bad upbringing and environment have corrupted them. It is bad social arrangements, unjust laws, despotic governments, that cause evil. Man is by nature good. If he were not corrupted by bad conditions, his natural goodness would out and make for a free society based on equality and justice.[5]

In saying as much, Rousseau was attacking not only the ideas of the ruling authorities, but the general assumption that inequality was natural and necessary. Such sentiments contrasted in a fundamental way to those of other Enlightenment theoreticians, such as Voltaire, who was far more concerned with highlighting the incompatibility between the discipline of the church and 'national prosperity'.

During the Enlightenment there was a long debate running between Voltaire and Rousseau about human nature and the problem of inequality. Rousseau was particularly concerned to reverse the individualist notion that people were inherently selfish and aggressive. He wished to show that inequality injured society as a whole. Voltaire, on the other hand, wished to show that equality would "injure property and destroy all industry" (Laski 1936:216). He believed that the laborer and the artisan "must be cut down to necessaries, if they are to work: this is human nature. It is inevitable that the majority should be poor; it is only not necessary that it should be wretched" (Laski 1936:222).

That Rousseau perceived the cause of wickedness to be 'bad social arrangements' meant that he was advocating not only the replacement of existing authority with a more humane system, but social revolution also. As far as Rousseau (1998:5) was concerned, the relations and conditions that led to inequality were based on nothing other than convention. For him, the fact that the lower classes accepted their

---

[5] This quote is taken from D. Thomson's *Political Ideas* (Thomson 1969:102).

position in life proved nothing other than their acceptance of convention. The compliance on the part of oppressed people, such as slaves, was for Rousseau the effect rather than the cause of the master-slave relation. As Rousseau (1998:7) put it, "slaves lose everything in their bonds, even the desire to escape from them".

Rousseau by no means bought into the individualist conception of freedom that was promoted by other Enlightenment thinkers. What he sought was the maximum individual liberty possible within political society. Insofar as he believed liberty to require equality of power and condition, he regarded the freedoms promoted by the bourgeois individualists as insufficient. As he saw it, the freedom demanded by the propertied classes depended for the most part on the slavery of the masses. On this basis he insisted that "the right which every individual has over his own property is always subordinate to the right which the community has over all" (Rousseau 1998:23).

Rousseau believed that property rights should never be allowed to override rights related to the preservation and good of society generally. He believed that the good of society as a whole, and the maintenance of civil liberties therein, were more important than the particular interests and related liberties of the bourgeois class. He recognized that perceived freedoms are always in conflict with one another. The unlimited freedom of one, such as in a monarchy, is based on the servitude of all. In the same sense, the unlimited freedom of one class is bound to impinge on the freedom of the lower classes. Freedom, like wealth, must either be shared around or it must remain the privilege of a select few.

Voltaire's Individualism

The freedom that Voltaire insisted upon was very different from that of Rousseau. It required that those with a store of capital, or land, must remain free to do with it what they wished. The individual owner must have, Voltaire insisted, "the powers of a king to use or abuse at his discretion". This was justified on the basis that "if the government deals with abuses of property, it will not be slow to deal with its uses as well. When that happens, there is an end to any true notion of property or liberty" (Laski 1936:217). The bourgeois class realized that in order to maintain control over resources, workers would have to be forbidden to strike. After the French revolution the government took measures to prevent the laboring classes from organizing. These were similar to the British Combination Acts of 1749–1800 (Laski 1936:229). The laboring classes could not be allowed to vent their strength, nor could they be allowed to have a say in the running of the new system.

Though Voltaire may have said that "man" should be free to comment upon public affairs, he considered private property to be a totally private affair. Therefore, the affairs of the country should be left to those that owned it. With regard to free speech, he believed that the masses ought to go unhindered, but thought that they should not be free to say things that were inappropriate. As Laski explained, the laboring classes would enjoy free speech so long as they said nothing radically different to "the kind of thing a stout bourgeois, whether in business or, like Voltaire, in letters, is accustomed to say" (Laski 1936:172).

The Enlightenment theoreticians all wanted the freedom denied them under the Church and 'unenlightened monarchs' (they were not necessarily opposed to absolute monarchy as such). But, as Laski (1936:165) pointed out, they had not arrived at any consensus about "what freedom is for, and upon what principles its limits are to be traced". Of course for Locke and Voltaire it was fairly simple. Freedom was treated as a function of property. It could only exist beside the force of the state and under the rule of law. Locke insisted that we are only free if we are free to compete against one another. As such, no one could champion freedom without accepting the inequalities that result. If persons were to be free they had to be free to be unequal. Inequality was accepted as the price that had to be paid for freedom. Individualists did not like to admit that their freedom was a measure of the social power that results from the concentration of wealth and the tendency thereafter for one group's freedom to infringe upon the freedom of others. They could not acknowledge that if the portion of the population that sells itself to another in order to survive is considered free, then their 'freedom' is really a synonym for economic domination. Though Voltaire, Locke and others may have entertained the above conception of freedom, Rousseau certainly did not. For Rousseau (1998:97), people can be free only at the expense of others. Therefore, the citizen cannot be completely free except when the slave is enslaved to the utmost.

The Development of Individualism

The Enlightenment can be regarded as a tradition only insofar as 'tradition' refers to opposition on the part of Enlightenment thinkers to prevailing conditions and relations. It was precisely the opposition to the excesses of 18th century monarchs that brought diverse groups of political antagonists and diverse styles of thought under one broad category, Enlightenment. Since unity existed only through opposition, that unity disappeared with the demise of the old order. Since there was no longer a common enemy to be vanquished, the various thinkers involved began to realize that they had little in common. Individualists took an uncritical view of the system that had emerged in the place of the old, whereas radical thinkers proposed that freedom needed to be extended to the laboring classes.

The diversity of views held by Enlightenment thinkers reflected the new interests that arose with further development of the capitalist system (Porter 1990:75). In spite of this diversity, there were some ideas that were shared by Enlightenment thinkers. For example, most of them believed that reason was the road to truth. Most of them believed that social progress and the emancipation of humankind could be realized scientifically. Enlightenment thinkers were sure that verifiable knowledge about the nature and needs of humankind was possible and that freedom could be attained through the proper application of humankind's rational capacities. They presumed that the best possible social system would be one that had been planned scientifically.

Those following in the individualist tradition put forward criticisms of authority in a selective manner, but this criticism ended when their immediate interests were realized. Individualists had found it necessary to entertain vague conceptions of freedom until the eve of revolution. This was necessary for the purposes of mobilizing bias against a political establishment that was perceived to be inhibiting the development of the market system. For the most part, bourgeois theoreticians reserved their greatest criticism for the economic restrictions suffered under the established order.

Individualist thinkers have been mainly concerned with the ideological maintenance of the relations underpinning the rule of capital. As such, once the bourgeois class had entrenched itself in power in England, France and elsewhere, and had established a code of law and tax structure that would ensure its continued control over the general population, individualist antagonists stopped producing subversive ideas. The theoretical contributions of subsequent generations were designed with the maintenance of bourgeois society in mind, not with revolutionary change.

The project of human emancipation through science and reason was not pursued further, at least not by the bourgeoisie after they had entrenched themselves in power. Insofar as capitalism was free to develop after the bourgeois revolution, individualists assumed that freedom had largely been achieved and opposed further emancipation on the grounds that it infringed upon the rights of the individual. The new ideologues had come to resemble the reactionaries they had displaced. Bourgeois individualists proved that they could be just as reactionary as those that had condemned them in the past. But as Lenin pointed out (over a century later), it has occurred more than once in history "that the conqueror took over the culture of the conquered".[6]

Under the banner of the Enlightenment there existed disparate groups of antagonists whose political views varied a great deal. That they have been lumped together is mostly for the convenience of modern analysts. Though some Enlightenment thinkers saw a need for greater equality of condition, some were concerned mainly with the removal of obstacles in the way of capitalist development. They did not think it necessary to ensure that all persons benefited from the wealth created in society. It was enough to ensure that all were formally free and had the same chance of growing rich as everyone else. It was presumed thereafter that society could not function unless some were rich and some were poor.

When dealt with in their historical contexts, the individualist doctrines expressed by Puritan and Enlightenment thinkers appear to have little to do with freeing people from control by collectives or the state. Instead, they appear to constitute part of a broader historical attempt to shape individual attitudes and behavior in accordance with the collective will of capitalism's investing classes.

---

[6] This quote is taken from Leon Trotsky's *Revolution Betrayed* (Trotsky 1972:99–100).

CHAPTER FOUR

THE THEORY OF POPULATION PRESSURE

As the capitalist system developed in the early 19th century, it became necessary to explain its observable consequences and to provide theoretical and moral justification for its advance. To this end, theories were developed that accounted for the human condition in terms of natural processes. The perceived necessity of cutting off services and provisions to the general population gave rise to appropriate doctrines. Among the most compelling theories serving such purposes was the principle of population, advanced by Thomas Robert Malthus. This theory explained poverty in terms of a supposed tendency on the part of all animated life to increase beyond the nourishment prepared for it (Malthus 1973a:5). The central idea was that all living creatures, including human beings, need subsistence to survive, but the capacity to subtract the means of subsistence from nature is finite; therefore, the number of human beings born into the world must have natural limits.

The principle of population drew upon established facts about existing levels of industry and the possibilities with regard to food production, and set this knowledge against population statistics. The difficulties faced by humankind were explained in terms of a "simple calculation applied to the known properties of land, and the proportion of births and deaths" (Malthus 1973b:26). Poverty was ever present because the means of subsistence increases arithmetically (1, 2, 3, 4) at best, while population is disposed to increase geometrically (1, 2, 4, 8). Once the number of people increased beyond the natural limits, a "surplus population" would emerge, bringing terrible consequences. Unless the production of a 'surplus population' was avoided by way of 'moral restraint,' population pressure would always give rise to positive checks such as famine and disease.

The main message that Malthus wished to convey was that there is a natural and inexorable tendency for populations to press hard against the means of subsistence. Though what Malthus had to say was not new, his theories were presented in such a manner as to give the appearance of mathematical certainty. The persuasive power of Malthus' thesis was, as D. Wells (1986:383) observed, due to the "apparent precision of his geometric ratio for population increase, contrasted to the arithmetic ratio for the growth of agricultural production".

Malthus (1973a:314) believed that subsistence determined the population of a country. "Corn countries," wrote Malthus, "are more populous than pasture countries, and rice countries more populous than corn countries". In every country, population increased right up to the limits of available food. As such, the growth in numbers of the settler population in North America was attributed to the abundance of food and space; of course, this space was afforded through the relocation and/or extermination of indigenous people (Wells 1986:382). The point was that wherever such favorable circumstances exist, pressure against the means of subsistence becomes negligible and population expands exponentially; it was set to double every twenty-five years (conditions permitting).

Once a country was well stocked, the population would come to realize that the ability of the land to yield means of subsistence was actually finite. They would discover that the *potential* increase in food would always be less than the *potential* increase in population. Until such time, the value of labor would remain high and the incentive to have large families constant. Adam Smith (1976:79), from whom Malthus borrowed a great deal, had already explained that, in North America, where labor was very well rewarded, "a numerous family of children, instead of being a burden is a source of opulence and prosperity to the parents". In such situations the prospect of having many children did not discourage marriage. On the contrary, where the value of children was recognized, it became "the greatest of all encouragements to marriage".

Both Smith and Malthus believed that if large families brought positive consequences, then large families would become the norm. With respect to the colonies, Malthus had to explain why the native populations of North America and elsewhere were not thick on the ground given the vastness and fertility of the land on which they lived (Malthus 1973a:32). The manner in which he did this involved employing an earlier version of Jeremy Bentham's pleasure/pain principle.[1] As far as Malthus was concerned, the fact that there was no rapid and continuous

---

[1] The idea that man's two masters are pleasure and pain was developed into a coherent system of thinking by Bentham. However the basic idea had already found expression in the works of earlier writers such as Thomas Hobbes (Hobbes 1998:6).

increase in numbers proved only that the conditions in which 'savages' lived were miserable. For reasons that will be outlined below, Malthus could not admit that the low population level among aboriginal communities was the result of forward planning, so he simply presumed that the extreme misery of their existence led them to lose all desire of having children (Malthus 1973a:29).

Supply and Demand

In Malthus's system it was in the interest of all laborers to provide only as many hands as were needed in industry at any given time. The productive classes would be best served if their growth and decline corresponded to the demand for workers. The property-less had to accept that an over supply of their commodity (labor power) would cheapen its value. Where there were many workers competing for few jobs population growth had to be curtailed one way or the other. Malthus borrowed this idea from Smith (1976:89), who had already explained that:

> the demand for men, like that for any other commodity, necessarily regulates the production of men; quickens when it goes too slowly, and stops when it advances too fast. It is this demand, which regulates and determines the state of propagation in all the different countries of the world.

The poor law system, which involved the provision of relief to the poor according to number of children, was considered a gross violation of these supposed laws of supply and demand. Malthus thought that since provisions were set aside for the redundant portion of the community, less was left for the rest of the laboring classes on which to survive. This interference caused the price of provisions to rise and spread poverty among a greater number of people than would otherwise have experienced it (Malthus 1973b:38–48).

In order to strengthen this point, Malthus (1973a:269) highlighted the improved conditions of the laboring classes in Scotland, which he attributed to an increase in the preventative check. It was suggested that the laboring classes there had developed a superior moral character, and that this was because they suffered the consequences of their own decisions. Since the people in Scotland were forced to be self-reliant, or were 'independent,' they had no choice but to adjust their numbers to suit the demand for hands. Malthus (1973a:273) explained that it was the lack and/or uncertainty of provision that had forced the poor in Scotland in a responsible direction.

From Malthus's point of view, relief needed to be scanty and precarious in order to encourage the common people to make greater efforts to avoid the day on which they must apply for such relief. If individuals did not perceive and anticipate negative consequences of having large families, they would usually have large families. If large families were provided for in accordance to their size, then no consequences would be felt and improvidence would continue as usual (Malthus 1973a:273).

Malthus presented his arguments in such a manner that they appeared to be based on concern for the laboring masses generally. As such, he explained that if the poor in workhouses were to live better than they did, the effect would be to "depress the condition of those out of the workhouses by occasioning an advance in the price of provisions" (Malthus 1973b:48). Only by controlling the supply of labor power could the laboring classes expect to better their conditions. But the poor laws, which acted as a spur to population, had created a supply of labor power where there was no demand for it. If they were abolished, the laboring classes would have no choice but to restrict the supply of labor power and their bargaining power would increase as a result.

The notion that the poor would not exert themselves sufficiently to better their conditions unless their conditions were truly terrible, was constantly stressed in Malthus's works. He thought that poverty could only be reduced if laborers worked hard, but they would only work hard if they were kept as poor and miserable as possible (Malthus 1973a:58).

The Context in which Malthus Wrote

Malthus's political/economic doctrines were developed at a time when the volume of capital invested in manufacturing enterprises increased at an unprecedented rate, as did the power to save and to reinvest (Ashton 1948:76). Therefore, an appraisal of Malthus's works must address the years of the industrial revolution (historians generally locate the industrial revolution between the years 1760 and 1830), which spanned the years of Malthus's own life (1766–1834).

The general rationalization of production in this period led to an unprecedented output of goods and commodities; but though endless improvement of the human lot may have been anticipated, private ownership over productive capital ensured that the costs of production would be socialized and the benefits privatized.

The accumulation and reinvestment of capital depended upon the willingness of laboring classes to enter into exploitative wage contracts. In order to ensure that they did so it was necessary to ensure that conditions of life forced them to submit to the will of employers. The propertied classes and their representatives realized that prevailing power-relations depended on the maintenance of particular conditions of life. As Arthur Young once put it, "every one but an idiot knows that the lower classes must be kept poor, or they will never be industrious".[2] Workers were kept at subsistence level throughout the industrial revolution.

During the years of the industrial revolution, machinery had been improved to the extent that one worker in the cotton mills could perform work that had required hundreds of workers a few decades before. But regardless of the time saved by technological innovation, the duration of the working day was never reduced and was sometimes even increased (Marx 1977:26). In spite of the potential to save labor and regardless of the profits realized on the part of capitalists, the laboring classes were still required to work a twelve-hour day or more (Engels 1958:191–199). It was clear that science and technology were employed in a manner acceptable to the owner of capital as against the worker, ensuring that part of the population would remain redundant.

Once the modern industrial capitalist system had firmly established itself, individual capitalists were continuously compelled to cut costs because competitors were always finding ways of doing so. Maintaining profit margins would be a never-ending problem due to ongoing competitive innovation and the increasing portion of an investment going into fixed capital rather than labor power. Producers found themselves compelled to increase the productivity of labor power through new techniques and economies of scale. Each had to find ways to cut costs and extend its market share and get its goods to those willing to purchase at a price that would permit a profit. However, a market can only bear so much, particularly if the working population lacks the ability to continue purchasing the goods that they produce. The limits of effective demand are invariably reached and periodic crises

---

[2] This quote is taken from R.H. Tawney's *Religion and the Rise of Capitalism* (Tawney 1948:270).

result. Since production depends on the profit motive and the system is anarchic, business has to be scaled down from time to time and massive numbers of people need to be thrown out of employment. The mechanics of this problem were worked out in the mid-1800s by Engels (1977:169), who insisted that, for as long as production continues in an unplanned manner and at the mercy of chance, "for just so long trade crises will remain".

In spite of working conditions and forced idleness, the industrial revolution brought with it a significant reduction in mortality rates. This was mostly due to the production of nutritious foods, improvements in public health measures (e.g., sewers and clean water), new medical knowledge and the establishment of centers for medical intervention. Population did increase, but not in consequence of births rates, which fluctuated over the course of Malthus's life.

The rise in population during the second half of the 18th century was clearly due to a reduced mortality rate, which was a measure of improved health across society. The fact that more people lived to maturity meant that they added to the normal span of life. In the worst years before 1750, up to 74 per cent of the children born in London died before they were five years old. This trend changed with the study of midwifery and foundation of maternity hospitals after 1747, which helped to reduce infant mortality rates drastically. In the latter half of the 18th century, death rates were reduced from 1 in 42 to 1 in 913 among the mothers, and from 1 in 15 to 1 in 115 among newborn babies. The discovery of inoculation for smallpox by Hunter, in 1740, along with the establishment of vaccination by Jenner, in 1798, helped to stretch survival rates for the rest of the population (Dietz 1927:15–16).

With respect to sanitation it may be said that the industrial revolution did have positive effects, even for the property-less. Malthus recognized these effects but explained them in terms of a supposed ratio between population and means of subsistence. He had no interest in the role of new medicines, improved sanitation and improved nutrition (Malthus 1973a:311). Malthus wished only to attribute conditions of life to population pressure, and the latter to individual foresight, which he regarded as a key factor leading to the economic development in Europe. The development of industry and the relative absence of famine and epidemic in Europe, which still plagued the 'savage' nations of the world, was thought to reflect the moral character, if not the intrinsic genius, of Europeans (Ross 1998:17).

Malthus and the Growth of Radicalism

Malthus (1973a:5) claimed that the aim of his investigations was to find out "the causes that have hitherto impeded the progress of mankind toward happiness". He claimed that his investigations were concerned with the causes of poverty, and with the possibilities that existed for the removal of those causes. It is quite obvious however, that Malthus was far more concerned with discrediting the various thinkers advocating 'Systems of Equality' (Devi 1986:337). Thinkers such as William Godwin had attempted to overturn the idea that poverty was natural, and had rejected the Puritan idea that poor conditions reflect poor moral character. Godwin insisted that such problems as face human societies were really the product of poorly designed human institutions. The view that over-population was the source of poverty was rejected since, in Godwin's (1985:769) view, "myriads of centuries of still increasing population may pass away, and the earth be yet found sufficient for the support of its inhabitants". Godwin (1985:759) was confident about this because he knew that the productive power of labor grew along with population. He was also aware that production would be further revolutionized with "complicated machines of human contrivance".

During the industrial revolution no one could say where such improvement would end; but it was becoming apparent to many that improvements in production techniques were not reflected in conditions of living for the laboring classes and poor. The reason for this, according to Godwin (1985:713), was that a portion of the community "have usurped the power of buying and selling the labor of the great mass of the community [and] are sufficiently disposed to take care that they should never do more than subsist".

A great number of other thinkers expressed similar sentiments at the time. That they were popularized during the period of industrialization is entirely fitting. The conditions thrown up in this age of seemingly boundless possibilities were wholly inconsistent with expectations. A particular impetus was given to revolutionary thinking and many theoreticians came to the conclusion that society could and should be ordered differently.

The inconsistency between potential and actual conditions of life posed serious problems for those hoping to maintain the status quo. It was in this context that Malthus set about producing his famous doctrines. They were developed in order to depict social equality as an absurd idea, and to prove all "systems of equality" unworkable and/or inconsistent with nature. As such, the first edition of Malthus's essay was subtitled *"With Remarks on the Speculations of Mr. Godwin and Other Writers"* (Ross 1998:367).

The problem with greater equality, according to Malthus, was that it would remove the 'goad of necessity,' which was supposed to have lifted humankind out of its 'natural' state of indolence and savagery (Ross 1998:10). Malthus believed that without the threat of poverty, labor would not be performed at all. He claimed that "if industry did not bring with it its reward and indolence its punishment; we could not expect to see that animated activity in bettering our condition which now forms the master-spring of public prosperity" (Malthus 1973b:254).

As with contemporary conservatives (especially those calling themselves libertarians), Malthus wished to encourage 'individual responsibility'. The propertied classes had always insisted that if people were ever to be responsible, industry would have to be rewarded. Of course this did not entail paying the laboring classes in proportion to the wealth that they created; raising the wages of workers would not improve the conditions in which they lived because, as Malthus (1973b:49) explained, "all that they earn beyond their present necessities goes, generally speaking, to the ale-house".

Malthus believed that the laboring classes needed to have responsibility forced upon them through the pressures of necessity. It was on this basis that he ridiculed Marquis de Condorcet's proposal to set up a fund for the elderly "produced in part by their own former savings, and in part by the saving of individuals who in making the same sacrifice die before they reap the benefit of it" (Malthus 1973b:3). Malthus believed that any fund established with the view of ensuring people assistance, even for those in their old age, would lead to improvidence, especially since the intention was to provide it in the name and under the protection of society.

The propertied classes and their representatives were bound to find fault with Condorcet's plans, which threatened to undermine the power relations between labor and the owners of productive capital. If Condorcet and others had their way there would be no destitute people left. The result would be to ease the pressure on laborers, who might not thereafter feel themselves compelled to enter into exploitative contracts. Insofar as they were controlled to the benefit of the propertied classes, the laboring classes were considered 'independent.' The greatest evil of all, as far as Malthus was concerned, was the 'dependence' of people on society. Of course the real fear was not that the property-less would become dependent but that they would become *less* dependent on the will of the propertied classes.

The inequalities that existed in the industrialized parts of Europe in Malthus's day were obvious enough to anyone that wanted to see them. Among those taking issue was Robert Owen. In order to convey to people what he thought was wrong with existing institutions he contrasted it with an uplifting vision of how he imagined society could be ordered in the future. Owen suggested that society would one day be organized according to the interests of the majority. He claimed that:

> One portion of mankind will not, as now, be trained and placed to oppress, by force or fraud, another portion, to the great disadvantage of both; neither will one portion be trained in idleness, to live in luxury on the industry of those whom they oppress... Nor yet will some be trained to force falsehood into the human mind and be paid extravagantly for so doing while other parties are prevented from teaching the truth.[3]

Malthus was appalled at this sort of assertion. He argued that a system of equality, such as that envisaged by Owen, would lead to an explosion in population and a decline in productivity. He was sure that in an egalitarian society there would be nothing to "prevent the division of the produce of the soil to each individual from becoming every year less and less, till the whole society and every individual member of it are pressed down by want and misery" (Malthus 1973b:25–27). Even if 'community in goods' did remove fear of want it would eventually spell disaster because people would become lazy and useless.

Malthus warned that all attempts to tinker with the conditions proceeding from natural forces could only spread poverty and immorality across society. The unequal relations between classes and sexes were considered natural and therefore any move toward egalitarianism would offend nature. The maintenance of this impression required Malthus to attack 'inflammatory' theoreticians, such as Godwin, Condorcet and Owen. He wished to consign all of their efforts to the dustbin of scientific enquiry (Ross 1998:6). Many believed that he had done so. The propertied classes certainly saw in the principle of population, which explained the human condition convincingly and conveniently, a ready means of discrediting all proposals for radical change. Malthus gave them further reason to believe that inequality was natural and

---

[3] This quote is taken from Hunt and Sherman's *Economics: An Introduction to Traditional and Radical Views* (Hunt and Sherman 1978:52).

beneficial to all involved. Systems of equality were thereafter considered "completely destructive of the true principles of liberty and equality" (Malthus 1973b:3).

Marx and Engels on Population Pressure

It took Marx and Engels to explain that the destitute and idle sections of the community, so often seen as superfluous by the population theorists, were really by-products of the economic system. To these thinkers, idleness and poverty had nothing to do with population growth. The capitalist system was said to depend on, and constantly reproduce, a 'reserve army of labor,' which was always needed to exert pressure, through its competition, upon the employed. Without this pressure the laboring classes would not readily agree to exploitative wage contracts and related conditions.

Marx (1953:92) explained that it is the employed who produce the surplus laborers through their over-work, and conversely, the unemployed through its competition, forces the employed to submit to over-work. The maintenance of a reserve was considered part and parcel of the maintenance of capitalist relations since it ensured that those in employment agreed to work long hours for a reward that would barely maintain them. The process that maintained the reserve ensured that no matter the intensity of production, huge numbers would remain in conditions of poverty and/or idleness. The main point was that the problems facing humankind were not technical or natural, but political.

Engels claimed that economists had invented population theory as a convenient explanation for the consequences of capitalism. As he saw it, pauperism was continuously reproduced as the capitalist market order developed and would remain a feature of that order no matter the size of population. The supposed 'surplus population' would still exist if millions more or millions less inhabited a country. A redundant section of the population would be reproduced so long as production was geared toward the profit of private owners rather than the needs of those that actually did the work. Engels (1977:171) claimed that economists "could not afford to admit that this contradiction is a simple consequence of competition". They needed population theory in order to obscure the relation between the extraction of surplus value and the redundant portion of the community.

Marx and Engels treated Malthus's famous *Essay on the Principle of Population* as part of a much larger attempt to counter radical interpretations. This work, which first appeared as a much smaller publication was, according to Marx (1953b:121) at least, "nothing more than a schoolboyish, superficial plagiary" (mainly of Adam Smith's works) and the sensation it caused was due to nothing other than "party interest". The theory offered no new insights but was highly valued because it appeared to justify existing privileges and simultaneously thwart egalitarian visions. His key principles were generally acceptable to all of the propertied classes (including the landed aristocracy and the Church) as against the workers and peasants.

Malthus's commitment to certain privileged sections of the community sometimes produced arguments that fell outside the normal scope of classical political economy. It was with a view to justifying the maintenance of the aristocracy, religious and other idle groups, that Malthus developed a theory of consumption, wherein the tendency for supply to outstrip demand and produce crisis was well recognized. This may have been the earliest theory of overproduction. Marx (1953:153) drew attention to the fact that it was supplied by the same thinker who insisted that it was impossible to produce enough food to feed people.

Though Malthus' contribution was conservative in the extreme, his recognition of an inevitable lack of demand makes him a forerunner of Marx and/or Keynes. This aspect of his thinking did not really interest the propertied classes. It was the notion that profligate humanity and stingy nature meant that humankind would be forever doomed to perpetual scarcity that drew the most attention and had the most lasting effect. It is for this reason that certain contemporary economists, such as William Dugger (2003:6), believe that it was Malthus who transformed economics into the dismal science that it is today.

For Marx and Engels, the growth of pauperism could not be understood without an appreciation of centralization of industry, the trend toward urbanization and the socialization of labor under the industrial system. They knew that pauperism grew as the ranks of the proletariat grew. They knew that the proletariat grew as the portion of the community with access to the means of labor diminished. They knew that independent crafts people were finding it increasingly difficult to make an independent living because those already possessing large amounts of capital could purchase labor power as a commodity, erect colossal factories and drive them out of business. In the face of the more efficient factory system, the smaller producer was poor competition. More and more people came to depend on large enterprises for employment.

The great migration to the towns was due to the fact that the market for labor power was concentrated in the industrial centres. Factory production required the existence of great numbers of people in one place, which is partly why the population of Lancashire increased tenfold in 80 years. The population of the towns grew because the factory system needed to be fed with labor power (Engels 1958:16).

With industrialization came great bursts of economic growth, which created a great demand for labor power and a rise in wages. In such times it appeared as though 'hands' were scarce. At other times it appeared as though there were too many workers, less of a demand for labor power, and wages were reduced accordingly. In order to maintain the value of labor power, advocates of the population doctrine thought it necessary to limit the supply of laborers in accordance with the changing demand. Marx (1953:94) quickly pointed out that even if wages did respond to the availability of hands, by the time an increase or decrease in the population was realized, the rise and fall of the economic cycle would have passed more than once. Unless the plan was to put newborn infants to work, the notion that the population can be made to obey the laws of supply and demand cannot be taken seriously.

Population Theory Applied: The Irish Potato Famine

Malthusian theory helped the propertied classes of the early 19th century to believe that no one could prevent a famine from visiting a people but the people suffering it. It was generally agreed that if levels of poverty increased it had to be the consequence of a greater increase in births and/or a decline in demand for labor power (Malthus 1973a:191). This belief was converted into policy during the Irish potato famine of the mid 1840s. The British authorities came to believe that if they alleviated suffering in Ireland it would encourage population growth, which was considered to be the source of the problem.

Malthus had assumed that insofar as abundance of food made possible the support of large families, the crops that were grown in different countries, such as rice, corn or potatoes, determined population size. He was not interested in the factors leading to the cultivation of these crops in the first place. Likewise, the Malthusians of the mid 18th century simply considered the populations of countries such as Ireland to be predetermined by the type and amount of food available.

It is true that population was increasing quickly in Ireland in the years prior to the famine. It is true also that the cultivation of the potato, which is a very prolific crop, created the means of subsistence necessary to sustain such a population. However, the cultivation of the potato in Ireland was a response to the industrial revolution in Britain. The laboring classes were forced to maintain themselves on tiny parcels of land in order to free up great tracts, which were then used to produce crops for export to the industrial heartland and to the colonies (Ross 1998:35–55). A great population was maintained, but the bulk of food, save about 50% of the potato crop, was produced for export.

The buying power of the Irish laboring classes was weak since there was little capitalistic enterprise in Ireland and very little opportunity for people to get access to any means of production on favorable terms. Of course the Malthusians believed that this meant there was an over supply of labor. As a consequence of this over supply (or the undersupply of means of labor), the price of labor power was reduced to almost nothing. The purchasing power of the Irish peasantry was far less than that of the industrial worker in Britain. It is this fact that paved the way for famine. People could not purchase alternative foods; so, if anything happened to the potatoes the result would be catastrophic. The famine would have been likely to occur in Ireland even if the population was half the size (Ross 1998:35–55).

The notion that potato blight caused the famine, which prevails to this day, is insufficient. Though blight did destroy the potato crop in the mid 1840s, it did not cause any shortage of food in the country. At the height of the famine there was enough food being produced in Ireland to feed all of Great Britain and Ireland twice over (Ross 1998:32). Up until the famine the peasants of Ireland were nourished sufficiently that they would continue to exist; but no matter how hard they labored on the land their purchasing power would never enable them to enjoy any of the comforts and luxuries as existed elsewhere.

The convenient explanation for the low reward for work in Ireland was simply that the price of labor was set, as every other commodity was, according to the demand for it. Of course, it would be more accurate to say that it was set at subsistence level, relative to the cultural level of the society in question. In pre-famine Ireland this meant that it was set at next to nothing. The price realized by laborers for the sale of their labor would never be enough to purchase manufactured goods. Accordingly, almost the entire population was condemned to live in huts and to eat only potatoes. They would never benefit from the export of crops even though it was they that worked the land. The majority were living hand to mouth, without the power to purchase extras to vary their diet or import manufactured articles. Insofar as they were wholly dependent on what was growing on their tiny parcels of land, one bad harvest would be enough to finish them. Ireland was a disaster waiting to happen.

When famine eventually took hold in Ireland, it was one of Malthus's own students, Charles Trevelyan, who was in charge of famine relief. Trevelyan took the same negative view toward poor relief as Malthus did. He considered that the provision of relief was the very source of poverty. At the height of the famine he insisted that the only way to end the suffering was to bring all operations to a close. In Trevelyan's view the famine was "a direct stroke of an all wise and all-merciful providence".[4] Trevelyan's attitude was by no means exceptional. The land agent, John Thornley, was just as well able to articulate the Malthusian perspective of the English and Irish ruling classes. He declared that "there will come some good out of the present misery, you may be sure. It is good for the country that the surplus population is driven away, even by stress of famine, to seek more prosperous homes elsewhere, leaving the land to be made the best of " (Keary 1979:123).

Many of the poor law guardians responsible for administering local relief at the time were landlords (Ross 1998:48). Most subscribed to the view that the poor would have to face the consequences of their imprudent ways. Poverty was regarded as nature's way of punishing imprudence. Malthus had held that "nature shows us the wrongness of an act by bringing from it a train of painful consequences" (Wells 1986:383). Insofar as it was individual failings that were blamed, it was not considered improper that people should be forced to mend their ways. It was not only the British ruling class that interpreted the situation in this manner. The ascendancy in Ireland took a similar view. Bishop Berkeley was dismayed to find "sturdy beggars" in receipt of poor relief. The famine was considered to be partly the result of the laziness of these individuals. As such, he thought it fitting that they be "seized and made slaves to the public for a certain term of years" (Keary 1979:123).

As famine took hold in Ireland, over one hundred thousand families were evicted from their homes. Though neither food nor shelter was in short supply, hundreds of thousands found themselves malnourished

---

[4] Quote taken from E. Ross's *The Malthus Factor* (Ross 1998:46).

and homeless. Though the needs of the domestic population had never been greater, the profit motive ensured that tens of thousands of heads of cattle and pigs, along with other foodstuffs, were exported for sale in England's markets (often to the benefit of absentee landlords). As a result of this system, coupled with Malthusian-inspired government policies, over one million children, women and men died as a result of the famine and over one million more were forced to emigrate. Though the exact figures are still questioned, what is certain is that in 1845 the population of Ireland was over eight million and by 1851 it was only around five million.

Population Theory Applied: The Old Poor Law

When the conditions that Malthus and his people had the opportunity to observe during the industrial revolution and concurrent imperatives of the propertied classes are considered, it is not difficult to understand why his *Essay on the Principle of Population* became so popular. Not only did it justify the conditions of the laboring classes, it also gave renewed impetus to the long-standing demand for the gradual abolition of England's Old Poor Law. Population theory was very useful to those that wished to forward utilitarian arguments against it (Malthus 1973b:25).

The arguments for abolition were usually made with reference to the Hobbesian conception of a fixed and permanent human nature. Malthus adopted the Hobbesian view that "man" is naturally selfish and aggressive, but for the purposes of his arguments, man needed to be naturally lazy also. As far as Malthus (1973a:59) was concerned, a state of "sloth, and not of restlessness and activity, seems evidently to be the natural state of man". This conception of man enabled Malthus to argue against the poor law system from the point of view that something must have brought man out from his natural state of indolence. It could be argued that whatever it was that lifted man from his original savage and lazy state had to be for the best. This was much the same tactic that was used by Hobbes (1998:126) to justify strong government and Locke (1980:123–25) to justify the unlimited accumulation of private property. Humankind's supposed nature was laid down in order that new and improved dispositions could be explained in the manner most convenient to the system of relations desired.

Malthus explained that humankind was brought out of a state of natural idleness only by the strong 'goad of necessity'. In order to avoid a decline in living standards, individuals would have to compete. Only for so long as this competition was maintained would the community prosper. The poor law threatened to undo all of this, preventing as it did the development of a competitive ethos among the property-less. As such, Malthus (1973a:273) declared that the Old Poor Law was dangerous, and was everywhere destroying the love of "independence".

Malthus sought to depict the Old Poor Law as a root cause of immorality. He insisted that the conditions of the people would improve only as their moral characters improved. Improvements of condition were in turn viewed as evidence of improved moral character, which improved wherever the poor were sufficiently encouraged in the direction of 'prudence' and 'industry.' Insofar as provisions for the poor had the opposite effect, it was not considered immoral to do away with them. If relief discouraged prudence, industry and 'moral restraint,' it also helped to "spread the evil over a much larger surface" (Malthus 1973b:38).

The Malthusians had been particularly concerned with a later amendment to the Old Poor Law, according to which relief was given to poor families according to the number of children they had. Relief was thought to spur on population and thereby create more paupers. At best, relief would postpone the inevitable, and at worst, it would make the consequences felt by a far greater number. Malthus, who insisted that it was necessary to be cruel to be kind, thought it far better to remove relief for the poor wherever it was likely to encourage early marriage and large families.

Malthus died around the same time that the Old Poor Law was abolished. With the passing of the *New Poor Law Amendment Act* of 1834, the Old Poor Law, proceeding from an act passed in 1601, was effectively reversed. When the Old Poor Law was in operation parishes had to support their own poor. The poor considered provision as a right rather than a charity (Engels 1958:322). However, industrial capitalism could not tolerate the poor law as it stood, or the morality attached to it. Advocates of the 'free market' saw that Malthus offered a new morality for the new society that was developing. They accepted his prescription for the betterment of the condition of the people and ignored the fact that it contradicted itself.

Malthus claimed that conditions could be improved if certain policies were implemented, which nullified his scheme, since improved conditions would inevitably lead to an increase in population pressure and the conditions associated with it. This is exactly what S.U. Devi (1986:340) suggested when he pointed out that the measures for which Malthus was the greatest advocate served only to strengthen that which caused poverty. In the course of his arguments, Malthus (1973b:4) had insisted that where people are sure of a comfortable provision for a family, they have families, and that "if the rising generation were free from fear of poverty, population must increase with unusual rapidity". As such, his argument boiled down to the nonsensical notion that the only way to alleviate poverty was to keep people poor. The argument was never put forward in such terms for obvious reasons.

Reproduction and Individual Morality

Malthus argued that humankind could replace positive checks on population, such as war, famine and epidemic, with preventative checks, such as 'moral restraint'. He insisted that the only moral method for keeping population in line with the means of subsistence, voluntarily, was moral restraint (repression of sexual drives). The immoral alternative was vice (contraception). Malthus (1973b:5) insisted that the only alternative would be "a promiscuous concubinage, which would prevent breeding, or to something else as unnatural". He favored the continuation of moral restraint, and rejoiced in the fact that in modern Europe "a much larger proportion of women pass a considerable part of their lives in the exercise of this virtue" (Malthus 1973a:315).

Since it was presumed that women were more inclined toward 'moral restraint' than men, it was left up to the female of the species to hold the line with regard to population. Promiscuous sexual intercourse was among the 'vices' held to be destructive to the moral character and to society generally. Of course it was the behavior of women in particular that was the focus of Malthus's moral indignation; little was made of the sexual 'immorality' of men. Malthus (1973a:13) did not think this unfair in the least since promiscuous sexual intercourse was bound to "degrade the female character, and destroy all of its most amiable and distinguishing characteristics". Of course when Malthus referred to amiable 'qualities' it may well have been the desired passivity and subservience of women that he had in mind.

It was necessary for the proper functioning of the capitalist market order to ensure that women facilitate labor (i.e., serve the man of the house) and turn out a new generation of 'hands' free of charge. Therefore, it was just as important that women be exploited in the home as in the factory system. The unpaid labor of women in the home would only be performed so long as women knew their place and did not neglect their assigned duties.

The relations facilitating domestic exploitation were necessarily accompanied by a system of sexual repression, which was legitimated by an extremely skewed sexual morality and related double standards. Malthus (1973a:13) believed that to relax the codes of sexual morality would be to "poison the springs of domestic happiness, to weaken conjugal and parental affection, and to lessen the united exertions and ardour of parents in the care and education of their children". Of course by domestic happiness Malthus meant the patriarchal arrangements that prevailed in the society with which he was familiar. The gendered roles that were reinforced by these codes obliged women to facilitate the exploitation of laborers in private enterprises. They legitimated the arrangements under which women reared up a fresh generation of laborers to be sold as a commodity for next to nothing.

Though the bourgeois class rarely had any problem treating labor as a commodity, they did not wish to consider how it had come to be prepared for the market. If they did so they would have to agree that this commodity was produced without payment. They preferred to support the 'domestic happiness' upon which the exploitation of women rested. Having explained the existing patriarchal structures in the convenient manner, Malthus (1973a:15) confidently proclaimed that "no person can doubt the general tendency of an illicit intercourse between the sexes to injure the happiness of society".

Malthus (1973b:29) found it necessary to insist upon "the impossibility of checking the rate of increase in a state of equality, without resorting to regulations that are unnatural, immoral or cruel". He thought it better to have the property-less face poverty and disease than promote 'immoral' practices. He was only prepared to entertain the long-term solution of preaching moral restraint. Of course if artificial forms of birth control were tolerated then there would be no need for the rich to preach industry and prudence, which were the character forms most conducive to bourgeois accumulation.

Though contraception was always the most rational and obvious solution to the supposed problem, Malthus would not accept it. The problem was not so much the case that contraception might cause injury to society, but that it offered a real solution to the supposed problem. If there was a solution to the problem, population theory could not be used as an argument in support of the existing system of relations.

Malthus had to rule out the solution to the very problem that he claimed to be so concerned about. If there were a ready means to ease 'population pressure,' then all of those justifications, which Malthus had so carefully constructed for the ideological maintenance of the relations and conditions produced in bourgeois society, would quickly fall to pieces. It would be a potential hindrance too for accumulation insofar as it would give the laboring classes some control over their own lives. He had no option but to declare all forms of artificial contraception immoral. As such, contraception is sectioned under 'vice' rather than under 'preventative check' in Malthus's system.

The Social Function of Malthusianism

It is not true to say that some theories are prejudicial while others are simply objective. Theories usually begin with a prejudice in mind (Cox 1986:204–254). The form that they take depends on what the theoretician decides to accept in order to rationalize them. The level of methodological or theoretical sophistication reached in the process of an enquiry does not alter the fact that the author begins from a prejudice. No matter the lengths to which an author goes to obscure things, the political component remains and the resulting theory serves some agenda or other.

For Malthus's part, the agenda involved portioning out blame for unpleasant conditions to those persons and institutions that stood in the way of capitalist development. Malthus created the impression that those who continued to insist that something should and could be done to improve the conditions of the laborers and paupers actually did them a disservice. The involvement of philanthropists was held to exacerbate poverty since it enabled the poor to bring more children into the world even though there was no room for them. More blame was portioned out to the poor, who, it was believed, were ultimately responsible for the conditions in which they lived. It was their imprudent ways that generated 'population pressure' and brought poverty upon their kind. As such, helping the poor only helped them to create more poverty. This position taken up by Malthus appears to be designed to dash all hopes of further human development.

Malthus and his followers attributed poverty to failures on the part of millions of individuals to anticipate the consequences of their actions. If the poor were to have a little foresight, that is, if they were to exercise 'moral restraint' and act prudently, they would not be faced with lives of poverty and misery. Of course this view was far from exceptional. Almost the entire intellectual wing of the investing classes believed that 'population pressure' and the conditions related to it, stemmed from the immorality of the people themselves. It was the moral failings of each individual that brought nature's positive checks (famine and disease) to each door. Malthus was stating nothing new when he suggested that riches follow virtue and poverty follows immorality and vice. He was following in the manner of John Locke, who, when speaking in his capacity as a member of the Commission on Trade in 1697, claimed that the growing number of unemployed was caused by "nothing else but the relaxation of discipline and corruption of manners" (MacPherson 1962:222–223).

It has always been important, for the sake of bourgeois interests, to encourage the poor to think and to act in the manner most compatible with the smooth running of the capitalist market order. Malthus realized how important it was to distribute the blame for poverty between the natural world and the human passions, while leaving some portion of blame for the individual human conscience. To his mind there were three factors working together to create the great misery experienced by the property-less. In the first place, the means of subsistence were finite and could only increase at a certain rate. Secondly, the natural passions between the sexes pressed population against the means of subsistence. Thirdly, there was the indolence, imprudence and vice of the laboring classes. All of these factors, mixed together, produced poverty, epidemics, wars and whatever else the propertied classes claimed to be concerned about.

The ideas formulated and promoted by Malthus and his followers found further expression among the classes that enjoyed a measure of economic independence, education, and a certain decent pride in their status. This portion of society was, according to R.H. Tawney (1948:202) at least, the most prone to display "contempt for those who, either through weakness of character or through economic helplessness, were less vigorous and masterful, than themselves".

The political element in population theory was buried under a great deal of statistically recorded material. As such, many 19th century thinkers, such as J.S. Mill (1992:132), were impressed by its apparent objectivity and exactitude. They were convinced that to bestow a life where there are little prospects for a desirable existence "is a crime against that being". Mill believed that those creating new life without visible means of support were committing a crime against their own class. This great liberal even suggested that laws forbidding marriage "unless the parties can show that they have the means of supporting a family" could not be considered violations of individual liberty (Mill 1992:132–133).

Mill did not recognize the social function of Malthusianism. He could not see that despite the claims made, population theory was not disinterested and did not reflect any objective reality, but was produced, as all theories are, to serve a particular purpose. Malthus was not attempting to calculate, as he claimed to be, the best means of improving the lot of the laboring classes. What he was actually doing was calculating the best means of turning out cheap and willing labor into the market, for purchase. Though Malthus's admirers have complained about the many criticisms that his works called forth, given the policy agenda that corresponded with his doctrines, it was probably inevitable that he would become "the best-abused-man of his age" (Devi 1986:337).

The central message conveyed by Malthus and his followers was that where social, political and economic phenomena could not be attributed to natural processes they could be explained in terms of the behavior and values of individuals. If individuals did not perceive and anticipate negative consequences of having large families they would have large families. If large families were provided for in accordance to their size then no consequences would be felt and improvidence would continue as usual. As such, if there was, at any time, an increase in the number of paupers, then the cause was already known. The severity of the misery produced reflected only the level of individual immorality and the extent to which the laws of nature had been offended. In short, population theory was an effective means for giving expression to long-standing individualist doctrines. It served to promote and legitimate individual (bourgeois) control, not only over resources that were individually possessed, but also over the communities depending on those resources.

CHAPTER FIVE

DOCTRINES OF SOCIAL EVOLUTION

In the *Origin of Species* Charles Darwin (1964:66) claimed that throughout the animal and vegetable kingdoms (in which he included humans), hardship acted as a spur to the process of procreation. Considering all that he observed in nature, he concluded that, "if an animal can in any way protect its own eggs or young, a small number may be produced, and yet the average stock be fully kept up; but if many eggs or young are destroyed, many must be produced, or the species will become extinct".

Darwin's demonstration that fertility levels increase with hardship should have represented a serious blow to the Malthusian idea of poverty as a check on population. It was clear to Darwin that since nature spares no expense when it comes to producing certainty, the harshest conditions must result in more seeds, eggs and young being produced. The implication of this was that in order to check the increasing birth rate and reduce pauperism, which Malthusians treated in cause and effect terms, it would be necessary to ease hardship, not maintain it. The remedies proposed by Malthusians could only exacerbate the supposed problem.

Insofar as Darwin's evolutionary theory was developed within the confines of an existing world-view, of which Malthusianism was part, Malthus is usually given a measure of credit for its emergence (Hawkins 1997:30). Even some later opponents of Malthusianism, such as Bertrand Russell (2001:151), were convinced that the ideas of Malthus led directly to Darwinism. It is easy to understand why the notion prevails. In the *Origin of Species*, Darwin (1964:63) modestly claimed that his theory was nothing more than "the doctrine of Malthus applied with manifold force to the whole animal and vegetable kingdoms". The first problem with this claim was that it was not actually Malthus that developed the doctrine of natural increase. The doctrine was actually borrowed from Robert Wallace (Bonar 1885:8–9). In any case, when Darwin applied this to the natural world he was introducing it into the only field in which it holds true, as the famous sociologist Lester Frank Ward (1970:279–280) pointed out. The doctrine for which Malthus may be given credit was nothing other than Wallace's doctrine plus the suggestion that human increase is set at a faster rate than are the various species of animal and plants upon which human beings depend for subsistence. This is the doctrine attributable to Malthus. It is a doctrine that was rejected by Darwin (1964:66), who explained that "every single organic being around us may be said to be striving to the utmost to increase in numbers; that each lives by a struggle at some period of its life; that heavy destruction inevitably falls either on the young or old".

Insofar as Darwin (1964:64) insisted that there is "no exception to the rule that every organic being naturally increases," he could not remain faithful to Malthus's model. It may have been that Darwin was unaware of the extent to which his system opposed that of Malthus. Marx (1953:124) claimed as much when he suggested that Darwin had overlooked the simple fact that Malthus's model depended on the opposition of Wallace's geometrical progression of human beings "to the chimerical 'arithmetical' progression of animals and plants". Insofar as Darwin highlighted geometrical progression in the animal *and* vegetable kingdoms, he destroyed the very exceptions upon which Malthusianism depended and overturned every doctrine that was unique to Malthus. Darwin was attempting to explain the struggle for existence in nature whereas Malthus was mainly concerned with depicting humankind's struggle against the existing socio-economic system as though it was a struggle against a naturally determined means of subsistence.

The idea of population pressure had, until the mid-19th century, enabled the ruling classes to dampen any optimism about further human development. With the development of industrial capitalism, evolutionary doctrines offered the means of explaining all of the destructive competition involved in terms of natural processes. Insofar as Darwin emphasized struggle and competition, his theory of evolution was analogous to the prevailing economic system. So prevalent are the terms and phrases of liberal political economy in the *Origin* that Oswald Spengler once complained that it "reeked of the English factory".[1]

Darwin's description of relentless competition between and among different species was quickly employed as explanation for the unequal fortunes presenting among the human species. Darwinism was incorporated into political doctrines and employed in such a way as to explain

---

[1] This quote is taken from D.P. Crook's *Darwinism, War and History* (Crook 1994:13).

the social inequalities. Individualists found that evolutionary theory mirrored the competitive economic framework. They were encouraged by some of Darwin's writings, especially those employing the terms profit, inheritance and competition. Of course Darwin not only used metaphors drawn from business, banking and industry to depict animal behavior, he also employed the language of British imperialism. For example, he liked to speak of one species "overmastering" another (Crook 1994:14). This language made it easy for individualists to read aspects of Darwin's theory into the competitive economic order. The idea of natural selection was, after all, modelled after the prevailing notion of competition in capitalist market societies (Merton 1973:37).

Genetic Inheritance and Evolution

In the *Origin*, Darwin explained that genetic mutations, which are the source of the variety within a species, are sometimes conducive to survival of particular members of that species. In his evolutionary model, competition and selection became the means of ensuring that beneficial characteristics would be passed on to the next generation. The struggle for life aided the development and improvement of the species as a whole. The mutations ensured variety and competition among individual members, which ensured that advantageous variations would be passed to the next generation. The survival of those that had adapted to their immediate circumstances would lead to successful genetic adaptation of the entire species to a changing environment. Darwin held that as circumstances changed within the natural environment, new species would emerge and others, insofar as they were ill suited to that environment, would disappear off the face of the earth. There was no preconceived plan. It was haphazard genetic mutations that led to the adaptations that were generally conducive to the survival of the species (Hawkins 1997:24). The Darwinian description of the evolutionary process was quickly employed as a means of bolstering the case for *laissez-faire* capitalism. Competition under the prevailing economic system was thought analogous to the healthy competition that existed in the animal kingdom. Those that failed to benefit from the capitalist system could now be labeled 'unfit' in the great struggle for existence. This was a ready-made argument, especially given that individualists took the existing capitalist economic relations to be humankind's natural environment.

Among the most famous theoreticians employing the above evolutionary ideas and/or biological analogies, were William Graham Sumner
and Herbert Spencer. These thinkers, along with those following their
example, are usually referred to as social Darwinists. They were called
social Darwinists because they attempt to derive laws of nature from
the Darwinian model and apply them to human societies. The concern
about population increase was not as important to this group of thinkers as it had been for the followers of Malthus. In fact, some stressed
how important it was for all species (including humans) to multiply
at a rapid rate so that there would be a great degree of variance. Social
Darwinists presumed that when nature was left to do its job, that is,
when the strongest were allowed to thrive and the weakest to die, the
species would improve. It was thought that any interference in the
process so described would lead to degeneration.

The insistence on the part of social Darwinists that the laws of nature
had to be respected, echoed the long-standing demands from advocates of *laissez-faire* that 'economic laws' (the relational imperatives
underpinning capitalistic accumulation) had to be respected. Insofar
as attempts to interfere with existing market relations were thought of
as attempts to interfere with nature's processes, the social Darwinists
viewed regulations inconvenient to the owners of capital, as offences
against the laws of nature.

Social Darwinists were less inclined to explain events in terms of
the moral characters of individuals. As with the Malthusians, they
thought that paternalism and/or socialistic legislation would undermine individual morality, but they were more inclined to believe that
those suffering hardships were always bound to suffer due to inherent
deficiencies. Though there was a difference of emphasis, social Darwinism involved no great departure from Malthus, who had also believed
that particular classes of people were inherently inferior. Malthus's
objection to Jenner's work on the smallpox vaccine was made on the
presumption that it would lead to people surviving regardless of their
"civic worth" (Ross 1998:61).

Progress and Competitive Struggle

The notion that the downtrodden section of the community was of lesser
worth reached a high level of sophistication in the eugenicist science of
Charles Darwin's cousin, Francis Galton, who proffered his system as

"the means by which the physical and moral attributes of a population might be improved by selective breeding" (Ross 1998:60). Galton was sure that the rich were successful due to inherent qualities that reflected genetic inheritance of traits favorable to individual survival. It followed that the cause of poverty was to be found in the genetic makeup of poor people. This individualist explanation interpreted the poor as inherently inferior and therefore incapable of manifesting the traits that had brought great fortune to others. Where Malthus had concentrated on indolence and imprudence, nineteenth century individualists attributed conditions to genetic blueprints which were thought to determine the lot of the individual from the very beginning of life.

The above explanation was used in arguments against all manner of social progress. It was argued that since poverty was produced by the inferior sample of the community (the poor), then relief could only exacerbate the problem because it rewarded inferiority. Socialistic legislation had to be opposed also, not simply because it was inconvenient for the owners of capital, but because it would lead to a "multiplication of morons". The social Darwinists and the eugenicists thought that democratic progress would destroy natural selection, and perhaps the human species with it. The message that these individualists wished to convey was that the poor are held down by nothing other than biological deficiency. Therefore any attempts at national salvation would require a system wherein the "better stock" would be preserved (Hofstadter 1944:163).

It was in order to arrive at conclusions that were inoffensive to existing privileges and which would lead to prescriptions conducive to existing power relations that nineteenth century individualists embraced evolutionary theory. Even though Darwin undermined the basis of Malthusianism, individualists employed evolutionary theory as a supplement to Malthusian individualism. Notions of moral failing were thereafter accompanied with evolutionary notions of maladaptation to a common environment. The general aims of these thinkers were not very different from those of Malthusian thinkers. Their social, political and economic analysis was very similar. They insisted that inequality was necessary, that the only choice available to humankind was plenty for some or misery for all. They set about creating an understanding of nature and of human societies that supported this idea. Like Malthus, they wished to create a concrete reality beyond which no alternative could be envisaged. And, like Malthus, social Darwinists insisted that the sacrifice of a portion of the community was necessary for the healthy development of the whole.

Social Darwinists treated individuals as though they were isolated beings in competition with one another and freely adapting to a common environment. Individual behavior and psychology were taken as given. The extent to which the conditions thrown up under the existing economic system shaped or debased individual characters received little attention. Rather than taking into account the various factors contributing to social problems, social Darwinists explained by way of analogy, and in such a way as to reduce the role of bourgeois institutions to zero. As such, poor conditions had to be treated as evidence of inferiority and/or the consequences of vice and improvidence.

Social Darwinists, such as Sumner (1963:81), insisted that poverty and misery "will exist in society just so long as vice exists in human nature". The conditions of life experienced by each individual were treated as a measure of moral character, which was thought the result of inheritance. Those that were more advanced mentally and morally would thrive while those living lives of vice and improvidence would perish. All conditions of life were depicted as stemming from efforts of the individual. And since conditions of life were thought to reflect the laws of nature, those experiencing circumstances that made it difficult to survive were simply receiving the fruits of maladaptation. It was never suggested that the materially successful were successful due to their physical strength. In Sumner's case at least, success was attributed to the inheritance of moral and economic virtues (Hofstadter 1944:57).

Though the inheritance of wealth was an obvious factor determining success or failure in a competitive industrial environment, it was not considered inconsistent with competition. Social Darwinists considered inherited wealth as accumulated effort rather than unearned income. It was not considered offensive to the supposed laws of competitive struggle and adaptation. On the contrary, it was said to ensure inheritance of the necessary 'economic virtues', which were regarded as a compliment to genetic inheritance.

Sumner thought in terms of social and moral evolution rather than physical. He explained that the "social equivalent of physical inheritance is the instruction of the children in the necessary economic virtues" (Hofstadter 1944:58). He chose to equate moral teaching of parents and subsequent development of children with the evolutionary adaptation of animals to their natural environment. This was consistent with the views of Darwin, who suggested that as far as civilized humankind is concerned, bodily evolution had become secondary to mental and moral evolution (Crook 1994:27).

For the sake of the arguments they wished to make, social Darwinists found it necessary to work the individualist concept of merit into explanations of social evolution. In order to facilitate this, Spencer developed the 'Law of Conduct and Consequence,' which consisted of the idea that "each individual shall receive the benefits and the evils produced in consequence of his own consequent conduct: neither being prevented from what his good actions normally bring to him, nor allowed to shoulder off on to other persons whatever ill is brought to him by his actions" (Taylor 1992:234). Spencer claimed that insofar as the state interfered with this law it created injustices. Wherever the actions of the state awarded advantages to those that had not earned them through their own efforts, the laws of nature were offended. Spencer had less to say about the exploitative capitalist relations maintained by the state through its coercive institutions. It could very well be argued vis-à-vis the categories of social Darwinism, that the extraction of surplus value from the worker in a free market economy creates injustice and infringes upon the rights of the individual, since that individual is denied part of the produce of his or her labor.

When Spencer expressed concern about socialistic legislation, it was on the basis that it would lead to the degeneration of the entire human species. He claimed that the government, which was, in his view, determined to aid the offspring of inherently inferior people, was the source of humankind's present and future misfortune. The mistakes made by government had the potential to produce a world filled with "swarms of good-for-nothings, fostered and multiplied by public and private agencies" (Spencer 1969:96). The only way to stop the world from being filled with 'good-for-nothings,' or 'morons', was to ensure competition, which would automatically ensure that the strongest thrive and the weakest die off.

If individuals were to get what they deserved, it followed that each individual had to receive no more and no less than the fruits of their own labor. No distinction was made between those selling labor power and those buying labor power and profiting from its use. Individualists avoided admitting that income derived from inherited wealth was unearned. They were less willing still to consider the wealth extracted from the labor power of others in a factory enterprise as anything other than the reward of effort. The relations between capitalist and employee were not regarded as exploitative and the inheritance of wealth was treated as the inheritance of accumulated effort. Individualists demanded that each individual should receive benefits proportionate to their efforts. However, this individualist notion of just distribution was underpinned by the view of wealth as evidence of effort (Taylor 1992:233). More broadly, inequality between individuals was regarded as the result of individual skill and effort. It was rarely considered worthwhile to look at the structure of the economic system for the causes of wealth and poverty. The few thinkers in the mid-19th century that did so, such as Friedrich Engels (1953:176), were quick to point out that "the difference between human and animal society is that animals are at most *gatherers* whilst men are *producers*". Engels claimed that this distinction at once made it impossible to transfer the laws of animal societies to human societies.

Individualists were not disposed to worry too much about any distinction between gatherers and producers. They employed evolutionary analogy to explain that the terrible conditions experienced by the laboring classes. These conditions were thought to be due to the maladaptation of the affected section to its immediate environment. The nature of the environment in which people actually lived was largely ignored. Free exchange and competition in an environment of common opportunity was simply presumed to exist. This ignored the fact that relations underpinning the capitalist market system ensure that a great portion of humanity must pay for access to the means of producing their own subsistence (Laurent and Nightingale 2001:24).

Though impressive theoretical models were constructed, and the arguments forwarded by Spencer and others may have appeared convincing, the social Darwinists could do little more than label those in control of the economy 'fit' and others 'unfit' in an arbitrary manner. It was presumed that the poor were rewarded by the market, and in a manner relating to the efforts they had made to help themselves. Their conditions were thought to correspond roughly to what they deserved. Engels, who knew well that the effort expended by an individual was only one of many factors determining remuneration, rejected all individualist notions of effort, reward and just deserts. Private ownership of the means of production was thought to skewed things considerably. New liberals acknowledged this also in the late 19th and early 20th centuries. Some of them, such as J.A. Hobson, came to consider private property (in land at least) to be incompatible with the rights-based individualist theory of justice (Taylor 1992:233).

Survival of the Fittest

The notion that the free market system enables the 'fittest' members of the human species to rise to the top, requires the presupposition that free competition prevails in human societies (as though all persons started in the same position). In reality, free competition, which the social Darwinists claimed to favor, would mean, as Taylor rightly pointed out, eliminating all of the advantages "conferred by the privileges and inequalities inherent in the existing social system" (Taylor 1992:73).

It is pointless to talk of survival of the fittest when a section of the community born with inheritance has great social power over whole sections of the species concerned before expending any effort or developing any of the necessary skills that success is said to require. When the social Darwinists spoke of natural selection in the context of human societies, they presupposed profits derived from property ownership and/or hereditary wealth. They were not prepared to admit that there could be no survival of the fittest unless all had equal access to productive resources.

It was in order to depict success in the capitalist market system as the result of free competition that the term 'survival of the fittest' was invented in the first place. This phrase was not coined by Darwin, but Spencer. Darwin only decided to use it in the 6th edition of his *Origin of Species* (Laurent and Nightingale 2001:19). This fact seems to have escaped Bertrand Russell (2001:151) who remarked that the phrase 'survival of the fittest' was too much for the intellects of those who speculate on social questions. Russell laughed so hard at the social Darwinists that he failed to notice it was they that had invented the phrase in the first place.

The notion that natural selection operates in human societies was also rejected by David Ritchie who claimed that in order to ensure natural selection in human societies it would be necessary to abolish all such institutions as inheritance, law and order, marriage for life and "everything that separates us from the animals" (Taylor 1992:91). Others, such as Lester Frank Ward (1970:264) suggested that if there were true competition in the industrialized world it would inevitably resolve itself into a competition between machines, so that instead of the fittest organism surviving it would be the fittest mechanism that survived.

The social Darwinists continuously ignored all such considerations. They continued to insist that competition needed to be maintained in order to avoid the possible degeneration of the human species. Nothing could convince them otherwise but that in nature there was a great plan, which was cruel, but necessarily so. There was no option but to let the strong survive and the weak die off.

In capitalist market societies it is almost always those that have the resources necessary to avoid competition that rise to the top. Those who co-operate (the propertied classes) generally thrive at the expense of those who compete (the property-less) (Ward 1970:239). Spencer and Sumner understood the process in a different manner. They assumed the capitalist system to be based on free and fair competition. As such, the hardships faced by the productive classes in modern industrial societies could be explained in terms of evolutionary failure. For them, human history was "heaped with the cadavers of evolutionary failure" (Spencer 1969:29). It could never be any different.

The form in which evolutionary theory was initially presented was such that it offered a ready platform upon which bourgeois theoreticians could justify all of the human consequence of the capitalist system. The economic terminology employed by Darwin throughout his work provided political antagonists with a means of furthering their own class interests. Darwin (1964:62) did supply a number of qualifications that were far from helpful for these antagonists. "I should premise," said Darwin, "that I use the term Struggle for Existence in a large and metaphorical sense, including dependence of one being on another, and including (which is important) not only the life of the individual, but success in leaving progeny". Statements such as this were neither consistent with, nor conducive to the social Darwinist efforts to give the force of natural law to the idea of competitive struggle in human societies (Hofstadter 1944:6).

Social Darwinists believed that the process of natural selection enabled human beings to adapt to their immediate environment (capitalist society). This process was considered to be the equivalent to the struggle for existence in nature. Nature was held up as a model to be followed by man and all were forbidden to 'meddle' with its operations. But though the social Darwinists appeared to worship nature, their reverence was really for bourgeois institutions. It was the interference with practices and institutions dominated by the owners of capital that was really forbidden (Ward 1970:250).

To create the impression that society was organized as it should be social Darwinists created the impression that the place of each individual in the social order was predetermined by genetic and/or cultural inheritance. It is this notion of a pre-determined social order that characterises social Darwinism. As contemporary commentators, such as Mike Hawkins (1997:31), have pointed out, Darwinism is based on scientific determinism whereas social Darwinism's "determinism extends to not just the physical properties of humans but also to their social existence and to those psychological attributes that play a fundamental role in social life". Social Darwinists explained individual behavior and circumstance in terms of inheritance and did all they could to downplay the role of class relations and related environmental conditions.

Non-individualist evolutionary thinkers such as Lester Frank Ward and Alfred Russell Wallace made none of the above assumptions. They believed that the evolution of human consciousness and reason must be understood in the context of human institutions. Though they did not deny that humankind might be evolving and adapting, they insisted that this evolutionary process was intelligible through examination of existing forms of social organization. Humankind adapted to changing circumstances through institutional and organizational processes. Unlike Spencer and Sumner, they believed that as human societies evolved they were raised above the senseless competition that characterizes the animal world (Ward 1970:261). The idea that the prosperous sections of human societies realized their prosperity through competitive struggle was rejected. It was understood that inherited wealth enabled one portion of the community to live idly off the labor power of others and thereby maintain their position in the order of things without having to compete.

The social Darwinists did not seem to mind if the wealthy were supported artificially. But they objected strongly to any state support for the working classes and poor. The effect, they claimed, would be to preserve the ill-suited genetic qualities that had made the weaker members weak in the first place. Welfare ensured that all of the poverty related character flaws would be passed on to the next generation. As such, it would call forth disastrous consequences up to and including the destruction of the human species.

The social Darwinists appear to have believed that the stronger members (the rich) were the ones that would ensure that the evolution of the species was in accordance with changes in the environment. Sumner, who considered wealth as the legitimate wages of superintendence, argued that the inheritance of wealth was a necessary means through which economic virtues and skills were acquired by the next generation. He regarded millionaires to be "the naturally selected agents of society for certain work" (Hofstadter 1944:58).

Since there is nothing in nature to maintain sections of a particular species artificially (such as owners of capital within the human species), it could be argued that the exploitative economic relations of bourgeois society, which are artificially maintained by the state apparatus, are inconsistent with 'natural selection' and the 'survival of the fittest'. It could be argued that the waste of human talent under capitalism offends the laws of nature. Of course any suggestion that capitalism is 'unnatural' would be just as groundless as the claims made by social Darwinists. All such claims can only be supported by taking prescriptions from nature and reading them into human societies in a prejudicial manner.

Family Ethics

When speaking of the progressive measures realized in the 19th century, Spencer claimed that they amounted to an intrusion of 'family-ethics' into the ethics of the state. This distinction between family ethics and individualist values enabled Spencer to argue that the latter reflected the cultural evolution of the human species as it adapted to a changing social and economic environment. Family ethics were altruistic, primitive impulses. In hunter-gatherer societies these ethics were valuable, but in market societies they stood opposed to individual self-interest and to public prosperity generally. Spencer explained that among different species in the animal kingdom the modes of behavior inside the family-group and outside were quite different. Inside the family group the weak are cared for. Outside the family group they are weeded out by means of the great struggle for existence. Since each system was designed for a specific purpose the intrusion of either mode into the sphere of the other would have to be destructive (Spencer 1969:137).

Spencer thought that family-ethics had no place outside of primitive social systems and that related sentiments should not be permitted to hold sway in modern societies. This objection was made on the grounds that it would undermine the struggle for existence and lead to the degeneration of the human species. It may also have had something to do with the tendency for altruism and/or solidarity to strengthen and equip the lower and weaker against the higher and wealthier classes of the community (Hofstadter 1944:100).

The problem with family ethics, as Spencer saw it, was its tendency to ensure the survival of members of the human race that should rightly perish. Only individualist values were consistent with an unhindered operation of the natural processes involved. As such, Spencer associated individualist values with modern industrial civilization and family ethics with primitive, tribal societies. He claimed that in primitive societies the well being of the state was considered more important than that of individuals, whereas in modern industrial societies the interests of individuals prevail. It was on this basis that he distinguished between primitive (militant) and modern (industrial) social systems. In his Book *The Principles of Sociology*, Spencer (1975:568–574) explained that there were really only two basic types of social organization. There was the militant type, in which the individual was owned by the state, and there was the industrial type, in which the individual is free to act, or not to act, under established rules. In militant societies, individuals were only free to pursue private ends if the state had no need for their services. Spencer explained that the militant system "does not simply restrain; it also enforces. Besides telling the individual what he shall not do, it tells him what he shall do". The two types of society were not thought of as separate systems that overlapped. They were thought to have found their 19th century expression in individualist ethics and family ethics respectively. As Spencer saw it, a new advanced type of society was evolving within the older 'militant' system. The behavior and morality ensuring individual adaptation to the common environment had to be different in the new 'industrial' society. There would no longer be any need for primitive moral precepts such as 'social justice'. The 'Law of Conduct and Consequence' would prevail in the 'industrial' society that was emerging, provided the human species was not prevented from evolving in accordance with its changing environment.

The militarist/industrial dichotomy served to justify the set of negative rights that enabled the owners of capital to maintain control over resources and over those that perform the actual work. It justified the processes through which competition among the laboring classes was maintained, along with the coercive measures through which collective action was prevented. As such, it justified the mechanisms through which the laboring classes were prevented from attaining their maximum development. This particular understanding of the social system was used in conjunction with social evolutionary doctrines in defense of the competitive order.

There were thinkers that were less willing to appreciate the merits of competition, such as Ward (1970:260–261), who insisted that the real effect of competition is "to maintain a certain comparatively low level of development for all forms that succeed in surviving". Ward knew that those members of a species that manage to avoid competition quickly outstrip those that cannot. For Ward, all human progress required humankind to "grapple with the law of competition and as far as possible to resist and defeat it". In contrast to Spencer, who believed competition (the industrial type) to be the basis of civilization, Ward believed that civilization progressed with the triumph of mind over ceaseless and aimless competition.

As Spencer denounced family-ethics and its consequences (reformism), he warned that disaster was on the way. He insisted that where reward is "great in proportion as desert was small, fatal results to the society would quickly follow" (Spencer 1969:137). The acts of parliaments of the 19th century were expected to produce the same consequences as the old poor law system had done previously. Spencer thought it essential to resist all reforms, the advance of the labor movement and any extension of the democratic franchise. All of the above would lead to socialism, which would act as a disincentive to healthy selection, "by cushioning the inferior from competition and stimulating their feckless breeding" (Crook 1994:71).

As far as Spencer was concerned, the liberal party under Gladstone was liberal in name only. It was interfering with the process of natural selection and, therefore, was actively promoting the "survival of the unfittest" (Spencer 1969:141). Gladstone, having granted reforms that would benefit the laboring classes to some limited degree, had offended the laws of nature. Given the proposals for reform that were made, Spencer came to the conclusion that legislators could not successfully prescribe for society unless they understood its laws. He thought that those prescribing for society must be able to properly chart "the normal course of social evolution...not to guide the conscious control of societal evolution, but rather to show that such control is an absolute impossibility" (Hofstadter 1944:43). In other words, legislators would never be competent enough to do anything unless they realized that they should do nothing. The free market was considered the only means of sorting out the good from the bad. If left to do its good work, it would leave the world stocked with those individuals that were best adapted to their environment.

Insofar as governments interfered with the natural struggle for life, they prevented people from exercising their natural faculties and this was expected to result in degeneracy. Within human societies, of which the capitalistic relations were thought a normal part, it was important to allow the forces of nature to weed out 'the weak' and make more room for 'the strong.' It was taken for granted that the strong were those that controlled the means of production and had managed to accumulate wealth off the back of the laboring classes (Crook 1994:43). Accumulation was part of a natural 'purifying process'. It was considered essential that the strong continue to shoulder aside the weak, and thereby ensure that the human species prevented the "multiplication of its inferior sample" (Spencer 1969:139). Spencer could not admit that the supposed inferior sample (the working classes) were actually the source of strength for those deemed most fit for existence.

Spencer had warned that the consequences of 'socialistic' legislation and related democratic progress would be disastrous. If the strongest (the owners of productive capital) were hindered in any way, or, if the weak (the working class, peasants and poor) were to be maintained artificially, useful variations would not be inherited by the following generation. As such, it was important to ensure that it was the individuals failing to adapt to their surroundings that suffered the consequences and not those that had adapted well. This would be in keeping with the 'Law of Conduct and Consequence' as well as supposed laws of nature and the process of natural selection operating within human societies.

Spencer reasoned that competition would need to be maintained if the human race was to remain healthy. Of course, the competition that was required was that between the laboring classes. Cooperation would always be necessary among the propertied classes. Ward (1970:264) recognised that this was how the system actually functioned. He complained that until the 19th century the chief difference between employers and employed was that the former used the 'rational method' while the latter used the 'natural method'. In other words, capital has always combined and cooperated while labor has only competed.

Insofar as radicals wished to make the economy subject to democratic control and demanded that production be planned in accordance with the well being of the people, radicalism was considered very dangerous (or even as a form of social disease) (Bentley 1987:61). The demands of organized labor were depicted as 'interference' with an otherwise free system, whereas, in reality, the labor movement demanded nothing other than the replacement of one set of regulations with another. The free market already operated within the confines of a particular set of regulations. Within that system the well resourced had a chance to make full use of their rational capacities. The laboring classes, who were necessarily kept in competition with one another since the free market system functions on that basis, usually did not.

In spite of the consequences that were readily observable in the social system, the political economists of the 19th century believed that competition produced the best of all possible outcomes for all involved (Ward 1970:264). Friedrich Engels (1953:185–186), who was among the few thinkers of the period to consider this system backward and destructive, suggested that Darwin "did not know what a bitter satire he wrote on humankind, and especially on his countrymen, when he showed that free competition, the struggle for existence, which the economists celebrate as the highest historical achievement, is the normal state of the animal kingdom". Engels insisted that competition and haphazard production would need to be abandoned and that only conscious organization could lift humankind above the rest of the animal world. He believed that competition, which exists among irrational animals, inhibited the potential development of a large portion of humanity. Ward (1970:262) took a similar view. He even suggested that all human civilizations had actually been built on top of cooperative efforts at the expense of competition. He claimed that all human institutions such as religion, government, law, marriage and custom were all simply "ways of meeting and checkmating the principle of competition".

These objections would make little difference in the end because market individualists were committed to the idea that competition was the mainspring of all civilization and prosperity. Spencer was one of the first to realize how useful it was to create the impression that competition served the same evolutionary function in human societies as it did in the natural world. This required him to overlook the fact that human societies develop in an artificial social environment that changes relatively quickly and therefore cannot be compared with animal life in a natural environment. The environment transforms the animal, while human beings transform the environment (Ward 1970:257).

The Language of Darwinism

The ideas of social Darwinists had really very little to do with Darwin's evolutionary theory. They became popular, not because they represented a scientific breakthrough, but because they highlighted the potential political uses of biological analogies. The propertied classes saw social evolutionary thought as the best available means of justifying existing power relations and related privileges. Spencer's system was widely adopted, not because it aided the study of social and economic life, but because it offered a means of dressing prejudice up as science.

Social Darwinism served mainly as a means of advancing proposed solutions to the problems faced by humankind that involved the removal of obstacles to capital accumulation. It did not matter that the arguments provided were baseless. What mattered was that, in the ideological climate of the day, it served to reproduce the long-standing individualist dictum: 'feed paupers and you will create more of them'.

It cannot be presumed that Darwin approved of the above speculation on social matters, especially those backed up by nothing other than biological analogy. Darwin was never content unless he could supply a great variety of evidence to support his arguments. And no one that studied the environment in which human beings lived could support the individualist notion that genetic deficiencies were the reason why particular people failed to achieve an adequate standard of life for themselves. Darwin actually believed that the "causes of progress seem to consist of a good education during youth whilst the brain is impressible" (Crook 1994:27).

It was not so much Darwinism as Darwinian concepts that attracted individualists. They saw that such concepts carried an aura of legitimacy and could be used to give the impression that the capitalist market system was ordered according to the laws of nature, that this was inalterable and that all designs to change things must lead to disaster. It was necessary to depict the capitalist order as something that had grown and evolved naturally. Using the phraseology of evolutionary science, the social Darwinists produced some convincing arguments as to how society *is*, but what they really wanted to do was convince themselves and others about how things *should be*. As with other commentators on social, political and economic phenomena they tried to disguise the moral and/or prejudicial content of their investigations and create the impression of disinterested scientific investigation. The manner in which human societies are understood provides the basis for speculation about how they should be organized. If a particular notion of what the world or human nature is like becomes 'common sense,' it can serve to legitimate social relations, opportunities, conditions of life, and distributions of wealth as they stand.

For his part, Darwin did his best to follow through with his scientific enquiries in a dispassionate manner, even if he did not like the results. That is not to say that his was a value-free analysis. There is no such thing. However, those claims for which there are good reasons to believe, need to be distinguished from those for which there is little or no evidence. The social Darwinists claimed to oppose state interference, but again, like all individualists, they could only really object to certain aspects of it. In order to maintain the impression that they stood for the individual rather than the state, they depicted the regulations from which the propertied classes benefited as something other than interference. They suggested that the various rules and regulations facilitating the rule of capital were formulated for the sake of individual freedom. Though the impression was created that individual freedom was demanded for the benefit of all people, it could not be, since, by individual freedom, individualists meant the freedom that depends on preserving for the owners of capital the right to dispose of property, along with the persons depending on it, in whatever manner they see fit. As with all individualists, social Darwinists supported state coercion for the benefit of the individual bourgeois as opposed to the individual laborer. They stood for rules and regulations relating to the collective will of the owners of capital as opposed to those relating to the collective will of organized sections of the wider community. They convinced themselves that they stood for individual freedom and stood opposed to collectivism. This dichotomy was used effectively by Spencer to argue against democratization and social progress generally. It was employed throughout the 20th century by theoreticians who wished to do the same.

CHAPTER SIX

INDIVIDUALISM AND THE QUESTION OF DEMOCRACY

The modern regime of liberal property ownership is characterized by a particular concept of democracy. That concept of democracy is bound up with the liberal concept of freedom, which is strongly influenced by the relations and conditions necessary for the proper functioning of the market system. Private property is considered the basis of the freedoms upon which democratic rights depend. Capitalist relations and democracy are considered to be part of the same package. Advocates of the free market highlight this connection, and with regard to early capitalism and democratization they are not wrong in doing so. The historical development of democratic forms corresponds to the historical development of the institutions facilitating production and trade based on the institution of private property. European capitalism provided the impetus for the development of liberal democratic systems in that part of the world, which produced multiple parties, facilitated elections and competition for office. The competition for office required a relatively free environment, and electoral politics in a free society was bound to call forth further democratic progress. In order for the liberal democratic system to function, even one with property and gender qualifications, it was necessary that freedom of association, freedom of speech and freedom to form political parties be established.

Though the development of democratic forms of governance has depended on the institution of private property, the extension and spread of democracy has been restricted by that same institution. To the extent that democracy refers to the capacity for people to influence the decisions that affect them, direct participation could well undermine the freedoms associated with private property. As such, any democracy promoted by advocates of the free market must be one subordinated to the dominant economic interests generated under capitalism. It must be a democratic form limited in such a way that it does not interfere with the continuous transfer of power from those with no access to capital to those with a ready access.

The form of democracy that developed in step with capitalist relations is closely bound up with the liberal mythology of private property, free markets and the rights and freedoms of the individual. Liberal democracy thrives under the protection of the capitalist state, which serves to facilitate compulsive transfers of powers from individuals unable to exercise their freedoms in practice to those with the capacity to do so (MacPherson 1966:50). The power-relations stem from the fact that those without resources must somehow gain access to resources owned and controlled by private individuals. Such access requires them to transfer control over their capacity to work, along with the product that results, on terms decided by others (MacPherson 1966:58).

The readiness with which people agree to sell their labor power has always depended on the extent and immediacy of their dependence on the will of the owners of capital. The laboring classes are pressured to sell their labor power in commodity form to the extent that those in control of productive capital are free to do with it whatever they please. That the owners of capital are free to destroy their own property means that they are free to destroy the class that depends on that property to produce their very means of subsistence. Insofar as capitalist regimes safeguard liberal ownership of productive capital, they positively facilitate the rule of capital over and above democracy. Liberal democracy is a form of democracy that prioritizes the accumulation of capital over and above public participation in political decision making.

The early liberals were certainly more concerned with the protection of property than with the extension of democracy. They never entertained the prospect of full manhood suffrage (never mind universal suffrage).[1] Though it was considered important to make governmental power subject to periodic elections, the franchise was restricted to free men (i.e., those with a store of capital). Those that sold their labor to individuals possessing capital did not qualify. Since they had allowed themselves to become dependent on the will of another they were no longer regarded as free men. Having renounced their natural freedom and independence they retained no independent will of their own, and were therefore in need of representation by others (MacPherson 1966:6).

---

[1] It is a common misconception that the levellers campaigned for manhood suffrage. They thought it best to exclude those in receipt of alms along with servants or wage laborers (MacPherson 1962:120).

The exclusion of the laboring classes and the poor from democratic participation was based on fears that they would make the 'wrong' decisions if included, and upset prevailing power relations. The exclusion of laborers hinged on the realization that the rule of capital could only continue so long as they had no real active part to play in the exercise of collective power.

Though the investing classes prefer to operate under democratic conditions, they insist that the power of any elected government must be limited. If the individual is to have the freedom to pursue his/her selfish interests (to accumulate capital), it is important to compel the entire community to respect property rights. With regard to such rights, people must not be given the opportunity to change the rules, and governments cannot be permitted to interfere with economic matters at their behest.

The continuous conflict between democracy, and what individualists called 'freedom,' was well understood by the great liberal, Benjamin Constant, who insisted that there could be no freedom to participate in the exercise of real political power. This, he suggested, was the kind of freedom enjoyed by the ancients. The liberal democratic system was, in contrast to this, designed to prevent people participating in the exercise of collective power. Constant (1988) celebrated the fact that there was no such participation in the capitalist market order. Individual independence from collective power was preferable to the freedom to participate in the exercise of collective power. He knew that the capitalist market order required independence from collective or governmental interference with the rights and properties of the individual (ruling-class freedoms). The important thing, of course, was that the owners of capital were free to control the lives of all those that depended on the use of their capital without any governmental regulation or public sanction.

Unlike many other individualists, Constant was up front about his position. He admitted that the political rights enjoyed in modern democratic societies, such as the right to vote, were not intended to give citizens any real power. He claimed that citizens "are called at most to exercise sovereignty through representation, that is to say, in a fictitious manner" and that the power that each individual has is "an ideal share in an abstract sovereignty" (Constant 1988:320). As such, democracy was transformed into something far removed from the literal meaning of the word. It had to be reinterpreted since there can be no 'rule by the people' in a capitalist market society. The citizen can play a part in the choosing of government, but cannot take part in the business of governing. As the modern economist J.A. Schumpeter (1943:284–285) explained,

> we simply do not mean by "democracy" what the word meant in pre-modern times: "democracy" does not mean and cannot mean that the people actually rule in an obvious sense of the terms 'people' and 'rule.' Democracy means only that the people have the opportunity of accepting or refusing the men who are to rule them…democracy is the rule of the politician.

The last part of Schumpeter's claim, that capitalist market societies are subject to 'rule by the politician,' though not incorrect, is somewhat problematic. While it cannot be denied that politicians do in fact lead and make decisions of great importance to large numbers of people, the relations between people, the conditions in which they live, along with all matters to do with investment, production and distribution, depend on decisions made in boardrooms. If it is accepted that these decisions have social, political and economic consequences then it must also be accepted that the dominant economic powers decide (though not necessarily by conscious design) if, where and when economic crises, wars and famines happen. The alliances made between nations and declarations of war depend, for the greater part, upon the augmentation of profits and damage done them, and not upon the whim of the politician. The role of the politician in all of this involves, among other things, the creative construction of pretexts. The extent to which the elected political representatives of big business are replaced by more representatives of big business (every four years or so), hardly effects the power relations constituting capitalist market societies. Politicians do not rule freely, but are subject to the same powers as are the laboring classes. As Constant (1988:310–311) admitted centuries past, "[t]he representative system is nothing but an organization by means of which a nation charges a few individuals to do what it cannot or does not wish to do herself. Poor men look after their own business; rich men hire stewards".

The Challenge of Democratic Progress

Freedom of speech and publication eventually caused problems for the propertied classes. As the capitalist system developed, the laboring classes grew. It was only a matter of time until they decided that they should have some say in the decisions being made that affected them. The fear that grew among the investing classes was that of broad democratic participation in political life, which could destroy their whole system. Since capitalistic accumulation depended upon the collective exploitation of the laboring classes, they would soon have to contend with efforts to undermine and eliminate it (MacPherson 1966:8). The fear that this might happen was once expressed by the great liberal Alexis de Tocqueville, who complained of a "depraved taste for equality, which induces the weak to desire to humble the strong, which brings men to prefer equality in slavery to inequality in freedom" (Bentley 1987:4)

It was important to ensure that the competition for political office was between parties representing different sections of the propertied classes only. Independent representation for workers needed to be discouraged because that level of participation would undermine the general task of the capitalist state, which is, of course, to maintain and promote capitalist relations (MacPherson 1966:9). It was necessary to ensure that those with a store of capital were able to use it to control the rest of the population. In order to maintain the dependent relations and to augment the existing means of economic coercion they needed to be in control of the political machinery. This meant that they were bound to oppose real political equality and real democratic participation.

The investing classes grew more worried as the class struggle within and against the liberal capitalist system took an organized form during the 19th century. The agitation of Robert Owen and his followers certainly exacerbated their fears. The types of reforms and regulations that Owen demanded were designed to limit the freedom of capitalists to employ and use capital and labor power as they wished. The businessmen and politicians of the day began to regard Owen as a troublemaker. When he was simply a philanthropist he was the most popular man in Europe, but, as Engels (1998:42–43) observed, his popularity waned when he identified the great obstacles blocking the path of social reform, which were, in his view, private property, religion and the institution of marriage.

The factory acts of the early 19th century placed uncomfortable restraints upon the conduct of manufacturers. The various regulations undermined the right of manufacturers to use or abuse their own property (including labor power with people attached to it), which was regarded as fundamental to their basic freedoms. As such, reforms that undermined the control of manufacturers were usually interpreted as infringements on the rights and liberties of the individual (Spencer 1969:71). The Chartist movement, with which Owenism overlapped, was considered to be particularly troublesome (Schwarzkopf 1991:208). The level of democratic participation demanded by this early socialist movement was feared more than any set of demands issued previously, since it threatened to completely undermine bourgeois institutions and practices.

Herbert Spencer

In the minds of individualists, the concessions granted the laboring classes by 19th century liberal politicians were completely offensive to the rights and freedoms of the individual. Herbert Spencer (1969:72), for example, regarded the decision to make it punishable to employ boys under twelve not attending school and unable to read and write, as offensive both to the economic laws of supply and demand, and the laws of nature. For Spencer, such legislation reflected how ignorant and backward-looking legislators of the day were. The reformism of the 'new' liberals and reformist politics of politicians such as Gladstone was understood as a throwback to Christian paternalism. Spencer (1969:151) protested that the "divine right of kings" was being replaced by "the divine right of parliaments". It did not occur to him that what individualists were advocating in their stead was the divine right of capital.

The message Spencer wished to convey was that democratic reformers were the new enemies of 'true liberalism'. As parliaments became responsive to the demands of the laboring classes, the freedom of the individual from 'the collective will' was diminished. There was no longer any guarantee that parliaments would not make inroads into the 'sacred rights of private property'. Indeed, if the pressure from the electorate was great enough, anything was likely to happen. As such, Spencer (1969:183) held that that the role of 'true liberalism' under such circumstances must be that of "putting a limit to the powers of parliaments".

Though 'new' liberals were considered dangerous, they were less of a threat than were the independent political organizations of the laboring classes. These demanded a measure of democratic control over the nation's resources and key industries. The pressure generated by these developments led some liberals toward compromise and reformist politics, and others to reaction. The more practical liberals saw the need to blunt the edge of class conflict.

As the ideas of socialism took hold, and the propertied classes were faced with an organized working class, many liberals felt that a compromise of sorts was necessary. Some even began to tolerate the idea of greater democracy. They began to entertain the idea of education for the working classes, labor laws and a whole host of progressive measures. Individualists were appalled at all of this. To them it was evidence that government was becoming responsive to the people in general, rather than just to the owners of capital. This situation put all ruling-class freedoms under threat. It was feared that society and the political machinery that had long-since facilitated class domination would never again be under the complete control of the propertied classes.

The investing classes realized that if the prevailing power relations were to be preserved only a democratic system that was well insulated from the will of the people could be trusted. The perceived threat of greater democratization plagued the ruling classes of the 19th century, which was really the heyday of capitalist market relations. Initially, it was the advocates of liberal ownership that had set the process in motion. Unfortunately for them, democracy began to outgrow the constraints they had imposed upon it. The class of waged laborers was growing more powerful as the economic system expanded, until it seemed as though the process of democratization was progressing in a similar fashion. The representatives of the ruling classes could no longer control such developments. They became analogous to Marx's sorcerer, who was no longer able to control the powers of the netherworld called up by his spells (Marx and Engels 1992:8).

Spencer was more sensitive than most to the dangers that social and democratic progress would bring. He feared that the market order might not survive the changes taking place in the 19th century. He thought it necessary to oppose all restrictions placed upon the bourgeois class, but for the sake of legitimacy, found it necessary to couch this opposition in language derived from the postulates of natural rights. Spencer did this to great effect. He insisted that all interference with the rights and liberties of the individual was interference with nature. The rights of the individual had to be protected from all threats, even those proceeding from democratically elected bodies. He claimed that such bodies were no more to be regarded as an unlimited authority than the authority of the monarch. He insisted that, "as true liberalism in the past disputed the assumption of a monarch's unlimited authority, so true liberalism of the present will dispute the assumption of unlimited parliamentary authority" (Spencer 1969:78).

The style of argument adopted by Spencer carried within it the illusion that social and democratic progress was opposed for the sake of key principles rather than class interests. The means through which the laboring classes might develop their intellectual capacities were also opposed under such pretences. The provision of free schooling supported by local rates was opposed, supposedly because it was inconsistent with liberal principles. It was said to be an infringement on the rights of the individual to 'compel' parents to send their children to school (Spencer 1969:73). But, of course, the problem that individualists faced was that the inhabitants of industrialized areas began to regard education as a right. They believed that it should be tax-supported and that it should be available to all. For Spencer, the prevalence of this belief was evidence that the 'true' principles of liberalism, set down by Locke, Constant and others, were being abandoned everywhere. He was incensed to find that people were beginning to denounce the payment of school fees as wrong (Spencer 1969:76).

Spencer realized that greater suffrage would bring about more of this kind of thing. Social and democratic progress only emboldened the property-less classes. Education would encourage them further. Moreover, if the working classes embraced the ideas of socialism they would settle for nothing less than a democratically controlled economy. As such, the task of 'true liberalism' thereafter had to be that of restricting the hand of the elected body.

Spencer did not believe that a general electorate would ever be able to choose representatives most fit for office. He complained of the established electorate that, "their selections are absurd" (Spencer 1969:243). Of course, he realized that if the laboring classes were given the opportunity to elect their own representatives then the existing mistakes would be replaced by worse ones. Therefore, it was necessary to prevent the property-less from having any say at all. It is "very dangerous," said Spencer, "to trust those whose interests are antagonistic to our own" (Spencer 1969:243–244). As part of an attempt to highlight the problems that democratic progress would bring, Spencer (1969:245) asked, "[w]hat should we think of a man giving his servants equal authority with himself over the affairs of his household? Suppose the shareholders in a railway-company were to elect, as members of their board of directors, the secretary, engineer, superintendent, traffic manager…should we not be astonished at their stupidity?"

The rhetorical questions supplied by Spencer were designed to play upon the most central prejudices and fears of the propertied classes. The above scenario was intended to convince them that further democratic progress had to be opposed. It was bound to have the desired effect because, for many property owners, the liberal state was regarded as something like a railway-company. Many considered themselves to be akin to shareholders with a stake in that company. From this point of view there could be no question of allowing the workers to have any say in the running of the state machinery. If they had any significant say in things then the rights and freedoms of the individual, as individualists understood them, would be short lived.

The political activities of the laboring classes did not begin with their involvement in electoral politics. They first began to vent their strength through defense organizations such as trade unions; but, since the working classes could not decide what laws they would be bound to obey, their organizations were generally pushed outside the confines of bourgeois legality. The hostility toward forms of working class organization has found some manner of expression in law since the earliest stages of capitalist development. The relations between capital and labor during the 19th century were maintained under extremely repressive legislation. In the U.K., this depended on an act that had been introduced in 1799, according to which any individual who joined with another to obtain an increase of wages or a reduction of hours was liable to be brought before a magistrate and face a sentence of three months in prison. This was the kind of legislation that was said to safeguard the freedom of the individual. There is no need to explain again what kind of freedom this was, who it was for, or what it entitled them to do (Ashton 1948:108).

As with the struggle for universal suffrage, the right to join a trade union was hard-won. Labor rights and universal suffrage were not realized in many industrialized societies until the early 20th century. The violent suppression of organized labor and other groups, such as the suffragettes, had to be endured up until then. The eventual granting of suffrage to the laboring classes in early 20th century Britain was, according to the Marxist author Ralph Miliband (1982:25), accepted by the ruling classes for the purposes of containing pressure from below rather than popular emancipation.

Spencer was not among those to recognize the necessity for reform. He knew that greater democracy would lead to the regulation and interference of business, and he was not prepared to accept this. Greater democratization would usher in laws limiting the hours worked by laborers in factories. There would be other interference such as provision of education to the children of laborers. The representatives chosen by the laboring classes would propose all manner of folly, such as public schools, welfare, pensions, and public health schemes. There would be no end to their attempts to order things to their benefit and to ease the conditions leading to competition in the labor market and prosperity in the community. Their interference would raise labor costs (something that is still viewed negatively) and thereby eat into the profits of investors. The laboring classes could never be given a voice in government because they could never fully appreciate, as individualists did, the 'sacred rights of private property'. Only the propertied classes could be trusted to cherish related rights and freedoms. As Carlyle once explained, "only the man of worth can recognize worth in men [and]...the worthiest, if he appealed to universal suffrage, would have but a poor chance". He continued by suggesting that, "if out of ten men nine are recognisable as fools, how...in the name of wonder, will you ever get a ballot-box to grind you out a wisdom from the votes of these ten men?" (Spencer 1969:249) The general point, of course, was that no good would ever come of universal suffrage. Greater democracy was considered a threat to civilization itself, since prosperity and freedom were thought to stem from the established regime of liberal owner-ship of productive capital (Malthus 1973b:3). If the full worth of the institution of private property were not appreciated, the consequences would be disastrous. For this reason, it was important not to permit the laboring classes to appoint deputies of their own choosing. Their deputies "will be truly representative," said Spencer, "representative, that is, of the average stupidity" (Spencer 1969:249).

Simple arguments to this effect were not enough to convince people of the error of their ways, which was why Spencer portrayed the market order as an outgrowth of human nature. He thought that if the capital-ist market order were understood as natural, people would no longer regard it as open to further manipulation by elected representatives (Spencer 1969:166). Unfortunately for Spencer, many did, and many of those that did, insisted on calling themselves liberals. These 'new' liberals began to promote all kinds of positive rights and freedoms, and sometimes even argued in favor of the extension of democratic control over the nation's economic resources. This was certainly the position adopted by later liberals, such as J.A. Hobson, which meant that in a few cases there was no longer a great distinction between those call-ing themselves liberals and those calling themselves socialists (Bentley 1987:93). Though new liberals seldom went this far, they were generally sympathetic to the demands for social and democratic progress and critical of the intransigence of individualists. They tended to accept that not all forms of collective action involved coercion, and, unlike individualists, they were willing to acknowledge that where the state provides public services, no one is compelled to make use of them, and no one is prevented from offering or availing themselves of the same sort of services on a private basis (Hobhouse 1911:75).

As far as Spencer was concerned, those that adhered to the reformist tradition (now associated with J.S. Mill) were advocating state coercion and not extended freedom as they claimed.[2] Spencer did not think of freedom as something that could be shared or equalized. The individual was free through ownership of his or her person, capacities and properties. Interference with any of these essential requirements diminished individual freedom (MacPherson 1962:148). Any attempt to equalize human potentialities, or, any interference from an elected body with the basic human rights of the individual undermined freedom.

It was not considered possible for the state to safeguard individual freedom and at the same time promote social justice. Spencer (1969:76) complained that the promotion of social justice brought with it "multiplying sets of regulations," which, when imposed, greatly restricted the "freedom of the citizen".

Democracy and Individual Freedom

In the minds of individualists, the capitalist market order provided the conditions of freedom wherein individuals could develop to their full potential. All persons were considered free to begin with because they were not prevented from entering contracts with one another freely. Insofar as they were free to live together as equals, they were also free to be unequal. Since there was no authoritative allocation of work, the deals made between individuals were considered the result of free choice. All individuals (men at least) had a legal right to own property; therefore, special privilege was no longer thought to exist (Patterson 1997:1).

---

[2] J.S. Mill recognized that the laboring classes in a market order were in fact forced to sell themselves as slaves. He insisted that the ability to alienate your own freedom was not freedom (Mill 1992:126).

The above interpretation could never change the fact that the relations between individuals in capitalist market societies are power relations, or the fact that the direction in which power is transferred depends on ownership of property. The conceptions of freedom and democracy that developed among individualists had to do with the maintenance of these power relations, related interests and prestige. These conceptions were born out of the realization that in order to safeguard the said power relations, the political system would have to safeguard liberal ownership over productive capital. Unless productive capital remained under the control of private individuals, surplus value (profit) required for reinvestment would not be extracted in a manner that left the propertied classes in control of the wider community (MacPherson 1966:7). It is for this reason that the individualist conception of democracy has always been narrow. It is for this reason that individualists use the word 'democracy' almost invariably in reference to the style of electoral politics that legitimizes the capitalist market system. It must be remembered that elections were first held for no reason other than to prevent one section of the propertied classes taking permanent control. In order for the capitalist market system to work, it was important to distribute governmental power among the various sections of the propertied classes. It was always assumed that the people that owned the country would have the greatest say in how it would be governed.

The early bourgeois democratic system was necessarily limited and responsible to different sections of the propertied classes. The function of liberal democratic government (wherever the laboring classes remained disorganized) was to promote and maintain liberal ownership rather than universal freedoms and class rule rather than democratic rule (MacPherson 1966:9). It required a measure of competition between different sections of the ruling class, which necessitated democratic freedoms. The right to free speech, freedom of assembly and freedom of publication for all citizens, along with other basic liberties, were established as human rights and were demanded *in principle* for everybody (MacPherson 1966:8).

Though they would not have the opportunity to vote, it was accepted that the working classes should have the same formal rights as anyone else. The granting of these rights to all was in keeping with the individualist notion that all are born with a set of basic rights and freedoms. Individualists saw no danger in granting the same formal rights to the working classes; they could have all the rights that they wished so long as they didn't try to exercise them. Of course the rhetoric was tested when the working classes began to organize themselves on the basis of their collective interests and began to demand all sorts of reforms, along with an extension of the franchise.

Ostensibly, individualists objected to an extension of the franchise in order to protect the individual from the 'tyranny of the majority.' In the 19th century, the notion that an organized working class would destroy 'freedom' generally prevailed. It was even entertained by progressives such as J.S. Mill, who was acutely aware that there was little opportunity for the laboring classes to better themselves under the capitalist market order. Though Mill stood at the foot of a separate tradition, he echoed the individualist claim that democracy carries with it the "peril of majority tyranny" (Gray 1986:21). Mill recognized that laborers, who in fact have "little choice of occupation or freedom of locomotion, are practically as dependent on fixed rules and on the will of others, as they could be on any system short of slavery" (MacPherson 1977:55). He was, nonetheless, won over by the scare mongering tactics of individualists. For the sake of 'liberty' this relatively progressive thinker proposed a system of voting that would prevent the laboring classes from having a majority voice in government. Nevertheless, Mill must be recognized as one of the first bourgeois democrats to entertain the idea of universal suffrage (MacPherson 1966:6).

Mill (1992:282) envisaged an electoral system in which there would be plurality of voting. He considered it fitting that the more intelligent (the propertied classes) should have more votes than anyone else. Liberty and individuality were thought to be at stake because the laboring classes were thought more likely to support tyranny than others. Until such time as strong democratic traditions and a love of freedom had developed among the masses they would not be ripe for participation in political matters.

To suggest that the property-less were not yet ready to have a say in the decisions that concerned them, was as good as saying that they never would be, since the conditions produced within the capitalist market order were hardly conducive to the development of a love of freedom and democracy. This did eventually develop among the laboring classes, but within their voluntary and defensive organizations; they did not learn it from bourgeois individualists. Of course, the conceptions of freedom and democracy formulated by the laboring classes were very different from those that had prevailed up until that point. They were not formulated in a manner in keeping with the unrestrained rule of capital, but according to the interests of the property-less classes. Their democracy was not compromised by the doctrines, institutions and legislation built up around the rule of capital; it was developed in reaction to the consequences of that system of relations. Unlike individualists, the laboring classes did not consider exclusive private control over productive resources to be the source of individual freedom (Althusser 1977:234–235).

In the 19th century, great sections of the laboring classes thought fit to exercise the freedoms they were supposedly born with. They began to seek representation independently of the owners of capital. This was something they were never supposed to do. As such, their actions were depicted as threats to the rights and properties of the individual.

Whether individualists realized it or not, another danger was on its way. Soon the struggle for greater freedom and democracy and corresponding threats to the system of bourgeois ownership was accompanied by scientific challenges to the ideology supporting the capitalist market system. These challenges reached their most sophisticated and coherent expression in the writings of Karl Marx and Friedrich Engels. These thinkers did more than any other to portray liberal ownership of productive capital as the source of deprivations experienced in industrialized societies. Their writings convinced many people that the only solution to the terrible conditions experienced by the laboring classes was social ownership and democratic control over the means of production. Insofar as such notions took hold, people came to believe that the suppression of socialism and democracy did not represent a *defense* of freedom but the *suppression* of freedom. Advocates of the capitalist market system detested Marxists due to the conscious efforts they made to reveal its exploitative nature. Their organizations were outlawed in many countries from the 19th century onwards.

Labor activists advocated the organization of labor on the basis of labor itself. The demands that labor organizations advanced could not be realized without beforehand undermining the social/political power of the owners of capital. As such, organized labor was treated as dangerous and aroused great fears in every capitalist market society. The potential of the collective power of workers to annul the continuous transfer of power to the owners of capital was well recognised. Individualists knew that in order for the capitalist system to continue to exist it would be necessary to prevent working class solidarity as far as possible. Historically this has been achieved by means of promoting collectivist ideologies that cut across class lines, such as nationalism (Bhaskar 1989:8).

The owners of productive capital can tolerate democracy in principle, but they must ensure that it is an elite game in practice. In circumstances where the subordinate classes manage to organize themselves in accordance with their own interests, the ruling classes must promote other interests in their stead (usually corresponding with nationalist, sectarian, racist, gendered, or other divisions). For the sake of the capitalist market system, anything is preferable to real democratic accountability. There is simply no place for it alongside continued accumulation of capital. In a capitalist market society, the key decisions must be made by a select few and according to the guidelines established in accordance with the rule of capital. A tiny minority of people must be free to decide how the society is to be run. The majority cannot be permitted to do much more than watch.

The contradiction between individualism and democracy was not diminished in the early 20th century when the advocacy of a broad democratic suffrage became the stamp of legitimacy (MacPherson 1966:1–10). Participation was still opposed, but individualists realized how important it was not to be seen to oppose it. Of course, it was difficult to defend the capitalist market order against the threat posed by democracy and at the same time express a devotion to democracy. Individualists soon realized that arguments against democracy needed to be presented as arguments against something else. Since they no longer wished to oppose democracy in an obvious manner, but knew that democratic progress put the freedom of the individual at stake, they focused their attacks on the progressive measures necessary for greater participation. They continued to treat the requirements for meaningful participation as attacks on 'freedom'.

Opposition to democracy was thereafter couched in terms of the supposed conflict between 'freedom' and democracy. Individualists emphasized the need to make a clear demarcation between the business of elected bodies and the business of the individual. If this distinction was made for the sake of universal (supra-class) freedoms then it would be perfectly reasonable, since those that cherish freedom must demand a demarcation between private life and the business of government. But this was not what individualists sought. They demanded the freedom that results from class domination and which depends on a lack of freedom on the part of the majority. They knew that the exercise of this freedom required private ownership of productive capital and the coercive maintenance of the unequal fortunes that result.

From the beginning of the 20th century, individualists have found it necessary to make a distinction between liberalism and democracy. This had to do with the difficulty of maintaining the basic power relations underpinning the capitalist system in the face of sharpening class antagonisms. The individualist thinker F.A. Hayek, who is dealt with in some detail in the following chapter, claimed that liberalism is concerned with the extent of governmental power, whereas democracy is concerned with who actually holds power (Hayek 1978:56). This distinction between abstracts was a means of avoiding a direct admission that private ownership and control over productive capital is incompatible with greater democratic participation. Hayek was in fact quite concerned to limit democratic participation. He lamented the fact that his own generation "talks and thinks too much of democracy and too little of the values which it serves" (Hayek 1991:52–57). While democratic forms were considered necessary for the efficient operation of a competitive market economy, democracy needed to be limited to that function. The free market had to take precedence over democratic accountability. In effect, this meant that regardless of the will of the mass of people, the great bulk of accumulated social power had to remain under the control of banks, big business and other unaccountable entities. Followers of Hayek, such as John Gray (1986:74), continued to stress the dangers, going so far as to insist that "no system of government in which property rights and basic liberties are open to revision by temporary political majorities can be regarded as satisfying liberal requirements" and that "an authoritarian type of government may sometimes do better from a liberal standpoint than a democratic regime".

The relationship between capitalism and democracy is burdened with conflicts. The compounding of the two in liberal mythology required the subordination of democracy to the set of rights that produce the necessary inequalities in freedom of choice (MacPherson 1966:7). As such, democracy is reshaped in a manner befitting the general prerequisites of capitalistic accumulation, which necessarily rules out mass participation in politics. It is not practical to advocate *laissez-faire* capitalism and also advocate the development of a democratic society. To insist that people must have the opportunity to influence the decisions that affect their lives is to insist that those in control of the productive assets upon which the entire community depends must be made accountable to the public.

CHAPTER SEVEN

THE IDEAS OF F.A. HAYEK

The course of events punctuating the first half of the 20th century made life difficult for those wishing to defend the unregulated variant of capitalism. Faced with disaster after disaster, people were beginning to regard the free market as a recipe for economic crisis, social unrest, imperialist wars, revolution and reaction. In the inter-war period, the more extreme individualist doctrines were overshadowed by theories paying closer attention to the crisis-ridden nature of capitalism, such as those offered by Keynes.[1] This change was not wholly the result of new insights. Keynes was not the first to challenge neo-classical economics. Many decades before, Marx had explained that "capitalism faces a strange new problem unheard of in previous societies: not scarcity of output and resources, but excess of output and resources relative to the effective money demand for them" (Sherman 1972:46).

Individualist doctrines went out of fashion for a considerable period in the 20th century. This shift in consciousness was partly due to the collective experience of worsening economic crises and war on a global scale. Even the political representatives of the investing classes realized that policy decisions could no longer be made without taking some of the immediate interests of the laboring classes into account. It was necessary to have the broadest possible appeal. The arrival of universal suffrage, along with the sharpening of class struggle in the early years of the 20th century, had rendered individualist doctrines impractical for the most part. Thereafter, individualism and the economic relations corresponding to its principles seemed to be on the way out.

Given the intellectual climate it is not surprising to find that the classical liberal, F.A. Hayek, was very much isolated among economists (Keynes dismissed him as "crazy", even though he considered his ideas

---

[1] In this case reality refers to the real relations and conditions that are readily observable. Keynes did not ignore the fact that the relations between people under capitalism meant that the purchasing power of the productive was so weak as to produce periodic crises.

to be "rather interesting").[2] For many people, the great depression had demonstrated the negative consequences of unfettered markets. However, for Hayek, unregulated markets remained the only means to realize beneficial effects for the wider community. He insisted that only free enterprise could properly facilitate the spread of knowledge (through the price mechanisms) such that the supply of goods and commodities would correspond with the preferences and needs of the consuming public. As Hayek (1982a:115–116) put it:

> The manufacturer does not produce shoes because he knows that Jones needs them. He produces because he knows that dozens of traders will buy certain numbers at various prices because they (or rather the retailer they serve) know that thousands of Joneses, whom the manufacturer does not know, want to buy them. Similarly, a manufacturer will release resources for additional production by others by substituting, say, aluminium for magnesium in the production of his output, not because he knows of all the changes in demand and supply which on balance have made aluminium less scarce and magnesium more scarce, but because he learns the one simple fact that the price at which aluminium is offered to him has fallen relatively to the price of magnesium.

Hayek (1991:12–13) pointed out that prosperity and progress resulted, not only from the unchaining of individual energies and the free use of new knowledge, but from the system of market relations, which spreads the relevant knowledge through changes in prices. It followed from this that all civilized life depended on individuals remaining free to utilize their knowledge in accordance with their own interests.

As with earlier economists, Hayek considered the free market as the highest pinnacle of human achievement. He was sure that where markets are free, and individuals are free to use detailed knowledge relating to their own enterprises in accordance with their own interests, the entire community benefits. For Hayek, there was no effective alternative means of enabling relevant knowledge to be spread and received by individual actors. It remained impossible for a public power to ever possess all of the knowledge required to meet the production and consumption needs of a complex civilized society (Gamble 1996:67). The market was considered to be the only adequate means for transmitting to others essential data about "the infinitely complex structure of preferences and resources in society" (Gray 1986:69).

---

[2] This quote is taken from Andrew Gamble's *Hayek: The Iron cage of Liberty* (Gamble 1996:2).

Hayek thought that it was precisely the prevailing assumption that production could be planned by a public power for the benefit of society that gave rise to the problems exhibited in the industrialized countries during the 20th century. He referred to this belief as the "constructivist fallacy" (Gray 1986:29). Anyone entertaining the 'constructivist fallacy' was treated as an enemy of individualism. Hayek went so far as to break all societies, past and present, into two kinds of order: 'taxis' and 'cosmos.' The word 'taxis' was used in reference to the types of order flowing from human will and intention, whereas 'cosmos' referred exclusively to 'the market order', which Hayek treated as a spontaneous order (one which no one consciously creates). Hayek thought that humankind had produced 'the market order' through trial and error. It was something that was stumbled upon as human societies became more complex. It was better than any system that could be set up by conscious design since it allowed for the knowledge and skill of all members of society to be utilized with the greatest possible efficiency. For the development of this system it was only necessary to ensure that individual rights and freedoms were recognized and respected (Hayek 1978:57). There was no need to plan and control things. On the contrary, this system could only function if knowledge was diffused among millions of economic agents and known in its totality by no one (Gray 1986:69). However, the very market operations that Hayek liked to contrast with conscious control of production was rapidly changing in and of itself. Though the market order may have at one time been dominated by owner-entrepreneurs making decisions on what to produce according to price signals, it was evolving, certainly from the beginning of the 20th century, into a system dominated by monopolistic firms working to check competition, organize production on a rational basis and control prices.

Since the capitalist market system presupposed liberal property ownership, it was necessary that everyone respected the private domain of the individual (private property). It was clear to Hayek (1982b:31) at least, that people would have to adjust their moral precepts to suit. There could be no large-scale pursuit of 'social justice.' Production and trade could not be subject to regulation for the sake of the perceived needs of society as a whole. It could not be rewarded according to perceptions of what was a 'just wage' for the labor performed. It was only necessary to abide by 'rules of just conduct', by which Hayek meant the rules that were end-independent and which aided the development of the 'spontaneous order'. The political movements that campaigned for social justice were treated as the product of outmoded and misplaced morality. The various strands of socialism were depicted as backward looking rather than progressive (Hayek 1982b:110–111).

To Hayek's mind the 'great society' (the capitalist contract society) was evidence of the continued evolution of the human species. The only problem was that it had run ahead of the instincts and emotions of the average individual, which, in Hayek's view, "are better adapted to the life of a hunter than to life in civilisation". He claimed that "human beings have become civilised against their basic instincts and emotions. In their hearts they remain socialists" (Gamble 1996:28). For this reason, Hayek considered it necessary to suppress such instincts and emotions in order to sustain the economic order and related prosperity. The new morality emerging within the market system was regarded as the product of social evolutionary progress since it enabled individual persons to develop the economic virtues most conducive to prosperity in a complex social order. Unlike many other individualists, Hayek did not suggest that humans were naturally cold, selfish and calculating, only that the competition generated within the market system made it necessary for people to act rationally. He held that the advantages that rational behavior confers on individuals ensured the related behavior would spread across society through imitation (Hayek 1982c:75). Since this was part and parcel of 'the market,' which was considered the basis of civilization, Hayek treated socialism as the greatest threat to human progress. It encouraged two of the most primitive moral instincts, solidarity and altruism (Gamble 1996:28).

One important distinction that Hayek wished to make was between the 'purpose-governed' organization of 'socialist systems' and the supposedly 'purpose-independent' liberal order (capitalism) which was thought to have emerged spontaneously. He thought that in a purpose-governed order each individual would be made to carry out some duty imposed by somebody else. In such a system, the individual would no longer be remunerated according to effort expended (which was assumed to be the case in the capitalist market order), "but according to how well he has, in the opinion of others, performed his duty" (Hayek 1978:68–69). Hayek claimed that the difference between a 'liberal order' and a planned system is that the former is impartial whereas the latter is moral. In a free market society, success and failure depend on a "mixed game of skill and chance". Insofar as people agreed to "play the game" and shared in the resulting prosperity they could not demand social justice simply because things were no longer going their way (Hayek 1978:68).

For Hayek, freedom simply meant the absence of coercion. He realized, of course, that in any civilized society there could never be a complete absence of coercion. As such, it was only possible to speak of freedom in terms of degree of independence from the will of others. Freedom required "the possibility of a person's acting according to his own decisions and plans" (Hayek 1960:12). Hayek (1960:13) insisted that freedom does not depend on the range of choices available to a person but "on whether he can expect to shape his course of action in accordance with his present intentions, or whether somebody else has power so to manipulate the conditions as to make him act according to that person's will rather than his own". In other words, people might have their choices foreclosed, but unless they were otherwise compelled to obey the will of another person, this could not be construed as coercion. Hayek insisted that freedom should be understood as *freedom from* coercion and not *power to* realize particular ends. The distinction between negative freedoms and positive powers enabled Hayek to treat 'the market' as a system of free and reciprocal relations between individuals. His critics, such as J. Viner (1991:112), were quick to point out that while it may be important to use different terms for "freedom from" and "power to" and not to confuse one with the other, "to discuss 'freedom from' in abstraction from 'power to' is futile, since the extent and practical significance of 'freedom from' is highly dependent on the extent and location of 'power to'". But the weakness of such categories mattered little since they enabled Hayek to deal with the market apart from the capitalist relations around which it had to operate, which could hardly be depicted as free or reciprocal. It was precisely Hayek's lack of attention to capitalist relations that enabled him to create the impression that the distribution of wealth across society was the result of fair competition, though he freely admitted that the results sometimes had more to do with chance than effort.

Hayek (1978:68) claimed that since nobody distributed income in the 'market order', as would be done in an organization, it had to be concluded that all talk of a just or unjust distribution was nonsense. He claimed that if risk does not rest with the individual there can be no choice (Hayek 1991:94). Though he may be right in some respects, the fact remains that the choice generally lies with the investing classes and the risk of falling into poverty generally lies with the property-less. As such, it is quite obvious that when Hayek stressed the need to preserve 'our liberty' he was referring to (though not necessarily consciously) a form of liberty that can be realized by a special section of society only.

Like other individualists, Hayek believed that any challenge to the economic power of investors amounted to an infringement on individual sovereignty. Not only did he oppose all proposed infringements, he actively worked to undermine the moral precepts justifying them, such as 'distributive justice'. He sought to replace these with moral precepts conducive to the rule of capital, i.e., those that take for granted state control over the laboring classes and/or justify related privileges. For Hayek, the 'market order' was not designed with the interests of particular people in mind. It was 'law-governed' whereas all other systems involved state coercion, which was always justified on the basis of some moral ideal. The idea of a 'moral' state as opposed to one safeguarding the individual enabled Hayek to depict existing privileges as the result of 'skill and chance' rather than the capitalist mode of production and related state coercion.

Theory, Method and Consequence

Hayek claimed that the direction in which ideas moved in a particular period could be traced back to the theoretical and moral positions taken by leading intellectuals of the day. The collectivist ideologies and movements of the 20th century were attributed to the conception of 'value to society'. Notions, such as that of 'social justice', were thought to lead to a personification of society, which inevitably led to collectivist movements. Hayek believed that wherever the collectivist mindset is absent and 'individualism' is present, a "spontaneous order of free men" emerges. Where collectivist ideas are accepted, all are made to serve a single hierarchy of ends. A society in which people were governed according to some ideal of 'social justice' would necessarily be totalitarian and personal freedom would be absent (Bird 1999:13). Totalitarian regimes were the consequence of a collectivist mindset rooted in the constructivist fallacy, which depended on collectivist theories and methods. For Hayek, an individualist mindset must proceed from methodological individualism and the collectivist mindset must proceed from methodological collectivism. The division is certainly not as clear-cut as Hayek imagined it to be. As Roy Bhaskar (1989:8) pointed out, collectivism in its right wing form:

is a complementary ideology to the market—it expresses the sum of...institutions, values and interests necessary to make the market work, from the inheritance of property to appeals to national interest...in its left wing form, it is a reactive ideology to the market—it expresses an array of social institutions, values and interests which allow the victim of the market to survive it.

The relation between collectivist thinking and the collectivist arrangements that characterize the capitalist market order was not something Hayek wished to dwell on. He preferred to deal in vague categories such as 'liberalism' and 'collectivism' and treat them as though they correspond exactly with capitalism and socialism, respectively. These were considered to be mutually exclusive, whereas fascism and socialism were considered to be products of the same movement of ideas. To Hayek, the world consisted simply of 'liberals,' who believed in freedom, and socialists (including fascists and new liberals), who wished to interfere with the rights and properties of the individual. Those valuing freedom were those opposing 'unnecessary' state intervention in economic affairs (Bird 1999:9). Fascists and socialists were considered part of the same movement on account of their 'common hostility to competition and their common desire to replace it by a directed economy' (Hayek 1991:30).

There is a grain of truth to this claim, though nothing more than a grain. It is true that there was widespread hostility to market competition in the years preceding the rise of fascism, but this hostility came from all quarters. The Weimar republic fell, largely because the Great Slump made it impossible to keep the tacit bargain between state, employers and organized workers, which had kept it afloat. Industry and government felt they had no choice but to impose economic and social cuts, and, as Eric Hobsbawm (1995:137) explained, mass unemployment did the rest. The working classes were well organized at the time and refused to accept depression cuts. This led to the collapse of parliamentary government and the rise of Hitler. The point missed by Hayek was that the conditions that produced hostility to 'the market' were produced by the capitalist market system itself.

Hayek's depiction of German fascism as a variant of socialism makes sense from an individualist standpoint. However, when attention is paid to the objective conditions giving rise to the movement and the functions that it ultimately served, the connection becomes dubious. Fascism emerged through the suppression of socialists, the elimination of independent labor unions along with other limitations on the rights of management to manage the workforce. In fact, the fascist 'leadership principle' was precisely that which bosses and business executives normally applied in their own businesses. As Hobsbawm (1995:129) explained, the fascists gave this principle "authoritative justification". Though the immediate interests of the investing classes were often overridden, in the long run, their interests were secured.

Hayek was not very concerned about the class structure of German fascism. He only wished to create a set of concepts that would enable him to condemn socialism by association and vindicate the market order in the same breath. He thought that the best way to do this was to undermine the popular belief that the fascist movement and related imperialist wars were rooted in bourgeois economic relations. Hayek claimed that fascism was just socialism employed in the service of a different class (the petit bourgeoisie). Of course this is like saying that monopoly capitalism is a sort of bourgeois socialism. But the claim was made in order to create the impression that individualists stand for freedom and that all other political traditions compromise freedom and rights to some extent. Those that questioned the wisdom of the capitalist market were generally grouped together under the heading of 'collectivist' or 'socialist'. The 'true' liberals were those defending the economic independence of the individual and collectivists were all those that wished to direct economic activity for the purposes of serving the greater good. This led him to believe that under socialism (i.e., fascism or interventionist/welfare state) the "individual is merely a means to serve the ends of the higher entity called society or the nation" (Hayek 1991:111).

Hayek's collectivist-individualist dichotomy enabled him to argue against the popular belief that fascism represented a reaction by those threatened by the advance of socialism. He suggested that rather than being polar opposites, fascism and socialism represented rival collectivist doctrines geared toward similar ends. All collectivists demanded planning of the economy as opposed to the free market system. This 'free market' was described as free because, supposedly, there were no attempts to realize any collective good or distributive ideal. The notion that 'the market order' is not organized according to any distributive ideal generally prevails among those with the power to decide the manner in which resources should be distributed.

The problem with Hayek's interpretation of fascism and socialism is that it does not correspond well with any facts or historical examples.

It was precisely the socialists, communists, social democrats, trade unionists, anarchists and other left wing groupings that opposed fascism consistently. Generally, when it came to opposing fascism, there was little sign of those he considered to be 'true liberals'. Hayek explained this away with reference to a supposed ideological battle between socialism and liberalism. He insisted that though socialists were the only significant opposition to the Nazis, this "meant no more than that in the wider sense practically all Germans had become socialists, and that liberalism in the old sense had been driven out by socialism" (Hayek 1991:6). Supposedly, liberalism in the old sense (individualism) had been swept aside by a general movement toward a collectivist mindset, of which fascism was part.

Followers of Hayek have continued to employ his individualist/collectivist dichotomy in political argument. It remains useful as a means of blurring the distinction between Stalinism, democratic socialism and fascism. In John Gray's book, *Liberalism*, this categorization is adopted at the expense of any analysis of the economic, social and political factors leading to the development either of fascist dictatorships or Stalinist bureaucracies. He depicted the system that existed in the USSR simply as socialism. He did the same with regard to fascism in Germany. To his mind, Stalinists were socialists, democratic socialists were socialists, left liberals were socialists and fascists were socialists. In a matter-of-fact fashion, Gray (1986:36) explains that "in Germany and Russia totalitarian socialist regimes came to power which inflicted colossal injuries on their own populations and stifled liberty over most of the civilised world". As with Hayek, the word socialism was used in reference to almost all forms of political thought and action that stood outside the individualist tradition.

Though Hayek thought of collectivism and the market system as mutually exclusive, the distinction had no basis outside of the conceptual framework he had built. He did not wish to admit that the market order (capitalism) actually gives rise to collectivist tendencies. The idea that collectivism was alien to the capitalist market order could never be entertained by anyone other than those wishing to obscure its workings. Drawing on Karl Mannheim's analysis, Andrew Gamble (1996:82–83) explained that collectivist tendencies arise from the way in which industrial societies are organized. He pointed out that modern factories and organizations are highly collectivist institutions. Their internal co-ordination does not depend on individualist market exchange, but on planning. In order to preserve the kind of individualist society idealized by Hayek, it would be necessary to positively restrict the size of organizations. It would also require an active promotion of small and medium-sized enterprises. Of course Hayek promoted nothing of the sort. There was always a considerable divergence between the kind of social organization that he and other self-proclaimed individualists claimed to advocate, and the policies actually advocated.

Hayek (1991:88) claimed that fascists and socialists were the same because they were in agreement with regard to the desirability of the state controlling all economic activity. It made no difference that they "disagreed with the ends for which the aristocracy of the industrial workers used their political strength". However, distinguishing between fascism and socialism in terms of the ends for which workers use their strength is pointless, particularly since a liberal democratic order, which symbolically legitimates the contract society, also depends on the support of the powerful organizations of the workers. Any serious explanation of fascism or socialism must be appreciative of the background conditions. In the German case this means dealing with the crises that developed within the capitalist system, but it also means recognizing that the commitment to democracy on the part of the propertied classes therein was greatly dependant on the leaders of the workers' organizations taking a centrist position. Trotsky (1963:236), who was well aware of this, explained that, "as soon as 'the normal' police and military resources of the bourgeois dictatorship, together with their parliamentary screens, no longer suffice to hold society in a state of equilibrium—the turn of the fascist regime arrives".

To treat fascism simply as a different end for which the workers use their strength is to ignore the simple fact that it is precisely through the annihilation of the workers' organizations that fascism entrenches itself in power. Fascism cannot depend on the "aristocracy of the industrial workers" to achieve this end. It derives its support from different combinations of the exploited classes than does liberalism or democratic socialism (Trotsky 1963:235).

Hayek was not worried about any of the details mentioned above. He was content to treat fascism as the 'socialism of the right'. He was sure that it was the very notion that things could be planned that was the root of all totalitarian systems. As such, he contested the view that fascism and/or the war that had broken out in Europe (WWII) at the time, had developed out of existing capitalistic economic relations and related conflicts between individuals, classes and nations. These developments were considered the result of one general 'movement of ideas' of which socialism and fascism were part. WWII was treated as an outgrowth of existing ideological conflicts, which were themselves rooted in theoretical fallacies, and isolated battles between values. Supposedly, Germany, Britain, the US, Japan, Australia and half of Europe went to war for the sake of abstract principles.

Hayek set himself the task of exposing the intellectual 'errors' and 'fallacies' that supposedly underpinned all illiberal doctrines and institutions. A certain mode of thinking underpinned socialism and the welfare state, and it was this that led to totalitarianism, nationalism, authoritarianism and the command economy (Bird 1999:7–8). It followed that there should be a theoretical or methodological solution to the said problems. That is to say, if people learned to think differently about the world in which they lived then the calamities associated with the collectivist mindset would never have arisen in the first place. If people would only get this notion of social justice out of their heads, think of themselves as individuals rather than as part of a collective, then the human lot would be the better for it. It is worth recalling Marx's attitude to this mode of reasoning. He continues to poke fun from beyond the grave, this time by way of the following story:

> Once upon a time a valiant fellow had the idea that men were drowned in water only because they were possessed with the idea of gravity. If they were to get this notion out of their heads, say by avowing it to be superstitious, a religious concept, they would be sublimely proof against any danger from water. His whole life long he fought against the illusion of gravity, of whose harmful consequences all statistics brought him new and manifold evidence (Marx and Engels 1976:24).

Hayek employed a similar approach to problems of the 20th century as did the 'valiant fellow' sneered at by Marx. He did not consider ideas as they were connected to the economic relations, conditions of existence and political events that developed concurrently. It was as though there were intellectual movements exerting an outside force, altering the course of history, which could explain the above developments. General movements of ideas were considered to be in consequence of individual speculation, especially that of economists. Hayek went so far as to suggest that if the effects of Ludwig von Mises' *Theory of Money and Credit* had been more rapid it might have prevented much of the suffering and destruction that visited the industrialized world. Since Keynes was considered to have altered the course of history, Hayek suggested that the world might have been saved much if only his German had been a little better (Klein 1992:131). If he had only paid a little more attention to representatives of the Austrian school of economics he might not have sent politicians on the wrong course. Of course, there is no reason to assume that the policies implemented, which were labelled Keynesian, were chosen by Keynes. It is more likely that the political and economic problems of the day chose Keynes.

With regard to fascist Germany, Hayek glossed over the social origins, the historical circumstances, the intellectual protagonists involved and the privileges that were in the end safeguarded. His entire explanation depended on the idea of 'collectivism' as a thing in itself and 'liberalism' as a thing in itself, and the notion that where individualist ideas were replaced by collectivist ideas, free societies are transformed into authoritarian ones. The emergence of totalitarian regimes was considered the result of turns in intellectual life and the promotion of particular values and principles over others. No explanation was offered as to why particular values and principles become attractive to people at particular times. It is well known that such regimes came into being in countries that were experiencing a serious economic crisis, and that these crises were by-products of the free market. The system defended by Hayek produced problems that were suffered by the population collectively, lending to the development of collectivist mindsets. It is the nature of those mindsets, whether they were geared toward the protection of existing privileges or not, that requires explanation. Certainly, that which developed in Germany in the 1930's was in no small way helped by the collapse of the economy. The effect of the crisis was such that appeals to working class solidarity achieved a widespread response. Radicals and reformists were poised to use this to their advantage. At the same time as these developments were presenting, the privileged sections of society, wishing to preserve their wealth and power, also began making appeals to working class solidarity. This involved appeals to the 'national interest', with nationalism thereafter employed as justification for imperialist expansion, wage cuts at home, the putting down of strikes that result, and much more besides.

Hayek did not wish to dwell on the extent to which the structure of the economic system facilitated the development of the collectivist mindset. He was convinced that the theoretical source of liberal values could be known and so could those underpinning totalitarianism, authoritarianism, socialism and fascism.

Appeasement and Reaction

The economic crisis in Germany had radicalized a great portion of the population, and the organizations of the working class were on the verge of developing a revolutionary strategy. It was for this reason that certain sections of the propertied classes realized that their interests would be best served by letting fascists loose on the population. Perhaps not wishing to spell out the interests that were served by fascism, Hayek made no attempt at all to explain what happened to the German individualists in the years running up to the fascist seizure of power. His book, *The Road to Serfdom*, which supposedly offered an explanation of where fascism came from, did not explain where individual fascists came from, or where the non-fascist individualists had gone. But of course if Hayek tried to explain what attracted people to fascism from other political persuasions, or indeed from positions of political apathy, he would need to highlight the context in which it happened. This would mean dealing with some of the utterances of its supporters and apologists. Doing this would mean highlighting the crossover between 'liberals,' 'individualists' and those he had labelled 'collectivists'. However, all that Hayek wished to do was create the impression that right-wing collectivists were part of the same movement of ideas as left-wing collectivists.

So where did the fascists come from? The sentiment expressed by Winston Churchill to a group of Italian journalists in Rome in 1927 (shortly after the fascist seizure of power), should offer a clue. Churchill stated frankly that, "if I had been an Italian, I am sure I would have been wholeheartedly with you from the start to finish in your triumphant struggle against the bestial appetites and passions of Leninism". He added that, "in England we have not yet had to face this danger in the same deadly form. We have our own way of doing things".[3] In other words, the rights and freedoms of the individual, the rule of law and democratic rights still had their place in England, but this would change in consequence of threats to the interests and privileges of the investing classes. Of course there was a potential threat. And this may partly explain why, as late as 1935, Churchill was still of two minds about Hitler. But this was before the interests of the propertied classes in Britain were threatened by Fascist expansionism.

---

[3] Quote taken from R. Miliband's Capitalist Democracy (Miliband 1982:47).

The Prime Minister, Neville Chamberlain, had rejected what honest journalists of the day were saying about the regime that had emerged in Germany in the 1930s as "Jewish-Communist propaganda". And though he feared that he might bring war, even Churchill expected that Hitler might "go down in history as the man who restored honour and peace of mind to the great Germanic nation".[4] The point, of course, is that the propertied classes and their political representatives are usually only liberal when it suits, democratic when it suits and internationalist only if and when it suits. To accept the argument that 'liberalism' had been driven out of Germany by 'socialism' ignores the interests that were at stake.

Hayek's dependency on categories of thought and related movements of ideas such as collectivism were not accidental. The concept 'collectivism', served as a means of political obscurantism, which enabled Hayek to deal with the development of fascism without questioning what happened to all the erstwhile exponents of 'true' liberalism. If Hayek investigated this delicate matter he would have had to explain whether they had been won over to the arguments of the fascists or those of social democrats, socialists and communists.

Though it was not expressed as such, Hayek's individualist theory of fascism made the claim that those building the organizations of the working class were part of the same movement as those that stopped at nothing to crush them. When stated in such terms it makes little sense. It even betrays an unwillingness to deal seriously with the subject matter. He appears to have been fixated with the task of establishing a link between fascism and socialism, while distinguishing both from liberalism. This meant avoiding the observable features and consequences of fascism and socialism that made this difficult. As such, he came to depend on obscure categories, such as 'collectivism.'

The tendency for control over resources to translate into political power is something that is rarely admitted by individualists (Hayek 1991:68). Likewise, individualists of the early 20th century were not willing to admit that it was the tendency toward monopoly, coupled with economic crisis that created an environment in which individualist principles became impractical and unpopular. It was in order to avoid such links that Hayek attempted to attribute collectivism to

---

[4] Quote taken from R. Miliband's Capitalist Democracy (Miliband 1982:49).

factors outside the economic system. There was little concern with the elements making up fascism, such as nationalism, anti-communism, anti-liberalism, along with the employment of street violence as a political tactic. This may have been because these features were also exhibited by non-fascist groupings on the right. As such, the many aspects of fascism that were supported by right-wing individualists, such as intolerance of independent working-class organizations and opposition to meaningful participation in political life received little attention (Hobsbawm 1995:117).

The point that needs to be stressed is that the propertied classes were staunch liberal individualists only where it was practical, such as in Britain, where they still insisted that each individual must enjoy the same legal rights and formal freedoms. This individualism is entirely in fitting with the requirements of the capitalist market system, provided of course that the property-less do not try to change things through the power of numbers. The capitalist system functions best if all people are guaranteed the formal freedom to buy, sell and accumulate capital. It is best that the laboring classes remain free to follow investment and to sell their labor power and even for some of them to accumulate capital for themselves (join the propertied classes). It is essential, however, that the propertied classes reproduce those social-economic conditions that enable them to use their wealth to maintain their privileged position in society.

Since individualists present bourgeois control as freedom, it is not surprising to find that in the individualist tradition collective action is treated as a threat to freedom. For some individualists, military dictatorship, which is sometimes required to keep a lid on things, is considered justified under certain circumstances. This is because, as John Gray (1986:74) has pointed out political majorities can sometimes undermine a liberal order and authoritarian rule is sometimes required to maintain it. In fact the rights and freedoms of the individual sometimes need extremely repressive regimes standing over them, such as that headed by Pinochet in Chile during the 1970s and 80s.

Racist Nationalism and Imperialism

Insofar as the German fascists ultimately protected the interests of the propertied classes, Marxists have sometimes explained fascism as though it were a sort of trump card that the ruling class uses wherever its system is threatened. The Marxist Historian, Alfred Sohn-Rethel (1987:32), claimed that "what united this conglomeration of despera-dos was the demand for dictatorial government directed against the organized working class in their trade unions and the social democratic and communist parties". He did not suggest that big business wished for a fascist dictatorship. The propertied classes were forced to throw their lot in with the fascists in the face of real social and democratic progress. Sohn-Rethel (1987:9–10) claimed that "the urban and culti-vated ruling-class of Germany, with great heart-searching and after all other options had closed, turned to the politics of fascism to preserve their place in the sun". He did give credence to the view that the roots of fascism in Germany were to be found in the collective mind, but insisted that the German economy and its structure also paved the way for the Nazi regime.

Hayek's explanation of fascism neglected the fact that fascists always seize power through opportunistic exploitation of the same frustrations, fears and hatreds as are created under the capitalist market order. As such, his claim that German anti-Semitism and anti-capitalism sprang from the same root may be regarded as a simplistic truism. What Hayek didn't say was that, in their 20th century forms, both were rooted in the relations underpinning the capitalist market order. His approach to the problem was designed in such a way as to avoid any evaluation of the similarities between fascism and other right-wing reactions to the advance of socialism and democracy in the 20th century (Hayek 1991:104).

No one can deny that political liberalism was in retreat for much of the first half of the 20th century, but as Hobsbawm pointed out, in Europe the threat to liberal institutions came exclusively from the political right.[5] Not all of the forces overthrowing liberal regimes in the period were fascist. Not all reaction was characterized by mass mobiliza-tion from below, since crushing the labor organizations did not always require the fostering of emotional nationalism, racist attitudes and/or cultivation of the fears and frustrations of the unemployed. Other right

---

[5] Hobsbawm did not mention the Stalinist bureaucracies of Russia and Eastern Europe in this regard. This may have been because he did not think that they posed a threat to the liberal institutions already in existence in Western Europe (Hobsbawm 1995:112).

wing reactions managed to get by with the traditional stress on national unity, the need for a strong leader and anti-communist propaganda.

The main difference between the fascist and the non-fascist right was that fascism existed, as Hobsbawm (1995:117) explained, "by mobilising masses from below". Fascism "belonged essentially to the era of democratic and popular politics" and it was maintained "symbolically in the form of public theatre". Hayek was not wrong to suggest that it depended upon a collectivist mindset. It certainly depended upon recognition of collectives such as the 'nation' the 'Germanic race' and so on. It is certainly the case too that mass mobilization from below included appeals to working class solidarity. The important thing to remember, however, is that the fascist appeal was such as to cut across the labor movement and its actions were such as to destroy it.

The insane emphasis on racial purity in the German case was such as to undermine all strands of socialist militancy. It must be remembered that German racist nationalism was used to justify repression when the workers put up resistance. It was used to justify war when it became evident that in order for capitalistic accumulation to continue, access to new markets and resources was needed. But of course since imperialism is something that is consistently opposed by all independent workers' organizations, such ventures often go hand in hand with the crushing of labor movements. Racist nationalism proved an effective means of mobilizing people toward achieving such ends. This is not to suggest that the propertied classes would not have preferred a traditional conservative government. However, at a certain point it became necessary to appoint a government that would put the necessary impetus and mobilization of resources behind the nation's overdue imperialist expansion (Sohn-Rethel 1987:47). With regard to this point, Sohn-Rethel (1987:48) pointed out that, "as early as October 1932, several months before the 'conqueror' Hitler had to be roused from his bed to be proclaimed Reichs Chancellor, an imperialist advance was made in Central Europe". The 'imperialist advance' mentioned refers to an 'unofficial' memorandum, which was drafted by the Mitteleuropaischer Wirtschaftstag (a business institute whose membership included representatives from all major sections of German Finance Capital) in association with the Foreign Office and the military counter-espionage. This memorandum, which was aimed at a violent overthrow of the postwar Central European order, was handed to Mussolini after the Volta Congress in Rome. It offered active German support to Mussolini, and included a detailed programme to partition Central Europe between Germany and Italy (Sohn-Rethel 1987:49).

As was the case under Mussolini in Italy, the pursuit of expansionist policies in Germany presupposed the pursuit of repressive anti-socialist policies. Of course, the putting down of strikes was a feature of fascism applauded by the ruling classes all across Europe, not least by those who were later to proclaim themselves anti-fascist. Individualists may have been appalled with regard to particular aspects of fascism but they approved of some of their measures. Likewise, fascists embraced individualist doctrines that suited. The Nazi attempt to purify the German race, for example, was carried out according to the doctrines of eugenicist science, which was originally developed by individualists as a means of legitimating the social consequences of the capitalist market order. The movement took an organized form, first in England and then in the United States (Hofstadter 1944:161). As was explained above, eugenicists and social Darwinists thought that competition was the necessary means to prevent degeneration of the species. German fascists took related social evolutionary ideas seriously, as did Churchill, who was a social Darwinist and a strong advocate of eugenicist science. For his part, Churchill tended to conflate the genetically inferior with political radicals rather than ethnic minorities (Ross 1998:66).

In spite of the strict dichotomy between collectivism and individualism, which was promoted by Hayek throughout his career, it is quite clear that collectivist movements were dependant upon individualist theory and methods (e.g., eugenicist science) and the supporters of liberal property rights were dependent upon collectivist ideas. Fascist thinking drew upon social Darwinism and emotional nationalism, both of which were enthusiastically advanced in reaction to social and democratic progress. It was the great individualist thinker, Herbert Spencer (1969:137), who claimed that a "society of men, standing towards other societies in relations of either antagonism or competition, may be considered as a species, or, more literally, as a variety of a species". Spencer (1969:137) had explained that any particular society "will be unable to hold its own in the struggle with other societies, if it disadvantages its superior units that it may advantage its inferior units". In Germany, such individualist doctrines were taken to their logical conclusion. They thought it essential to ensure that the Aryans were not disadvantaged as regards facing down some competing species. They too were determined to keep the inferior units (the working class) in their place. In short, it may be said that the Fascist mindset bears a far closer relation to the tradition to which Hayek belonged than it did to the so-called collectivists that received his condemnation. Hayek paid no attention to the individualist component of fascism. But the arguments made in this regard had less to do with explanation than they had with ensuring that atrocities carried out under fascist rule, show-trials and the gulag system, came rushing to mind at the mere mention of the words 'collectivism,' 'socialism' and 'social justice' (Christman 1994:6).

Individual Rights and Freedoms

Hayek thought fit to link socialism, social democracy and fascism because each represented an attack on freedom as he understood it. In Hayek's writings, freedom refers to an absence of coercion. Positive regulations that interrupt capitalistic accumulation are considered coercive and so represent an attack on freedom. Freedom reigns when the economic system is free from human orchestration. A 'liberal order' is said to require only 'negative' or 'formal' freedoms, in other words, the legal right to act. These freedoms, which are derived from legal rules, can be extended to the laboring classes since the economic constraints are sufficient to render these rights ineffective. Any demand above that of formal freedom would mean that property rights would sometimes need to be overridden for the sake of other rights. This is unthinkable for individualists, who spend their time warning people not to forget the vital role of private property and the free market in constituting and protecting the basic liberties of the individual. But those familiar with the individualist terminology know that this is like saying that private property plays a vital role in protecting private property.

The implication of the individualist tradition is that freedom prevails to the extent that the ruling-classes are in control of economic and political life. Hayek was certain that "free markets represent the only non-coercive means of co-ordinating economic activity in a complex industrial society" (Gray 1986:62). The maintenance by force of private control over the livelihood of entire communities was not regarded as coercive. John Gray might as well have been speaking about the so-called free market system when he complained that "unless the requirement of self-ownership is satisfied, human beings are chattels—the property of another (as in the institution of slavery)". Gray (1986:63) claimed that, "if I lack the right to control my own body and labor, I cannot act to achieve my own goals and realize my own values: I must submit my ends to those of another". This would make perfect sense if not forwarded in defense of private dictatorial control over resources under capitalism. Though it may be the case in capitalist market societies that free laborers have the legal right to control their own bodies and labor, they are in the end forced to sell themselves to those who have economic control over them. This point was raised by Andrew Gamble, who claimed that Hayek's greatest 'failure' was that he neglected the problem of private power. It was suggested that while Hayek was prepared to denounce state interference, he had 'overlooked' private coercion. Gamble (1996:190) complained that Hayek:

> endorses negative liberty over positive liberty, and defines negative liberty almost wholly in terms of the liberty of property-owners. Since on his own account the majority of citizens in the market order cannot be property-owners, and since he proposes no measures to enable them to become so, he appears to accept that there can be no return to the kind of liberal order which he favors.

However there is no reason to regard this neglect as a failure. It may be argued that nothing was overlooked, that he did not fail to consider private coercion, but used the term 'individual freedom' in reference to it. It may be argued that private coercion was exactly what Hayek defended, that the necessary control exercised by property owners over the majority of citizens actually underpinned Hayek's conception of liberty. His approach involved the building of conceptual categories that would aid his defense of the capitalist market order and aid his attempts to discredit its critics. He tried to fit the world into these categories, but since it did not fit he had to remain at the level of the abstract individual. The failures and prejudices underpinning Hayek's works are intelligible through examination of his individualism. For him, 'true' individualists and/or 'true' liberals were those that did not fall for the constructivist fallacy.

Hayek was sure that the market (capitalism) was free and spontaneous and that any socialist system would have to be imposed from above by force. It was clear to him that socialism was authoritarian at heart, but somewhere along the way chose to ally itself with the "forces of freedom" (Hayek 1991:18). Any directed economy, or 'socialism,' would force the individual to "serve the ends of the higher entity". In claiming as much, Hayek (1991:111) ignored the fact that it was precisely the desire to escape this condition that led ordinary people to demand the socialist transformation of society in the first place. Under capitalism, the individual worker serves the ends of a higher entity called capital. Though Hayek worried that ordinary persons might be enslaved, he depicted the mechanisms that constrain people in their everyday lives as the source of their freedom.

In many ways Hayek's individualism resembled that of Locke. He was not so much fearful that rights and freedoms would be lost, but that they might be given a universal quality. The demand underpinning his work was the fullest freedom to accumulate property. Insofar as each individual required property in order to gain independence, the benefits of freedom were still limited to the investing classes. The individuality championed was not that which could be enjoyed universally. It was to be realized by the few at the expense of the many (MacPherson 1962:255). As such, the social order championed by Hayek cannot be thought of as a spontaneous order of free and equal individuals. It cannot be considered an individualist order in a literal sense either, since the free development of individual human potentialities was sacrificed in defense of the capitalist system of economic exploitation.

There is a certain tension between Hayek's definition of freedom and the nature of the 'Great society,' which he actively promoted. By freedom, he meant freedom from coercion, that is, "from the arbitrary power of other men" (Hayek 1991:19). Of course, what was advocated in practice was the freedom of the individual (owners of productive capital) to exercise power over other men and women through their greater wealth. This must always be the case in an economic system that requires that some people have accumulated capital and that the vast majority have none. There must be an inequality in freedom of choice. Formal freedom may be safeguarded for everybody, but as C.B. MacPherson (1966:7) pointed out, when it comes to the exercise of freedom "all are free but some are freer than others".

The capitalist system presupposes the control of the well resourced over all those that must go through them to gain access to the means of production. Regardless of the principles upheld and values expressed, individualists are always in the business of defending and/or trying to extend this control over individuals. They do this at the expense of genuine individual freedoms (freedoms that could be exercised by the average individual person). This power may be attained through inheritance or through the accumulation of capital. It is only when the means for the exercise of arbitrary power is other than that of economic wealth that individualists object to it. They object to hereditary rule, to arbitrary government, and even to government by the people where it interferes with the freedom of investors.

Hayek's arguments reflect the fact that the ability of the propertied classes to control and direct the lives of subordinate classes depends on the defense of property at all costs. His arguments also reflect the fact that the greatest threat to these perceived rights is democratic progress. The propertied class would lose all importance in a democratically controlled economy since production and distribution would depend on decisions made by an elected body. Instead of wielding economic power and exercising control over the dependent population, the propertied classes would only have the same say as everyone else.

Though Hayek's individualism was incompatible with democratic progress this was exactly the charge that he levelled against socialism. He claimed that 'socialism' was authoritarian to start with and that democracy was something alien to it (Hayek 1991:18). Of course it makes little sense to categorize the earliest socialist movements as authoritarian or libertarian without considering the environment in which they emerged or the other traditions with which they were mixed.

The individualist objection to democratic progress is usually made on the basis that 'freedom' is at stake. For his part, Hayek attempted to convince people that further democratization would mean that the ruling authorities would realize complete control over every aspect of people's lives, as in totalitarian states. Of course, he did not supply any reasons why people should accept that the normal exercise of control by un-elected capitalists left people free. He simply asserted that if the economy were to be controlled by a staff of experts they would have complete control over people. He did not like to admit that this was the reality of life for the majority of people under capitalism. Hayek ignored the political nature of economic power until such time as it suited his arguments. It was suddenly recognized when it came to denouncing planning. On such occasions Hayek was prepared to admit that economic control is not control of a sector of human life that may be separated from the rest, but control over the means for all ends. When it came to private power Hayek maintained that no such control existed. But he was willing to recognize that it did exist in order to show how much control planners would have and how it could be abused (Hayek 1991:78).

The problems relating to economic control over the ends of individuals were precisely what socialists had consistently complained about. They did not agree that a privileged minority should decide conditions of life for the entire community and remain accountable to nobody. Socialists did not deny that, at a particular stage in its development, capitalism had been progressive. They did not even need to object to Hayek's (1991:78) claim that "the evolution of capitalism with its free market had been a precondition for the evolution of all our democratic freedoms". The early capitalist market system certainly had been the genesis for the development of bourgeois democracy and the liberal state. It also had much to do with the extension of democratic freedoms to the laboring classes, since it produced an organized work force that would inevitably demand them. However, socialists were bound to take issue with Hayek's (1991:78) claim that freedoms would disappear with the abolition of the capitalist market system. As far as they were concerned, the only freedom to be lost would be that of the propertied classes to control, alienate and exploit the rest of the population.

The demands of individualists, such as Hayek, can generally be reduced to the demand for freedom on the part of the owners of capital to invest without inconvenient conditions and to buy and sell labor power as a commodity without interference. The types of regulation that are inconvenient in this respect are those that are expected to put the freedom of the individual at stake. But it is precisely in accordance with the necessary opposition to these inconveniences that individualist doctrines were designed in the first place.

CHAPTER EIGHT

NEOLIBERALISM AND CAPITAL ACCUMULATION

Throughout the history of capitalist development, the capacity for populations of the world to develop local forces of production and benefit from such development has become more and more dependent on the operation of global markets. The 20th century has witnessed the growing dominance of international capital and the continued centralization of control over markets. The rules of trade have become more uniform, and more and more countries have to abide by trade rules set down by institutions such as the World Trade Organization. National economic policies have also become more uniform, and policies designed to free up the process of capital accumulation are pushed by institutions such as the International Monetary Fund and The World Bank.

Contemporary capitalism is characterized by a renewed enthusiasm to create opportunities for unhindered accumulation on an international basis. The demand for such opportunities gave rise to neoliberal policies and a revamping of liberal individualist doctrines to rationalize their implementation. The component parts of this body of policy prescription and ideology largely amounts to an adaptation of the tenets of liberal individualism and neoclassical economics to the conditions required for the valorization of capital under current monopoly conditions. This strategy and ideology of monopoly and finance capital is often referred to as 'market fundamentalism' or 'neoliberalism' (though few politicians, academics or pundits accept these labels). The commitment among its advocates to unrestricted competition is necessarily weak, as is the opposition to pro-corporate regulation.

For most of the course of capitalist development its corresponding liberal ideology has been expressed with competitive owner-producers in mind. The ever-increasing utilization of money capital and the ever-growing attempts to establish monopoly prices has meant that the extraction of surplus value is difficult to justify in such terms. Accumulation under contemporary capitalism does not simply involve the expansion of production and the increased exploitation of labor power. It also involves the creation of opportunities for money to make more money without investors having any involvement in value-adding activities. Accumulation is realized through means that are productive, but also, and to an increasing degree, through means that are not. The efforts to create more opportunities for unproductive forms of accumulation have been pursued relentlessly from the final decades of the 20th century up to the present. In reference to this tendency, Naomi Klein (2007:242) has claimed that today's investors see "government programs, public assets and everything that is not for sale as terrain to be conquered and seized". This is not simply a matter of eliminating government participation in the market. Opportunities to accumulate are increasingly realized, as Klein (2007:242) explains, by "enlisting the state to put a patent and a price tag on life forms and natural resources never dreamed of as commodities". The interests involved here differ considerably from those of owner-entrepreneurs and are to some degree reflected in neoliberal practice and free market doctrine.

Contemporary accumulation depends in large part on price-fixing, monopolies, financial organization and new forms of property that facilitate the extraction of wealth. The state and collectives of various kinds are becoming more and more central to the processes of capital accumulation. Despite this set of conditions the emphasis on 'the individual' and 'competition' has persisted.

As demonstrated in the previous chapter, F.A. Hayek (1991:111) never strayed from his conviction that individual freedom is only possible under a free market system and that under all alternative systems the "individual is merely a means to serve the ends of the higher entity called society or the nation". After Hayek's death, Chicago economist Milton Friedman worked tirelessly to keep these ideas alive. As with Hayek, Friedman was sure that no other kind of economic organization other than the free market could be regarded as consistent with individual freedom because it alone "separates economic power from political power and in this way enables one to offset the other" (Friedman 1982:9). To the end of his days (in 2006), Friedman insisted that the world works best when each individual is free to pursue his/her own individual interests.

The free market doctrine employed in the justification of neoliberal practice is often traced back to these two economists. Their ideas were used to justify the policies designed to facilitate accumulation on the part of corporations or money capital. The authority of their theories and doctrines was evoked by advocates of neoliberal 'market reform,' even where strict adherence to the principle of individual freedom was lacking.

Though the organization of the capitalist system changed over the course of the 20th century, the classical individualist doctrines have remained useful. Investors and their representatives still needed to rationalize the removal of obstacles to capital accumulation, such as progressive taxation, public ownership of resources, government programs and inconvenient regulations. The ideas of Friedman were particularly helpful in this regard. He explained that prosperity and stability were only possible where markets are permitted to operate without interference. With the aid of classical economic principles Friedman developed a market model, which was thereafter used to explain all economic problems in terms of 'distortions.' Following Hayek's example, he explained that in a free market, price signals can be transmitted freely and accurately to all involved in production and consumption, bringing the market into balance and maximizing efficiency in the process. It was held that if markets were permitted to operate freely, persistent economic problems would be drastically reduced.

Friedman's model was useful for those that wished to shift state expenditure away from social programs and public infrastructure. In order for Friedman's free market to exist it would be necessary to do away with government participation, along with price controls and other inconvenient regulations. The power of trade unions would have to be severely curbed. Workers would have to sell their labor at the price determined by supply and demand on the labor market, which would ensure that they receive the appropriate (market determined) wage. The expected result of all of this would be that employers would realize the appropriate return on their investments. Goods would be produced at just the right prices, and since the incomes of wage earners would also be determined according to market forces, everything produced could be purchased and consumed.

This abstract model of the market system imagined and supplied by Friedman worked perfectly in theory. In the absence of human interference in the market, the economic forces of supply and demand found their balance and presented, as Naomi Klein (2007:50) put it, "an Eden of plentiful employment, boundless creativity and zero inflation".

Those that considered Friedman's perfectly functioning free market as something to aspire to tried to identify the obstacles preventing the market from operating effectively. For those who believed that a market without distortions was possible, the problems of the real world were thereafter explained in terms of government participation in production, regulation of private producers and the demands of collectives such as trade unions. In order to bring the market society closer to this perfectly functioning ideal it was considered necessary to deal with the supposed distortions, which meant privatization, deregulation and the cutting of publicly funded services.

One of the problems with this was that Friedman supplied a pure market ideal with little relation to the capitalist system. It was a description of how he imagined markets could work if free of all interference. However, these ideas had great appeal on account of their capacity to justify the political strategies serving the needs of industrial and finance capital. Followers of Friedman used this pure market ideal to rationalize the implementation of neoliberal policy agendas the world over. This was done notwithstanding the fact that the ideal free market situation imagined by Friedman has never existed anywhere.

The idea that a market can be freed of all so-called distortions is in itself unconvincing. The idea that a market without such distortions would result in peace, democracy, prosperity and happiness is even less so. These are really faith positions. Wherever the imposition of conditions close to Friedman's ideal free market has been attempted, such as in Chile under Pinochet, economic conditions worsen for the majority of the population. In Chile, the country's debt exploded, there was hyperinflation and unemployment reached 30 percent, which was ten times higher than it had been under a market that was completely "distorted" by the Allende government (Klein 2007:85).

In her recent work, *The Shock Doctrine*, Naomi Klein (2007) draws attention to the anti-democratic implications of Friedman's prescriptions and doctrines. Klein highlights the popular opposition to Friedman-inspired 'market reforms', which is evident across the world. Against this opposition Friedman is said to have developed a shock strategy, which involves keeping free market ideas alive and available until a crisis of some sort disorientates the population, making their implementation possible. The title of Klein's book refers to Friedman's assertion that "'only a crisis—actual or perceived—produces real change'" (in Klein 2007:6). The fact that free market policies tend to provoke mass opposition means that the opportunity for the desired 'reform' is only open for brief periods. Awareness of this led Friedman to the conclusion that the changes need to be implemented with great haste. As Klein (2007:140) has explained, for a brief period, such as in time of crisis, "leaders are liberated to do whatever is necessary (or said to be necessary) in the name of responding to a national emergency.

Crises are, in a way, democracy free zones—gaps in politics as usual when the need for consent and consensus do not seem to apply".

The Friedmanite shock strategy was employed in many countries deemed ripe for market reform, from Latin America to South Africa to Eastern Europe. All across the world neoliberal policies have been relentlessly pursued by big business organizations such as the International Monetary Fund, pro-business think tanks, the World Trade Organization and the World Bank. In every corner of the world new opportunities to invest and accumulate have been created. Everywhere, governments have been pressured to abandon public or collective control of productive assets and spending on universal services. Private control over essential assets has been sought everywhere, markets have been imposed everywhere and opportunities to invest and accumulate have been created wherever possible. Policies leading to financial deregulation, to the advancement of private health as opposed to public and to the degradation of public services and social security, have all been pursued in the name of 'reform.' The resulting policies have all been justified in classical terms of freedom, efficiency and progress.

Oftentimes the focus on the individual and individual freedom is absent among ideologues working to justify neoliberal policy agendas. To an ever greater extent those pursuing 'reform' emphasize the free market over and above concern for individual freedom and competition. As corporate and financial interests are served even the devotees of Hayek and Friedman neglect such principles. This is partly because it is difficult to justify the monopolistic tendencies of contemporary capitalism in terms of the freedom of the individual. The policies that neoliberal doctrinaires advocate do not serve the individual owner-entrepreneur. They accelerate the concentration of capital, along with the merging of money, commercial and industrial capital. No amount of rhetoric about 'the individual' or 'competition' could alter the fact that neoliberal policies further undermine both.

The last decades of the 20th century have seen the imposition of policies that greatly facilitate forms of accumulation that take place apart from the expansion of production. Multi-national organizations and financial institutions accumulate by means of acquiring assets and rights once regarded as universal, such as water, services or particular forms of knowledge. Neoliberal doctrines are selectively employed and expressed in such a way by political and economic actors as well as pundits as to provide justification for the necessary practices. What is most important to representatives of investors is that the conditions for the accumulation of capital are met. As such, the emphasis on free trade increased every decade from the 1970s. It was considered necessary to foster and justify the kind of relations in which large investors exert maximum power regardless of where in the world they happen to operate.

Neoliberalism is not so much about the removal of obstacles to capitalist development (for which there is little scope in underdeveloped countries) than it is about accumulation on the part of the dominant industrial and financial actors. If the imposition of neoliberalism in Latin America is taken as an example, it becomes apparent that market 'reforms' have hardly facilitated real industrial development at all. They have greatly facilitated unproductive accumulation by enabling investors with little intention of actually supplying commodities and services that people want, to simply use their wealth to accumulate more wealth. The privatization of water in Bolivia, for example, involved handing over the service to Aguas del Illimani, which is mostly owned by France-based Suez (Prashad and Ballve 2006:153). This 'liberalization' led to a worsening of the service in many parts of the country. In order to ensure a profit for the investor the authorities made it illegal for people in the town of Cochabamba even to collect rainwater. This policy change was so unwelcome that its implementation required brutal state repression, including a massacre of citizens in El Alto in October 2003 (Prashad and Ballve 2006:140).

Though the above example is extreme, neoliberal policies have generated popular opposition more often than not. The regular opposition and the regular reliance on state coercion has a great deal to do with neoliberal methods of accumulation which involve the removal of rights once held, services once considered universal and assets and resources once publicly owned. The rise of unproductive methods of accumulation has led certain authors, such as David Harvey (2005:159–169) to explain accumulation under neoliberalism in terms of Marx's "so-called primitive accumulation". However, since the term "primitive accumulation" creates the impression of a particular historical point, and Harvey uses it to refer to a long drawn-out process spanning centuries, the term "accumulation by dispossession" is employed instead. The point made is that, through various forms of dispossession, the neoliberal policies imposed across the globe have created greater opportunities for international investors to realize a return. In addition to dispossessing people of tangible resources this has also involved the removal of people's creative capacities. The World Trade Organization's TRIPS agreement, which established wide-ranging intellectual property rights to the benefit of the world's large monopolistic firms, is one outstanding example of this. It is difficult to justify such policies in terms of individual freedom, particularly since they severely restrict the capacity of people to act as they wish and employ their own initiative in an unhindered manner (Perelman 2002:9–15).

The freedom of individuals to use available knowledge and make the best use of their individual capacities has long been championed by individualist advocates of the market. The investing classes once considered such capacities to be as sacred as conventional forms of property. Now, insofar as the appropriation of knowledge offers a means of guaranteeing a return to the largest enterprises, exclusive control of particular ideas and techniques is considered more important (Perelman 2002:8). This has led to an increasing tendency for conventional forms of property to give way to intellectual forms. The rights safeguarding ownership of productive capital now operate alongside an expanding regime of intellectual property. The freedom of isolated individuals to employ their mental capacities to their best advantage in a competitive market is abandoned by advocates of the latter.

Accumulation on the part of the monopolistic firms oftentimes depends less on using new knowledge to develop new innovative techniques than it does on the prevention of other producers from doing so (Perelman 2002:8). Control must be extended over that knowledge and that control must be justified in some way. As such, the impression is created that the ideas underpinning a new invention have an identifiable originator. Ideas that increase the potential to create wealth are considered to have been produced by an individual or individual-like entity and can be treated as 'property.' Patent laws are broadened and extended as large enterprises seek to purchase and monopolize knowledge underpinning particular innovations. Though this leads to ever more interference by the state in economic life and to ever more regulations preventing individuals from using their efforts and intelligence to their best advantage, it is promoted because it facilitates accumulation. Since it needs to be facilitated, this interference with individual rights and property is interpreted as the protection of individual rights and property. The protection of patents and copyrights, even when held by monopolistic firms, is explained in terms of freedom. Such rights have to be rationalized in some way because large firms need to be able to accumulate important knowledge and technique in a similar manner to wealth or regular commodities. With the concentration and centralization of capital, accumulation increasingly requires the privatization of ideas and techniques, either to exclude competition, or to extract royalties from those that actually produce goods and services that people need or want. In response to this need, advocates of the free market tend to favor the imposition of strict patent laws, which amounts to government regulation. This concession to government participation in economic life is by no means a deviation on the part of contemporary advocates of the free market. The same arguments are to be found with the most principled of libertarians. Ayn Rand (1967:128–139), for example, explained that patents and copyrights are "the legal implementation of the base of all property rights: a man's right to the product of his mind". The individual granted the patent on a new product was thought of as the 'originator' of the ideas that made it possible. The labor power expended in producing the new product was not thereafter considered the source of its value. That value was thought to be created by the new ideas. As such, for Rand, by granting a patent or copyright government does not extend a gift or a privilege to a business, it merely certifies the origination of an important idea and protects the owner's exclusive right to intellectual property (Rand 1967:128–139).

Part of Rand's justification of the patent system requires her to replace the real recipient of a patent (e.g., a multinational pharmaceutical company that manufactures drugs to treat victims of HIV) with an imaginary recipient of a patent (e.g., 'the individual'). Whatever the merits of Rand's various arguments, intellectual property rights amount to direct interference by government in the business of private individuals (including small to medium-sized businesses) and are difficult to defend in terms of voluntary exchange between free and equal producers (Perelman 2002:106). Incomes derived from intellectual property rights are based on little other than government interference. The accumulation of wealth by such means necessitates obstacles to free exchange.

Government interference that serves to safeguard returns on investments is rarely depicted as such. This blind spot leads to double standards. This is not simply true of the more practical representatives of capital. Even the most utopian of free market advocates does not appear to oppose government regulation of markets in a consistent manner. Regulations that benefit those with the capacity to invest are generally welcomed while regulations that obstruct accumulation, such as those protecting worker seniority rights, pay and conditions in productive enterprises are opposed. That advocates of the free market treat knowledge as private property indicates that the freedom they advocate has little to do with unshackling individuals in order to make their own way in the world.

The unproductive accumulation mentioned above requires arrangements different to those required by the owner-entrepreneur, and requires rationalizations that are not easily provided by long-standing individualist principles. It is clear that as more ideas become commodities and market relations extend further into the realm of culture, the individual is constrained to a greater and greater degree. As such, ideologues must concentrate less on 'the individual' and 'competition' and instead make a fetish of 'the market.' If liberal individualism placed 'individual freedom' as the primacy concern, the drumbeat of contemporary capitalism is 'market freedom.' The change in emphasis is intelligible in terms of the emergence of giant capitalist enterprises which continuously work to undermine competition.

The way in which related ideas facilitate capitalist accumulation in the present, requires at least some attention to the nature of modern capitalism. It must be kept in mind that capitalism, as a mode of production, has undergone continuous change for the few centuries it has existed. It has been continuously revolutionized in terms of scale, technique and organization. The surface configuration of classes has also been subject to continuous change. The emphasis of the free market and the decline in emphasis on 'the individual' and 'competition' among free market doctrinaires should be understood in this context.

The Changing Structure of Capital Accumulation

It is clear that by the beginning of the 20th century the concentration of capital in particular industries had reached such a level as to undermine its own competitive processes. Attention was drawn to the most salient developments in this regard by Rudolf Hilferding as early as 1910. In his famous work, *Finance Capital*, Hilferding (1981:21) identified the emergence of cartels and trusts in industry as a distinguishing feature of "modern capitalism". The process of concentration described by Hilferding continued nonstop throughout the 20th century and beyond. Free competition led to an ever-increasing concentration of capital, which actually worked to eliminate free competition in the long run. The tendency toward cartelization involved the establishment of production quotas and central sales agencies, designed to guarantee profits through the elimination of competitive pricing (Hilferding 1981:205). Time and again the enterprises devoted to particular industries became larger in scale and less in number. This concentration in the means of production was continuous because competition necessitated economies of scale, initially through the introduction of new technologies and equipment designed to further abridge labor. The process is also advanced through mergers and acquisitions. The resulting concentration increases possibilities for the elimination of the anarchy of production in more areas, control over prices and the maximization of profits.

Hilferding anticipated the long-term results of this process. He understood that in more and more industries the investment required was becoming too large for individual owner-entrepreneurs to assemble on their own. The emergence of the joint-stock company, as a solution to this problem, involved, as Hilferding pointed out, "the liberation of the industrial capitalist from his function as an industrial entrepreneur". The joint-stock companies that emerged involved the investment of money capital by investors that had nothing to do with what use is made of it in production. In order to realize the potential of money capital, associations were formed, where most contributors of money capital had no say thereafter. The majority of shareholders had no need for full property rights over the means of production as previously demanded by owner-entrepreneurs. Under these circumstances all that is required is "a limited form of property which simply gives the capitalist a claim to surplus value, without allowing him to exercise any important influence on the process of production" (Hilferding 1981:127). The investment of money capital requires a return, but does not presuppose control over the means of production requiring investment (Hilferding 1981:107). The proportion of such investments in industry consisting of money capital has since continued to increase and the demand for exclusive individual control over property is of less importance to a growing number of investors.

The competitive owner-entrepreneur, represented by liberal individualism, has always required and demanded individual control over the means of production. This is necessary because the return is realized through owner-management of the enterprise in which the investment is made. The investor in this case has a different role than the money capitalist. The money capitalist requires nothing more than to have claims to income secured, whereas the owner-entrepreneur requires full and exclusive control of the process of production in order to secure a return. The relationship between the owner-entrepreneur and the capitalist enterprise is close and usually long-term whereas the money capitalist has the capacity to "withdraw his invested capital in the form of money at any time, and to transfer it to other branches of production" (Hilferding 1981:140).

Though Hilferding did not state it, his analysis implies that the sway of the individual owner-producer must decline in consequence of the decoupling of ownership and management in productive enterprises. Shareholders oftentimes know nothing of the operations of the enterprise they are involved in, only that they have claims to the surplus value extracted. What matters to shareholders is that the shares representing such claims yield the maximum return. For the running of the biggest enterprises, control is required by the management and by key shareholders (these may or may not be the same people), whose interests are not identical to the interests of the majority of shareholders, and certainly not to those of owner-entrepreneurs.

Where the liberal individualist champions competition in the same breath as freedom, the cartel magnate demands, as Hilferding (1981:220) explains, that competition gives way to "the effective organization of production and the elimination of unproductive costs". Where it does not further accumulation, competitive anarchy in production is no longer idealized. Therefore, the ethical code required on the part of cartel magnates cannot be expected to be consistent with the classical principles of liberal individualism. With regards to the interests of finance capital, the day of the individual is over. Production must be organized and controlled on a rational basis. To the mind of the magnate, "the most heinous crime is a breach of solidarity, free competition, secession from the brotherhood of monopoly profit, for which social ostracism and economic destruction are the appropriate punishment" (Hilferding 1981:221).

If liberal individualism has served the function attributed to it in previous chapters, the changing nature of capital investment can be expected to undermine particular tenets of that tradition. Individualist doctrines are closely linked to the demand for exclusive individual control over productive property and unhindered management of the process of production. They are bound up with the imperatives of competitive capitalism, which continues to give way to monopoly finance capitalism. With regard to the latter, the facilitation of capital accumulation is not so easily conflated with the interests or freedom of the individual as opposed to the demands of collectives. The boards of directors of large corporations, along with large and small shareholders, are in fact component parts of collectives. The conditions required for accumulation on the part of corporations differ from those required by the individual owner-entrepreneur. The evolution of ideas attendant to capitalist accumulation is intelligible in terms of the progressive rise of unproductive methods of capital accumulation, which requires people to be further constrained, for fear that they may in some way hinder accumulation or the free movement of international capital.

The Neoliberal Concept of Freedom

Contemporary free market ideology consists of a body of principles, arguments and moral precepts derived from liberal individualism. The goal of both is the emancipation of capital. However, for classical liberal individualism, accumulation is facilitated through the emancipation of the individual entrepreneur with access to a store of capital, while for the neoliberal advocate this means the opening up of investment opportunities for syndicates, trusts, and hedge funds, which operate independently of shareholders on a trans-national basis. The ideology of the 'free market' is designed to justify accumulation under current conditions, and is useful to the extent that it helps maintain the impression of equal freedom under law, as promoted by individualists for the past three centuries.

In spite of the decline of the individual owner-entrepreneur, the principle of 'individual freedom' was continuously emphasized up to the end of the 20th century. This was partly because the example of Russia and Eastern Europe was conducive to such an emphasis. The fact that non-capitalist regimes did not guarantee individual rights and freedoms allowed scholars, such as Hayek and Friedman, to associate all such rights with the free market system. To them it appeared that the individual was free to the extent that markets were free. However, with the collapse of the USSR it became possible for the free market ideology accompanying neoliberal policy to become main-stream. Free market ideologues were confident that people everywhere would now appreciate the benefits of the free market system. Francis Fukuyama (1992:xi) identified what he saw as a "remarkable consensus concerning the legitimacy of liberal democracy" and went so far as to describe this as the "end of history," that is to say, the end of all credible alternatives to the free market.

After the fall of the various Stalinist regimes, the free market and competition were again forcefully championed across the world as the master-spring of public prosperity. However, there was never any intention to remove pro-corporate regulations or reintroduce competition into monopolized industries. Policies aimed at 'liberalizing markets' involved privatizing services and public enterprises that represented an opportunity for investors to get a return. They involved the removal of non-corporate regulations only.

The scramble to privatize, deregulate and lift constraints from the flow of capital produced disastrous consequences for working people across the world. The expected trickle-down effect materialized almost nowhere. Even in the leading power of world capitalism (the USA), conditions deteriorated in the last decades of the 20th century. This trend continued into the next. By 2008 there were six million more Americans below the poverty level than there had been in 2001. Family incomes declined more often than not. Where income levels were maintained it was usually because people worked longer hours. In general, the working day increased but wages were kept low as the labor market was 'liberalized.'

The removal of protections for workers has increased job insecurity significantly. Though this is bad news for workers, it is often viewed positively in business circles.[1] The same is true with respect to the conditions faced by workers in different countries and how these countries are viewed by international investors. The political representatives of the investing classes express concern about rights and freedoms and judge different regimes and governments accordingly. However, these values are understood in such a narrow fashion that they are almost synonymous with unhindered private control over production, labor power, trade and finance. The publications of the Heritage Foundation (a free market think-tank) show that freedom is used in reference to market freedom, or more accurately, markets with pro-corporate regulations only. Freedom is understood from the standpoint of concentrated and centralized capital rather than the individual owner-entrepreneur. According to the opportunities for unhindered accumulation, different countries are categorized on this basis as "free," "mostly free," "mostly un-free," or "repressed" (Heritage 2009).

---

[1] In explaining the economic conditions of the 1990s the head of the Federal Reserve Alan Greenspan was among those to credit "job insecurity" for continued growth and prosperity (Herman 1997).

One of the interesting things about the Heritage categorization of 'free' and 'repressed' countries is that it appears to be relatively independent of the conditions of democratic freedom, such as the right to free association, freedom of speech or the position of women in society. In spite of intentions, this index actually highlights the loose connection between free markets and basic individual rights and freedoms. It is evidence that under certain conditions the unhindered capacity to accumulate requires the degradation of those social institutions most conducive to individual freedoms and formal democratic rights (Monbiot 2001:8–14). The index champions a form of freedom that is attendant upon the accumulation of surplus-value. As such, it is little more than a measure of the extent to which socioeconomic conditions are tailored to the benefit of multinationals and finance capital.

CHAPTER NINE

ECONOMIC DOWNTURN AND DECLINE OF FREE MARKET DOCTRINE

The ideology of the free market has dominated in the industrialized world well into the first decade of the 21st century. Though the consequences of neoliberal 'reforms' usually involved cuts in services, job-cuts and increasing insecurity for workers, they were continuously advanced in the name of freedom and prosperity. Free market ideas were promoted all across the industrialized world for as long as they functioned to justify the kind of deregulation and privatization that facilitated capital accumulation under conditions of concentration and centralization.

The promotion of neoliberal policies did not really amount to the removal of every possible obstacle to competitive pricing. Markets were generally considered to be free once there was an absence of the kind of government interference that conflicted with the interests of the largest industrial and financial firms. Government regulation and interference, where it facilitated accumulation on the part of such firms, was not considered a hindrance to markets. As Michael Perelman (2007:55) has pointed out, "although business demands that the government avoid regulatory interference in business affairs, it expects government to underwrite businesses own activities through subsidies, tax write-offs, and protection from competition".

The political representatives of big business developed an understanding of a free market that was favorable to the interests and demands of the largest firms. The policies demanded by big business were not always consistent with the free market, yet they were promoted in free market terms. The policies fell short of the principles used to justify them. Neoliberal 'reforms' did not lead to minimal government interference in the market system. Neither did they lead to an overall decrease in state expenditure. This was because the neoliberal policy agenda was not really about reducing government involvement in economic life. The aim was that of ending government involvement that served the general population, while at the same time strengthening or extending government regulation and participation where it served the process of capital accumulation. As such, decreases in existing state expenditure were more than matched by increases in pro-corporate state expenditure. But as far as policy makers were concerned, lower state expenditure simply meant shifting it away from social programs and infrastructure improvements (Mandel 1993).

Enthusiasm for privatization and financial deregulation was quite strong up until the end of the first decade of the 21st century. George Soros referred to the body of principles and assumptions underpinning this enthusiasm as "market fundamentalism". For Soros (2003:4), market fundamentalism was underpinned by the belief that "markets tend toward an equilibrium that assures the best allocation of resources and that it is only government interference that stands in the way". Public policy in the United States and elsewhere was thought to have been guided according to this thinking.

What Soros called market fundamentalism really amounted to the application of old ideas about the efficiency of competitive markets to recent practice. Free market advocates had long insisted that the market must be left on its own to iron out any problems that arise. The free market requires that investors be permitted to go about their business unimpeded, to invest as they please, to take risks, to profit when the market rewards them and to take a loss when it doesn't. The market was thought to reward skill and effort and to punish inefficiency in an impersonal manner. Following Hayek (1978:68), market fundamentalists insisted that those playing the game had no business complaining or expecting government assistance when things didn't go their way. This ideology served the process of capital accumulation quite well until conditions deteriorated in 2007–2008.

The enthusiasm for the free market evaporated by the end of the first decade of the 21st century as economic conditions declined. This was not exactly a consequence of the decline in living standards that followed neoliberal deregulation. Instead, it was largely a response to the decline in opportunities for profitable investments. Neoliberal policies were relentlessly pursued and enthusiastically promoted according to individualist free market principles when the consequences were limited to ordinary working people. However, when the consequences manifested themselves as a financial crisis, there was a sudden change of mood. It was nowhere more sudden or dramatic than in the United States of America.

By the final year of the Bush administration, the United States federal government was forced to organize a $700 billion dollar bailout of the financial system (The Economist 2009). The largest banks and mortgage companies had to be propped up, which required large-scale government intervention. Though no justification for this could be gleaned from free market ideology, it was organized by policymakers that were wedded to it. The necessary measures were supported by the same politicians who had spent years insisting that markets were self-correcting.

The collapse of the financial sector was triggered in the United States by irresponsible lending practices. Various kinds of credit, loans and mortgages had been marketed aggressively in the previous years. The subprime portion of the mortgage market had been expanded considerably and this increased the risk of default. More and more mortgages were granted to home buyers with little or no steady income. The discipline of the market had done nothing to prevent this. In fact, financial deregulation only encouraged those involved to organize as many subprime loans as possible. The risk was no longer a problem since the loans could be repackaged and sold off quickly in the form of derivatives with considerable mark-ups. The profit motive ensured that the sub-prime portion of the mortgage market would continue to grow. This growth accelerated after 2003. There were more than $635 billion in subprime loans in the United States by 2005. Another $600 billion of subprime loans was added in 2006 (Rasmus 2008:13).

At a particular point it became evident that borrowers were having difficulty making repayments. Toward the second half of 2007 it was estimated that there could be 2–3 million potential foreclosures in the following few years (Rasmus 2008:13). Many banks failed to get rid of their 'toxic debt' in time and were left with a great deal of it on their books. This left questions over their solvency and banks became reluctant to lend to one another. They became determined not to take on further bad debt and even became reluctant to lend to otherwise profitable businesses that needed credit.

The financial crisis brought problems that had been developing in the real economy (this term refers to the productive side of economic life, as opposed to banking, insurance, share dealing, property speculation and so on) to the fore. On the eve of the financial crisis, productive capital was finding it difficult to sell enough products to make worthwhile returns. The purchasing power of the public was already facing a brick wall. Living standards had been declining in the United States for years, if not decades, before. According to the US Department of Agriculture (USDA), in 2007, 36.2 million people lived in households considered to be food insecure.[1] Unemployment and underemployment had already been on the rise. Real wages had been stagnant or in decline for about thirty years but consumption had continued to rise (thanks to an expansion of consumer debt). Those that have paid attention to this problem, such John Bellamy Foster (2006), have pointed out that "the ratio of outstanding consumer debt to consumer disposable income has more than doubled over the last three decades, from 62 percent in 1975, to 127 percent in 2005". Given the growing consumer debt relative to income, it was perhaps inevitable that industries, such as auto, would eventually experience a drop in sales.

The financial crisis exacerbated problems in the real economy and by November, 2008, General Motors had revealed that it was likely to run out of cash by the end of the year. Soon after, Ford and Chrysler, the other two major players in the auto industry, indicated that they were also in trouble. The government had to choose between stepping in to save these firms or see them face bankruptcy. Under such conditions, free market principles had to take a back seat. As with the banks and mortgage companies, it was well understood that the collapse of the auto industry would have widespread economic repercussions. In explaining this, David Cole, from the Centre for Automotive Research, estimated that if Detroit's production fell by 50%, the first year would see 24,000 direct layoffs, followed by 795,000 job losses among suppliers and 1.4 million more from other firms indirectly affected. The thoughts of such a scenario helped convince legislators that it was necessary to grant bailouts to the tune of tens of billions of dollars (The Economist 2008).

The free market principles that had been so convenient from the 1970s onwards could do little to justify the scale of intervention that needed to be organized by the government. But the consequence of the largest banks or the largest corporations going under was too much to contemplate. The former advocates of *laissez-faire* were well aware that enterprises that were profitable could be brought down with the unprofitable. For this reason, the largest banks and the largest corporations were recognized as being too big to fail. This was certainly the case with the mortgage companies Fannie Mae and Freddie Mac. These

---

[1] Of these 36.2 million, 23.8 million were adults (10.6 percent of all adults) and 12.4 million were children (16.9 percent of all children) (Food Research Action Center 2008).

could not be permitted to fail since together these giants own or guarantee nearly half of the nation's $12 trillion worth of home mortgages. If they collapsed, there was no telling how far the real estate market would plummet (Goodman 2008).

Faced with the reality of economic collapse, policymakers and key ideologues were forced to abandon the very notions thought to justify the 'reforms' of previous decades (i.e., that risk takers should suffer the consequences of their own bad decisions). The financial crisis and economic downturn meant that government intervention was now compatible with the interests of investors. The representatives of capital found themselves having to accept policies that were incompatible with the free market and reject policies that were compatible with the free market. The changing conditions led to a changed policy agenda, which necessitated a shift in outlook.

When the financial crisis and economic downturn spread beyond the United States, governments in other countries responded in a similar manner. Free market policies and doctrines were abandoned. Again, this had little to do with the hardships endured in consequence of privatization and deregulation. Governments went for intervention when share values collapsed, when credit tightened up, when businesses stopped investing for fear of losing money, and when banks and whole industries faced bankruptcy. It was this that led the practical political representatives of capital to call for state intervention in the market. They discovered that the survival of the financial system and the largest firms was far more important to them than their free market principles.

Prior to 2008, investors required deregulation in order to grow their investments, but after 2008 government control and support was needed in order to protect them. State intervention would be necessary for capital accumulation to resume. The investing classes and their political representatives had no intention of sticking to their principled positions where they no longer served that purpose.

By 2008, even the most principled free market advocates lost confidence in the market. Ayn Rand's loyal devotee, Alan Greenspan (former head of the US Federal Reserve), who, until that time, had been uncompromising in his insistence that the market knows best, thereafter acknowledged the necessity of government regulation. At a congressional hearing in 2008, Greenspan admitted that his presumption that the economic system was best served by the self-interest of organizations, such as banks, had turned out to be erroneous. Greenspan told the House Committee on Oversight and Government Reform that those "who have looked to the self-interest of lending institutions to protect shareholders' equity, myself included, are in a state of shocked disbelief" (New York Times 2008). After decades of market fundamentalism, Greenspan suddenly doubted the capacity of markets to self-regulate. Across the world, politicians, academics and pundits who had long insisted that government cannot interfere with the operation of markets, now called for immediate government intervention. But this was to be expected because, as David Harvey (2005:19) points out, "when neoliberal principles clash with the need to restore or sustain elite power, then the principles are either abandoned or become so twisted as to be unrecognizable".

Free market doctrines were relentlessly promoted for thirty years largely because they rationalized practices that facilitated capital accumulation. No matter the extent of hardships created by these policies for working people, there was no thought of abandoning them. They were not widely reconsidered until the so-called credit crunch and economic downturn threatened to undermine capital accumulation. Thereafter, former believers in the free market advocated interventionism on a massive scale. It was no longer possible to insist that the market be left to solve its own problems. It became necessary to demand guarantees, bailouts and all manner of government interference in the economy. Such necessary measures could not be justified in terms of the merits of free enterprise and individual entrepreneurship. This meant that it was no longer beneficial to continue repeating Friedman's (1982:9) claim that greater competition for wages and profits would lead to greater prosperity and freedom for all. The free market mantra, TINA (there is no alternative), had to be changed to TINABN (there is no alternative to bank nationalization) (Hadas 2008). The process of capital accumulation had to be preserved, even at the expense of such cherished beliefs.

Besides deregulation and privatization, the policies implemented over the previous decades involved a great deal of tax cuts for big business. This was justified according to the expectation that it would lead to greater prosperity in the next business cycle. The greater capacity to invest was presumed to lead to more investment in the real economy, more production, more jobs and a general increase in wealth creation to the benefit of society in general. However, the result of tax cuts to business was quite different from these expectations. There was no trickle down of prosperity. There was only a trickle up effect. Inequality continued to increase in the United States from 1970 up to the new millennium. The incomes of the top earners consistently increased. By 2006, leading Wall Street firms—Bear Sterns, Goldman Sachs, Lehman Brothers, Merill Lynch, Morgan Stanley—were awarding an estimated $36 billion worth of bonuses in one year to their employees. The bulk of this money went to the top 1,000 people, and two executives received almost $100 million (Perelman 2007:5).

The tax cuts introduced from Ronald Reagan to George W. Bush led to the accumulation of vast amounts of wealth by relatively few individuals and corporations. This wealth was not all invested in the real economy because there were not enough investment opportunities for such vast sums. By the end of the 20th century, the amount of money in desperate need of investment opportunities amounted to tens of trillions of dollars. Any commodity that appeared to be likely to increase in value attracted speculation, creating speculative bubbles in the process which collapsed one after another (Talbott 2008). Further deregulation was required to create the reinvestment opportunity for the resulting surplus of personal savings and corporate profits. The difficulty of realizing returns on investments in the real economy gave impetus to the vast growth of financial instruments. Since there were fewer productive outlets available, speculative channels had to be found (Ticktin 2007; Livingstone 2008). Free market ideology was employed as justification for the creation of such opportunities.

Sharp drops in prices usually follow sharp increases in prices where they result from speculative activity. This is because speculation does not involve the creation of any additional wealth. That depends on production in the real economy (Ticktin 2006). The creation of wealth requires long-term investment in production, which only happens when capitals are likely to get a return. The investors must be sure of ending up with more capital at the end of the process than the amount with which they began. By 2008 corporations could just barely sell their products and goods to consumers at volumes great enough to realize a profit. As such, those with the capacity to invest were often more inclined to trade in shares or derivatives, such as those backed by subprime mortgages, and other speculative, casino-like pursuits. Long term investment in the real economy is less attractive because it is less lucrative (Ticktin 2006).

Since the current downturn runs much deeper than the mass marketing of subprime loans, it is necessary to deal with it in the context of capitalist production. Ultimately, the decline in real wages relative to production is decisive and productive enterprises are among the first to notice when this leads to a drop in demand for real commodities and services. Once this means that a worthwhile return is unlikely, they abstain from investment. To the extent that the purchasing power of the public is the issue, no amount of tax cuts for the wealthy can solve the problem. As Livingstone (2008) points out, the 50 corporations with the largest benefits from Reagan's tax cuts of 1981 reduced their investments over the next two years. Likewise, the George W. Bush administration granted further tax cuts to the wealthy between 2001 and 2008 but investments in productive enterprises are (in 2009) being scaled back across the board.

The current world economic crisis has occurred at a time when scientific and technological change has drastically increased the capacity to produce. The needs of people are great, the capacity to meet those needs exists in abundance and there is no shortage of people willing to do the necessary work. In spite of these conditions, even the most advanced industrialized societies are faced with the spectre of mass unemployment and underemployment. Such a contradiction arises in consequence of a continuous shift in wealth to investors away from the working population and the consuming public generally. This has been the trend across the industrialized world.

Automation, Profit, Employment and Income

The last decade has seen a significant increase in productivity among workers, but this has not been matched by an increase in income (Mishel and Bernstein 2007). The innovations that increase the productivity of workers, and which are copied by other producers in an industry, have decreased the number of laborers needed for commodity production in many of the major industries. Competition ensures that producers must keep pace with all technological innovations. They must try to cut wages, produce more with the same number of workers, or produce the same amount with fewer workers. A good example of an enterprise that has been successful in this regard is General Motors. According to Mark Brenner and Jane Slaughter, there were 466,000 GM hourly workers in 1978 and by 2006 there were only 112,000 (Brenner and Slaughter 2007). Today (2009) the number of workers employed by General Motors is around 75,000 and continues to drop.

With automation, fewer workers are needed to produce the same products. That fewer workers are needed does not mean that the remaining workers see a benefit. The wages that are saved are not shared among those who keep their jobs. The working day does not decrease, either. It may even increase. The gain is realized on the investment side. The portion of an investment that needs to be spent on wages is less than it was before.

Given the saving in overall investment it would be reasonable to expect a rise in the profit margins for companies that manage to reduce the number of workers through automation. The reality is different however. Even though General Motors has managed to produce more and more cars, with fewer and fewer workers, it still struggles to maintain profitability. At present, plants are being closed, workers are being laid off and those remaining are facing wage cuts and the loss of benefits. Even with government intervention the company remains in trouble.

With the view to explaining such apparent contradictions, Marx (1976:241–262) thought it important to distinguish between 'constant capital' and 'variable capital.' Marx pointed out that competition between capitals changed the ratio between constant capital (plant, machinery etc.) and variable capital (the portion devoted to wages). Along with the tendency for the concentration and centralization of capital, Marx observed a definite and continuous trend with regard to this changing composition of capital. The portion of constant capital continuously increases relative to the portion of variable capital. After every business cycle the number of workers shrinks in relation to the magnitude of commodity production, and likewise, the percentage of total investments spent on wages is less and less (Mandel 1971:162–166).

When workers are replaced through automation, or in some other way, an increasing fraction of the annual product is used to maintain the existing stock of capital, while a decreasing fraction is devoted to wages (because there are fewer workers to be paid). With fewer workers, the portion of capital that serves to increase the value of the stock decreases (Mandel 1971:167).

Marx explained how he thought this trend undermines the capacity of investors to realize a sufficient profit. According to Marx (1976), the prices of commodities are determined by the value contained in them. One commodity is thought to contain more value than another when there is, on the average, more labor time required in its production. For example, if the cost of plant, machinery and materials are the same, a commodity that takes on average ten hours of labor power to produce will be more valuable than a commodity that takes two hours of labor power to produce. That is not to say that the value and price of a commodity is determined by the actual number of hours that goes into the making of that individual product (Marx 1976:238). Average levels of technological sophistication and an average levels of productivity among workers are presumed. On the basis of these theoretical averages Marx developed the concept of 'socially necessary labor time.' The price of a commodity is determined by the *average* amount of labor time necessary to produce it in a particular market society at a given time. All factors being equal, commodities contain more or less value according to the socially necessary labor time required to make them. To the extent that this socially necessary labor time is reflected in the market-determined price of commodities, the latter is thought to drop in consequence of the decline of the former (Mandel 1971:162–167).

When the price of the commodities produced drops, it becomes necessary to increase the volume of sales, and/or to cut costs of production, relative to the overall investment. A failure do this in the face of a continuous decline in market-determined prices, inevitably undermines profitability (Mandel 1971:162–167). With labor saving automation, the labor-time required to produce commodities decreases. As enterprises work to reduce the portion of capital devoted to wages, they also collectively reduce the amount of socially necessary labor-time in commodity production relative to the overall investment.

If only one producer manages to reduce the labor-time required to produce a commodity then that individual producer will realize a greater return. This advantage only lasts if the other enterprises fail to employ the same innovation. So long as other producers in the industry fail to do so, the value contained in the commodity is undiminished and the market price does not drop. The innovative enterprise profits because the commodity still requires, on average, ten hours to produce and can be sold at a price that reflects ten hours of socially necessary labor time, even if it has actually been produced with far less labor hours. Since less capital has been advanced for the payment of wages, the profit margin can increase.

Since individual enterprises are primarily concerned with their profit margins, they innovate in whatever way is most likely to increase returns relative to overall investments. The producers that innovate early, realize greater returns, but cannot rest easy having done so. Their innovation forces the other producers in the industry to do likewise, or better. The competitors realize that if they do not innovate they will be priced out of the market. The return on the overall investments may drop to a level that no longer justifies the continuation of production.

The competition between producers can lead to the number of people employed in an industry dropping, relative to the aggregate capital investment and to the total commodities produced and consumed. When this happens, there is less socially necessary labor time, that is to say, less value contained in the commodities produced.

The advance of the necessary capital for the production of commodities only makes sense to investors if the sum advanced is preserved and yields a worthwhile return. To ensure this, individual producers attempt to reduce the variable part of the total capital invested. Where this is generalized in an industry, there is a decline in value contained in the commodities produced (Mandel 1971:162–167). This eventually results in a drop in price, which means that individual producers can only maintain profits in the following business cycles by shedding more jobs, cutting wages and/or increasing sales. The increase in sales is sometimes realized by an increase in market share on the part of the strongest enterprises as weaker ones fail. The remaining enterprises must continue to cut costs in one way or another. The desire to find new ways of shedding more jobs is continuous, as is the drive to cut wages and benefits. There are limits to what can be done in this regard. In industrialized countries at least, wages cannot usually be reduced beyond the level required for the reproduction of a sufficiently educated and healthy working class (Marx 1976:340–360). Moreover, where wages continuously decline, consumption is eventually affected in a negative manner. With less effective demand, investors in the real economy are eventually faced with shrinking profitable opportunities. In the US, this problem was averted for a considerable period through the extension of consumer credit (Rasmus 2008). Across the country, GDP per person doubled between 1973 and 2007 while real wages (i.e., the real capacity for wages to purchase commodities and services) started to stagnate and decline from 1970 onwards. Eventually, people stopped saving and began to spend every penny of their incomes week by week. For big purchases, more and more people had to rely on credit. In order to keep consumers spending, enterprises found it necessary to devote an ever greater portion of the total capital invested to advertising. Consumers could not be permitted to rest (Bauman 1998:83). In order to keep spending, many people borrowed against the value of their homes, which rose in consequence of speculation, but would eventually have to drop. At a critical point, growing anxiousness and cautiousness affected people's behavior as consumers, first in small numbers and then in the millions (Financial Post 2009). In consequence of this, many enterprises found it increasingly difficult to sell enough products to maintain profitability. The tightening up of credit was the straw that broke the back of many enterprises. Those already faced with falling sales and declining profit margins edged closer to bankruptcy.

It is important to make a distinction between the sub-prime problem and the economic downturn that followed. The downturn was developing in and of itself. A sharp drop grew more and more likely as producers found it more and more difficult to sell their products. Ultimately, downturns occur when consumers cannot purchase and when capitals (accumulated wealth) cannot find profitable opportunities for investment. In order for investment opportunities to exist, whatever is produced on a mass scale must be bought by capitalists or a consuming public. If effective demand declines and commodities cannot be bought, then profits decline and production has to be scaled down. Ultimately it is the purchasing power of the populace that underpins this problem (Sherman 1972:83–90).

With the decline of real wages, to keep up long-standing consumption habits people had to work longer hours. The length of the working day increased fairly consistently in the United States over the last three decades. According to the International Labor Organization (ILO), US workers logged more work hours per year than almost any other industrialized nation. In 2002, the working year averaged at around 1,815 hours, whereas in major European economies it ranged between 1,300 to 1,800 hours. The hours were no longer even exceeded by Japanese workers (ILO 2003). These conditions worsened and hours continued to increase right up to 2008.

Since there are only so many hours in the day one worker can work until he or she becomes exhausted, maintaining consumer demand could not depend on increasing the working day indefinitely. At the start of the 21st century many US workers were living beyond the limit of their earnings. A drop in consumption was always likely because working people had accumulated a significant amount of personal debt and many would eventually become anxious and act accordingly. This happened when the level of concern people felt about their personal circumstances became greater than the capacity for advertising to make them ignore it. When this happened, people stopped spending, production had to be scaled back, workers had to be laid off and consumption was further undermined, provoking a greater scaling back of investment, more job losses and so on, until the house of cards came crashing down.

Government leaders of the industrialized countries appear to have been very surprised by the rapidity of events. For the most part, growth was expected to continue, investors were expected to maintain profits and workers were expected to keep their jobs. This was certainly the case with British Prime Minister Gordon Brown, who freely admitted that he never saw the downturn coming. Though he could not adequately account for its occurrence, he still refused to accept that he had failed in his pledge to end Britain's boom and bust economic cycle (Lea and Fleming 2009). The expectations of steady growth and prosperity were shared by policymakers in the United States. Even when the financial crisis was well underway, President George W. Bush rejected claims by economists that the U.S. economy was entering a period of recession. Bush insisted that the system was basically sound and that the financial problems were the result of nervousness. The main thing to consider, as far as Bush was concerned, was that the economy was growing, productivity was high and trade was continuing. Businesses were still operating, people were still working and whatever problems and weaknesses arose could be resolved in short order (Hunt 2008). As it turned out, they could not. Nervousness continued to increase and confidence continued to decline as the scale of the problem was revealed. Credit tightened as uncertainty about the amount of 'toxic debts' on the books of particular banks made them very reluctant to lend to one another or to businesses (McIntire 2009).

Falling confidence and growing nervousness are the result, rather than the cause, of economic problems. Attempts to restore confidence fail where there is little reason to be confident. Boom-period confidence cannot be expected in slump-period conditions. If the economic system consistently maintained enough secure jobs and decent wages, that is to say, if the public was not periodically priced out of the market, confidence would not be a problem. To expect a return of confidence among the consuming public is to expect people to be reckless and foolish with their hard-earned money, and to place themselves in ever more vulnerable positions. The same is true with regard to investors. It doesn't matter how much they are encouraged to do so, they do not develop the confidence to invest until it looks like profit margins justify it. Likewise, banks cannot be encouraged to trust one another when the amount of 'toxic debt' on their books remains unknown.

The decades-long transfer of wealth away from workers to investors, and the subsequent decline in effective demand, precipitated the current problems. As demand continues to drop, production continues to decline, more people lose their jobs, more businesses go bust and credit remains tight. As with downturns of the past, the current slump is ultimately underpinned by the incapacity of people to purchase what has been produced. In contemporary industrialized societies, this means that the cost of car loans, mortgages and basic commodities and services became increasingly difficult for people to deal with.

Just how long and deep the current downturn is going to be is still uncertain. Whatever the case, those investors that are best positioned will eventually enjoy a fresh burst of accumulation. The strongest monopolistic firms are likely to increase their market share. They may acquire plant and machinery at well below its previous value. The largest enterprises will begin the next business cycle amid a plentiful pool of unemployed workers and devalued necessities, both of which permit a reduction in the cost of wages. Through increases in market share, coupled with the drop in costs, some enterprises will see an increase in returns relative to overall investments (Marx 1976:359–365).

The downturn creates anew the possibility to extract surplus value. However, as soon as the upturn begins, so too does the competition between the capitals remaining. Periods of expansions and periods of crises are part of an ongoing cycle of capital accumulation and creative destruction. Some capitals are destroyed so that others may grow. Value is destroyed until the rate of profit once more reaches a level sufficient to attract investment. After an economic crisis new opportunities to accumulate eventually emerge. But as soon as the process begins, competition leads to renewed attempts to increase the productivity of workers and to reduce the numbers employed. As Marx (1976:363–364) explained:

> The stagnation in production that has intervened prepares the ground for a later expansion of production—within the capitalist limits. And so we go round the whole circle again. One part of the capital that was devalued by the cessation of its function now regains its old value. And apart from that, with expanded conditions of production, a wider market and increased productivity, the same cycle of errors is pursued once more.

The Libertarians

The degree of government intervention that the current downturn has provoked has caused a good deal of dismay among the remaining devotees of the free market. In Britain, libertarians see the response of the British government to the financial crisis as 'socialist.' That the British government considered it necessary to take significant stakes in the leading banks in order to re-capitalize them is regarded as a step away from capitalism (Heffer 2008).

For libertarians, any government intervention in the market system, under almost any circumstances, is portrayed as the introduction of socialism into economic life. As was the case with Hayek and Friedman, the term socialism is used in a very general way to refer to government intervention in the economy or regulations that hinder the transmission of price signals. This is contrasted with 'capitalism,' which is thought to be about productive enterprises freely supplying commodities that fulfill existing needs and wants. These conceptions are particularly widespread in the United States. As such, the bailouts and stimulus packages organized by the Bush and Obama administrations are regularly depicted as socialist. Democratic representatives are derided as socialists for advocating a wide-ranging stimulus package. And support for this on the part of some Republicans is considered evidence of their adherence to socialist ideas. In reference to these measures the *Ayn Rand Centre for Individual Rights* (2008) asks, "What is socialism, if not the idea that the government should seize citizens' wealth and control industry in the name of creating jobs and growing the economy?"

For libertarians in the United States, the activity of Federal Reserve is thought to represent government control of economic life. That control has long been depicted as socialist. When the Federal Reserve interferes with the supply of money and manipulates interest rates, this is considered government interference with the market system. Such 'socialistic' interference is thought to underpin the ongoing economic problems. According to libertarians, attempts on the part of the Federal Reserve to stimulate the economy undermine the laws of supply and demand, which would otherwise regulate the price of money. By keeping interest rates artificially low, the Federal Reserve is said to have encouraged leveraging and all manner of speculative activities (Brook 2008). These actions are presented as outside interference with the market even though the board of the Federal Reserve is made up representatives of the largest banks, which work relatively independently of government.

The interests underpinning government interference with competition and the effective transmission of price signals are presumed to originate outside of the market system. Since it is government that intervenes in the economy, and since it is government that implements the regulations considered to be harmful, libertarians claim that economic problems that emerge have nothing to do with capitalism. As libertarians see it, individual producers create wealth through the competitive market system, and the government, which is treated as an outside force, is thought to prevent them from doing so effectively.

There are a number of libertarians that have called for the abolition of the Federal Reserve. As with Texas Congressman Ron Paul, they believe that through the Federal Reserve System the government steals people's hard earned money. According to Congressman Paul, citizens of the United States are being taxed unawares through this system, which is thought to create all kinds of economic difficulties. After devaluation, people find that their savings have less value than they had before. If the dollar is devalued by 10 percent then, according to Paul, people have been robbed of 10 percent of whatever they had (Poor 2008).

Whatever the merits of such arguments, the libertarian understanding of 'the market', 'government', 'capitalism' and 'socialism,' and the links between each, leaves much to be desired. For libertarians, socialism and government are almost synonymous. Socialism is not used to refer to the interests of working people. Likewise, the suggested advance of socialism in no way indicates an extension of democratic control over the economy. The libertarian conception has nothing at all to do with the aspirations of socialists, or with attempts on behalf of workers to gain control over the wealth they generate. Instead of this, the term is employed in reference to the long-term practices of government institutions and the more recent abandonment of free market policies and principles on the part of the representatives of big business. The actions of the Federal Reserve, along with bailouts organized for mortgage companies, insurance companies, bankers and shareholders, are equally considered examples of socialist intervention (Ridgeway 2008).

To the extent that supply and demand is still expected to iron out all problems in the market, libertarians are the most reluctant to acknowledge that the current downturn developed within the market system itself. When problems arise they are regularly considered the result of factors external to the market. They are considered to arise in consequence of interference by a particular institution or bad policy decisions. As far as libertarians are concerned, capitalism would work to the benefit of the vast majority if left alone, without interference.

Since a completely unregulated market system based on voluntary exchange relations does not exist anywhere in the world, it is always possible to point to government interference when problems arise. This is exactly what libertarians do. Whether a downturn follows a period of regulation or deregulation makes no difference. That it happens amid some degree of government interference indicates to them that government interference is the source of the problem (Brook 2008).

With regard to the current downturn, libertarians consider it significant that it began with industries that were subject to government regulation, such as banking and housing. They contend that the financial problems occurred because government interfered with loans and with the housing market. The government tried to enable those on low incomes to buy their own homes. For libertarians, this was the reason the housing market grew rapidly and then suddenly dropped (Brook 2008b). They insist that for the capitalist system to function properly there can be none of this. There must be a separation of government and economy. There must only be unimpeded voluntary exchange between producers. The provision of all needs must be left to private enterprise and individual investors must be left alone to pursue their own selfish interest and to generate wealth in the process. Since the government plays some role in economic life and since investors are never completely free, the libertarians claim that the problems that arise in the economy cannot be attributed to capitalism. Brook (2008) has even gone so far as to claim that "whatever one wishes to call the unruly mixture of freedom and government controls that made up our economic and political system during the last three decades, one cannot call it capitalism". The system that exists is considered to be a mixed economy. There are said to be elements of capitalism and elements of socialism, or in libertarian language, elements of individual freedom and elements of government control.

Libertarians defend capitalism in its idealized form rather than capitalism as it actually exists. What they defend is an unrealized condition of free exchange between equal individuals (Klein 2007:50). The free market is defended and promoted even as it fails to serve the function for which business leaders value it. *Laissez-faire* is advocated even as the preservation of the process of accumulation requires a departure from it. In an earlier period, Keynes was quick to deride the intransigence of his free market contemporaries as "unduly conservative". With regard to the devotees of capitalism of his own day, Keynes considered their approach to be counter-productive. He explained that they attempted to defend capitalism by "rejecting reforms in its technique, which might really strengthen and preserve it, for fear that they may prove to be first steps away from capitalism itself " (Keynes 1933:321).

Since libertarians defend capitalism in its idealized form and consider the development of the market system and the development of government to be separate, they cannot adequately account for the interests underpinning government intervention. The fact is that market competition leads to concentration and centralization of capital and this creates economic interests consistent with control and regulation. The libertarian explanation of economic problems in terms of government interference it based on a false dichotomy between the interests and intentions of government and those generated through the market.

For libertarians, the divide between government and market, and what each represents, is clear. On the one side there is the market, which represents individual freedom. On the other side is government, which represents government control of the individual. Government is depicted as a force outside the market that imposes regulations that prevent the market from operating effectively. Those individuals (or individual-like entities) involved in the production and supply of goods and services in the trading world are credited with wealth creation, whereas government is thought to hinder the process through excessive regulation, and thereafter robbing and exploiting the public through taxation.

Wherever problems arise in the capitalist system, libertarians argue that government has caused them. Since the source of existing and future problems is already known, so are the standard solutions: the lowering of taxes, the dismantling of public enterprise and the removal of inconvenient regulations on businesses. The interpretation of the problems and the solutions are built around an understanding of capitalism that consists of economic arrangements under the rule of law with minimal government interference. Like the liberal individualists of the 19th century, the extension of markets is thought to involve little more than the extension of voluntary exchange relations. The world of actually existing capitalism is replaced by an imaginary system of spontaneously emerging voluntary relations of exchange (Amin 2004:41).

One of the consequences of this is that libertarians do not fully appreciate the relationship between the capitalist system of social relations and government intervention. They cannot appreciate the extent to which government interference results from changes in the manner in which investments are made. As the capitalist system grows, it evolves, and different arrangements are required for the realization of returns as it does. The capitalist market continuously generates interests and policy agendas that depart from the system idealized by libertarian scholars.

Regulations that appear to contradict the free market are condemned by libertarians. The government is criticized as something that exists above and beyond the society governed. It is treated as such even though the relevant policymakers are, more often than not, made up of the representatives of business, and the parties to which they belong are funded by financiers and industrialists.

In reality, the market system is always well represented by government. However, government policy may well be more responsive to particular sections of the business community (e.g., the largest banks and the largest industrial enterprises) than others (e.g., small to medium sized businesses). As such, it is unlikely to defend free competition in a consistent manner. It must serve competitive capitals but it must also serve the monopoly power that has resulted from competition between them. Government is pulled between demands for deregulation and demands to impose regulations that facilitate the accumulation of capital on the part of the largest corporations (Baran and Sweezy 1966).

Though the minds of libertarians are occupied by an imaginary capitalism, their thinking is often influenced by the interests generated under existing conditions. Though many stray from the right-wing consensus, when it comes to foreign military adventures they very often tolerate those regulations and interventions that facilitate capital accumulation. As Perelman (2007:56) has observed "libertarians who emphasise the defense of property rather than personal liberties often turn a blind eye to corporate welfare". Some libertarians consistently defend the competitive system, but these are relatively few.

The investing classes in the main and their political representatives are more inclined to recognize that there is a compromise to be made between free market principles and the conditions required for capital accumulation. They cannot consistently stick to free market principles because the need for compromise grows larger in consequence of the concentration and centralization of capital, which leads to the pursuit of policies that undermine competition and distort price signals. However, the relationship between the two is not sufficiently appreciated. Government policy is treated as though it is independent of the market system and the actions of each are analyzed separately. The policies government implements are often responsive to the new conditions required for accumulation as the market system evolves.

The Global Downturn and its Ideological Consequences

Though libertarians are a very useful component of the right-wing, no amount of their moralizing can stop the shift toward government intervention in the economy. They can do nothing about the abandonment of free market principles on the part of the political representatives of capital. This has been recently captured by the quip: "just as there are no atheists in foxholes there are no libertarians in a financial crisis" (Christie and Murray 2008). At present (2009), the scale of government intervention in the United States and across the world has made free market principles almost redundant. The shift toward interventionism and abandonment of free market principles is quick, relentless and global in scope. This is to be expected since a downturn in US capitalism means a downturn for world capitalism. The United States leads many countries in terms of domestic policy, foreign policy and the promotion of attendant doctrines. It also leads this global economic downturn. Its consequences (contraction of credit, home repossessions, job losses, bankruptcies and innumerable social problems) appear first in the United States, but inevitably carry through to other countries. This is partly because the United States consumes 25% of the world's resources and partly because the largest US firms are global enterprises, with branches, distributors and sales agencies in dozens of countries.

In addition to this the conditions underpinning the US downturn are present all across the industrialized world. Real wages have increased almost nowhere. Consumer debt has increased in many countries. Speculation in the housing market has been practiced the world over. In 2001, house prices in Britain were about five times the average annual earnings. By 2007, they had reached about nine times the average annual earnings. Significant numbers of young working people have had to take on enormous mortgages set to last thirty to forty years. In Ireland, the increases were even sharper. For several years leading up to 2008, house prices increased by around 30,000 Euro per year. In the years leading up to the property crash the yearly price increase was often as large as the average industrial wage for one year. Due to unrestrained speculative practices, many potential first-time buyers were simply priced out of the market (Global Property Guide 2008).

Though productivity has increased in most countries, almost nowhere has this been matched by increases in real wages. According to the International Labor Organization, between 1995 and 2007 there was a distribution of wealth away from wages to investors in three quarters of the countries in the world. The deregulation of financial systems was a worldwide process that created an upward redistribution of wealth through speculative activities (Harvey 2005:161). It is partly as a result of this that productive enterprises have been finding it increasingly difficult to find markets for their commodities. In most industrialized countries productivity has increased but sales have fallen. Manufacturing activity has been falling for years and people have been losing their jobs. Firms are in trouble all across the industrialized world. They struggle to maintain profits in Germany, France, Italy and Spain, in Japan and Hong Kong even though the share of gross national product that goes to wages has in each case declined while the share going to capital has increased (International Labour Organization 2003).

Given the interconnectedness and the fact that conditions are similar across the world, if a serious downturn is triggered in the United States it quickly follows in other countries. The abandonment of neoliberal policies has likewise been prompt as each government has been forced to intervene. Rhetoric about the free market has been abandoned across the world partly because banks and businesses everywhere require bailouts of different kinds and magnitudes.

Drastic shifts in policy were necessary in many other countries all across the industrialized world. In each case, proponents of *laissez-faire* began to argue the opposite to what they had been arguing for years. Once the threat of global economic downturn began to undermine investment opportunities, the governments concerned responded with state intervention and a shift away from market fundamentalism. This has been the case even with governments that have spent their entire terms in office extolling the virtues of the free market. It has not mattered how often deregulation has been justified on the basis that the investors are the 'wealth creators' or 'risk takers.'

The disapproval of a minority of libertarians shows that although right-wing ideologues are unified in their defense of capitalist relations, the right-wing consists of distinct strands of thought. Libertarians represent only one. There is no agreement on policy or principle among these strands. Michael Perelman (2007:55) has explained this division in an interesting way. According to Perelman, the right-wing consists of libertarians, cultural conservatives and class-warriors. The interests of investors are mainly represented by the latter, but the involvement of libertarians and cultural conservatives is crucial. The libertarians function to provide broad ideological justification for deregulation, privatization and tax cuts when and where the process of capital accumulation requires. They keep visions of a capitalist utopia alive and find convincing ways of presenting the right-wing agenda as though it represents freedom and prosperity for all. The cultural conservatives help by fostering public debate about issues such as abortion, gay marriage and family values, thereby diverting people's attention away from their real economic interests. The main representatives of capital (conservative class-warriors) work on the basis of the support generated. When they get to power this support is rewarded by means of conservative policies on gun control or stem cell research for instance. However, they are mainly concerned with implementing policies that facilitate capital accumulation even if this is opposed by other strands of the right-wing (Perelman 2007:55).

The principled libertarians condone everything that conservative class-warriors do where it results in lower taxation, less government intervention in the economy and less interference or supervision of the actions of investors. They look on disapprovingly, but quietly, as those who talk about free market principles go on to impose all manner of regulation that undermines competition and the price mechanism (Perelman 2007). To their disappointment they find that for the majority of the representatives of capital, free market principles are little more than a fig leaf. The economic crisis that unfolded further in 2008–09 finally revealed that the individualist free market principles were not valued in themselves but in their function as justification of the policies of finance capital. Most of those that had appeared to hold fast to the idea of a self-regulating market began to argue the opposite of what they had argued only a few months previously. The only concern was that of minimizing losses on investments. When the free market policies failed to deliver returns to the largest financial and industrial concerns, as they had done previously, the justifications were abandoned along with the policies.

CONCLUSION

Individualism cannot really be about the interests of the individual. Properly speaking, there is no such thing as individualism and there is no such thing as an individual. As Harry Jaffa once pointed out, the word 'individual' is an adjective, and "an adjective ain't nothing... till there's a noun to which it is attached. It is an attribute without a substance".[1] If there is no such thing as an individual, it should follow that the 'freedom of the individual,' as championed by advocates of the free market, never really had any precise meaning. For this reason it has not been possible to deal with individualist thought as a fixed set of ideas and principles. It is necessary instead to focus on its uses in the environment in which it develops and show it to be subject to change concurrently with changing potentialities for, and obstacles to, capital accumulation. The individualist styles of thinking that developed with the efforts to undermine prevailing feudal relations and related worldviews, were different to those of individualists faced with the workers' struggles of the 19th century. Neoliberal doctrines emerged as a further transformation of liberal individualism, but in all cases the key principles and ideas were rooted in the advocacy of minority control over resources vital for wealth creation.

The first few chapters explained that though individualism initially emerged as the foe of privilege, it was quickly employed in the ideological defense of the set of privileges that emerged with the growth of moveable capital, which grew in importance with the new techniques of production made possible by modern science. These techniques had an effect on the relations of production, since rationally planned production necessitated the transformation of labor power into a commodity, such that manufacturers could purchase labor power in individual units. Formal freedoms were advocated at this point. It became necessary to create and legitimate arrangements in which labor power was habitually treated as a commodity.

From the beginning, the freedom demanded by individualists went hand in hand with demands for independence on the part of those

---

[1] This quote appears in Machan's *Capitalism and Individualism* (Machan 1990:7).

with control over the necessary resources from the community that depended on them. As such, it was a freedom to be enjoyed by the investing classes only. It was a freedom closely bound up with the need to ensure that labor power was sold in the labor market as a commodity. Freedom required that the laborer had no say in its use thereafter, or in the distribution of the value generated in its exploitation. In order to legitimate the appropriation of labor power, individualists have always considered it to be wholly alienable from the individual. From Hobbes onwards, labor power has been treated as something to be bought and sold as any other commodity (MacPherson 1962:62). From the mid 18th century individualists (following in the manner of Adam Smith) tended to conceive of the laboring classes as merchants selling a commodity (labor power) at the price prescribed to it by laws of supply and demand (Hunt 1995:44–49). The capitalist market order was considered to be one in which no one was without anything to sell and all were in competition with one another to get the best bargain possible. A specific set of moral precepts emerged concurrently. All had to bear the responsibility for their own lot because all were free to make the best of what they possessed. Insofar as all were considered free to enter contracts, success and failure were thought to depend on effort expended and/or individual skills employed.

The bourgeoisie were inclined toward scientific argument, opposing it to the superstition of the existing society. As soon as the class with the capacity to invest first attained control of state power, its method of scientific analysis was transformed from a tool for advancing revolution into a tool for consolidating its rule. This did not happen across Europe in a uniform manner. Though in England the bourgeois class had achieved full political recognition by the 17th century, in other countries, such as France, they had not. The concerns of the French Enlightenment thinkers indicate that the rise of the bourgeoisie was resisted with greater success in France than England. All throughout the 18th century, thinkers such as Voltaire were keen to see bourgeois virtues triumph in France as they had done in England many decades earlier. Voltaire's principled opposition to aristocratic privilege, for instance, was linked to economic considerations. Such privileges, along with the monastic system of the church, were considered a drain on the resources of society. The absence of aristocratic interference was expected to herald a spontaneous order in which all could act according to their interests, and all could live in peace and prosperity (Laski 1936:173–174).

The social and political implications of the French Revolution caused much concern among the propertied classes in England. This concern was well articulated by political theoreticians, and many individualist thinkers adopted a reactionary attitude to the revolution and to the mood for change to which it gave rise. The example supplied above was Malthus's theory of population pressure, which provided the propertied classes with a reason to internalize the convenient belief that aiding the poor made them poorer in the long run. It justified the reaction to social and democratic progress that was taking place elsewhere. The status of the theory was a measure of its effectiveness as a means of rationalizing the powerlessness and deprivation wrought by bourgeois institutions upon the property-less. It rationalized the convenient presumption that resources were distributed just as they should be within the existing social system.

The problems facing the bourgeois class of the mid 19th century provoked similar efforts. Evolutionary science was partly an attempt to prevent the glaring realities of the mid 19th century from undermining the legitimacy of the capitalist market system. It also provided counterreformers with a means to condemn 'socialistic' legislation. Darwinism applied to society appeared to give scientific weight to the attitudes and prejudices already present among the investing classes, their apologists and representatives. What attracted the well-resourced was the potential therein to hide self-interested ideological distortions and the potential to obscure the consequences of the existing system. It was not a coincidence, as Donald Macrae (1969:48) pointed out, that social Darwinist ideas were supported mainly by businessmen, lawyers, administrators and legislators, and in that order of decreasing conviction.

The events of the early 20th century had shaken the world and the intellectuals in it. The shock was such that the reality of the politico-economic structure and its consequences could no longer be ignored. Those that continued to do so (e.g., Hayek) were regarded as cranks. It was obvious to most that an unplanned economic system generated enormous social problems. It was obvious that the development of this system required increased control over resources, including those beyond the confines of the nation state. This led to conflicts between the nations of the world, which brought with them an enormous human cost. The incredible waste caused by world war forced people to recognize that there was an underlying problem that needed to be addressed. It was partly for this reason that Keynes' (1933:312) argument against the neo-classical assumption that private and social interest always coincide, eventually triumphed. The rise of Keynesianism and the wholesale abandonment of the uncompromising principles of *old* liberal individualism, led F.A. Hayek to warn of an encroaching collectivist mindset. There was nothing novel about his claim that 'freedom' would disappear with the abolition of the free market. What distinguished Hayek was that he defended 'the market' through the creation of a strict dichotomy between 'individualism' and 'collectivism'. His defense of the market system was aided no end by the comparisons between the rights and freedoms enjoyed in Western Europe and elsewhere with those absent in the Stalinist countries. When compared with the authoritarian state bureaucracies that existed in Russia and Eastern Europe, or with elite theocratic rule as exercised in many parts of the world today, the democratic credentials of advanced capitalist countries appear obvious.

Though the ideas of the various individualist thinkers mentioned above are unique in their own way, each plays a twofold function: that of providing justification for the removal of obstacles to capital accumulation where they exist, and that of explaining the human condition in a manner consistent with that purpose. As such, the problems facing human societies have regularly led individualists to provide explanations, but without any connection between social deprivation and the process of capital accumulation. This disconnect spans the history of individualist ideas. For the earliest individualist thinkers, who wished to realize state protection for private contracts, the emphasis was on human nature. For these thinkers, the calamities faced by humankind were a measure of how ill-suited particular arrangements were to the supposedly inherent desires and drives of human beings. At the beginning of the Enlightenment period, superstition and/or bad government was the perceived problem. Soon after, there was great emphasis on the evils arising from religious intolerance. Later, immorality and population pressure were said to be the cause of the problems facing human societies. Later still, it was held that pauperism existed only because paupers (who, in the minds of social Darwinists, could never be anything else) were maintained. The supposed problem at that point was degeneracy.

Each stage in the development of individualist ideas also involves a renewed attempt to link the lack of social progress with the obstacles to accumulation. As with the earlier individualist thinkers, Hayek explained the calamities of the 20th century apart from the profit motive, while attempting to link them to the obstacles to capital accumulation. As such, 'collectivism' and the so-called collectivist mindset became the source of all evils faced.

Individualist explanations were not advanced so easily in the 20th century. The unprecedented destruction and crises resulting from the pursuit of total war had the effect of raising consciousness about the nature of national economies as well as the world economic system. For a number of decades in the 20th century, governments of the most advanced industrialized nations saw fit to regulate economic life and guarantee minimum standards for citizens. Individualists railed against 'big government,' which they regarded as incompatible with freedom (Beetham 1992:40). Though by the 20th century individualists did accept the principle of universal suffrage, they still insisted that the rights of property had to be guaranteed in advance. However, the history of the same century shows quite clearly that wherever individualists believe real and fundamental change to be on the cards they support authoritarianism and abandon democratic principles. The extent to which this happens cannot be explained in terms of any abstract principles or values promoted. It can only be understood in terms of political and economic conditions. The owners of capital and their individualist representatives have, over the course of modern history, invariably attempted to minimize democratic participation and advance private dictatorial control over economic life. This effort has gone hand in hand with efforts to maintain competition among the property-less. Just as the propertied classes have endeavoured to avoid any relaxation of the pressure on people to work for a wage, their representatives in political life have opposed social and democratic progress every step of the way. Individualists do not support democratic governments for the love of democracy, but because it is the most efficient form of capitalist rule. That being said, they do not oppose further democratization for the love of authoritarian rule, but to ensure that those to whom profits flow under capitalism maintain an upper hand with regard to the running of society. The commitment of individualists to democracy is tested wherever the property-less develop an appetite for real and fundamental change. Today (in 2009), this is far more evident in Latin America than it is in Western Europe or the United States. In the case of the former, there appears to be a greater capacity on the part of working people and peasants to attempt to seize political power or force change through massive civil disobedience. Faced with this possibility, market individualists are transformed from advocates of democracy into advocates of authoritarianism. Where they have no option but to maintain their system through coercive means, this is exactly what is done. Wherever the accumulation of capital is put in danger, the commitment to democracy melts away. These conditions also underpin bourgeois foreign policy. If democratic regimes are supported and dictatorships condemned, this is usually evidence of interests promoted by democratic forces and the harm done them by dictatorship. The reverse order is not uncommon. The interests of international investors are regularly safeguarded by despotic regimes and regularly threatened by democratic forces that seek to challenge the status quo.

The explanation of individualism in terms of the principle of individual freedom is wholly insufficient. Individualist theories (along with attendant values) change and evolve in such a manner that they may be squared with the changing interests of the investing classes. Even the continued advocacy of free market principles depends on what is needed to maintain and promote the accumulation of capital. On occasion, as in the current world economic downturn, the preservation of capital requires state intervention rather than *laissez-faire*. To the extent that it does, free market principles have been abandoned.

Considering the theories and arguments dealt with above, it may be fair to say that the individualist theoreticians under scrutiny have, always and everywhere, interpreted freedom to mean individual control, not only over what is individually possessed, but over those persons that require access to privately held resources and services. There is, of course, a secret that every individualist theoretician from Hobbes to the present has known, but none has yet stated explicitly. The secret is that the freedom of the individual 'to pursue one's trades and calling' was never really desired at all. That would be wholly insufficient. Individualism has always been more concerned with the freedom of investors to accumulate, to have a powerful state apparatus to protect the assets accumulated, and to shape and control individuals so that the process may continue. The freedom demanded by investors has always meant, and will continue to mean, forcing individual persons to obey the collective will of those with the capacity to invest. For this reason the capitalist market order cannot be regarded as a 'spontaneous order.' In presenting it as such, Hayek and others ignored the private power relations constraining people. The notion depends on the assumption that the state plays no role, that markets do not need to be imposed (they simply emerge) and that all individuals enjoy the same degree of freedom to choose the contracts that they enter into. The geographical extension of corporate and financial control, sometimes referred to as 'globalization,' is similarly depicted as a natural process. It is only understood as such because advocates deal only with 'the market' and overlook the actual structure of social economy and the coercion underpinning it.

Individualism, past and present, consists of doctrines, principles and ideas that are, as explained above, rooted in the advocacy of exclusive private control over a society's resources so as to extract a return. Individualism is so-called on account of the traditional emphasis on the individual and continuous claims of adherents to stand for individual freedom. Claims relating to the individual have been made to the extent that they have aided the development of an ideology attendant to the interests generated under capitalism. The concentration and centralization of capital has rendered such claims less credible. Likewise, the current economic downturn, which has necessitated unprecedented intervention in economic life on the part of national governments across the globe, has made a great number of the principles, theories and arguments constituting liberal individualism redundant. However, the ideological justification for extended private control over resources is still required by investors. As such, individualist doctrines are still employed, albeit with a declining emphasis on the interests of the individual. This has long been evident among neoliberal ideologues that see no reason for any strict adherence to the principle of individual freedom. In the end, individualism can do without the individual. The individual existed merely as a convenient tool employed by bourgeois ideologues to legitimate the processes of capital accumulation. The focus on the freedom of the individual has always been a means to an end and never an end in itself.

BIBLIOGRAPHY

Althusser, L. 1977. *For Marx*. London: Unwin Brothers Ltd.

Amin, Samir. 2004. *The Liberal Virus*. New York: Monthly Review Press.

Andrews, Edmund L. 2009. Economy Shed 598,000 jobs in January. *New York Times*, 06 February, p. 1 (consulted 09 March 2009): http://www.nytimes.com/2009/02/07/business/economy/07jobs.html.

Ashton, R. ed., *The Works of John Robinson Vol. II*. London: Reed and Pardon.

Ashton, T.S. 1948. *The Industrial Revolution*. Oxford: Oxford University Press.

Ayn Rand Centre for Individual Rights. (2008) Republican Socialists. Press release, 31 December (consulted 02 March 20): http://www.aynrand.org/site/News2?page=NewsArticle&id=22206&news_iv_ctrl=2703.

Baran, Paul and Paul Sweezy. 1966. *Monopoly Capitalism: An essay on the American Economic and Social Order*. New York: Penguin.

Bauman, Z. 1998. *Globalisation and its Discontents*. Cambridge: Polity Press.

Beetham, D. 1992. "Liberal Democracy and the Limits of Democratisation", in David Held ed., *Political Studies: Prospects for Democracy*. Oxford: Blackwell.

Bellamy Foster, John. 2006. The Household Debt Bubble. *Monthly Review*, 58 (1) (consulted 12 February 2009): http://www.monthlyreview.org/0506jbf.htm.

Bentley, M. 1987. *The Climax of Liberal Politics*. London: Edward Arnold Ltd.

Berman, Harold J. 1994. The Origins of Historical Jurisprudence: Coke, Selden, Hale. *Yale Law Journal* 103:1651–1738.

Bhaskar, R. 1989. *Reclaiming Reality: An Introduction to Contemporary Philosophy*. London: Verso.

Bird, C. 1999. *The Myth of Liberal Individualism*. Cambridge: Cambridge University Press.

Blair Bolles, E. ed., 1997. *Galileo's Commandment*. New York: W.H. Freeman.

Bonar, J. 1885. *Malthus and his Work*. New York: Harper.

Brenner, Mark and Jane Slaughter. (2006) What Does a Dying U.S. Auto Industry Mean for the Rest of America? *Washington Spectator*, 01 August 2006 (consulted 02 March 2009): http://www.washingtonspectator.com/articles/20060801endoftheroad_1.cfm

Brook, Yaron. 2008. Stop Blaming Capitalism for Government Failures. *Ayn Rand Centre for Individual Rights* (consulted 20 February 2009): http://www.aynrand.org/site/PageServer?pagename=media_topic_property.

——. 2008b. The Government Did it. *Forbes.com*, 18 July 2008 (consulted 02 March 2009): http://www.forbes.com/2008/07/18/fannie-freddie-regulation-oped-cx_yb_0718brook.html.

Bullock, A. 1985. *The Humanist Tradition in the West*. London: Norton.

Christie, Rebecca and Charles Murray. (2008) Paulson Hit by Investors as He Seeks to Halt Crisis. *Bloomberg.com*, 16 July 2008 (consulted 02 Mar 2009): http://www.bloomberg.com/apps/news?pid=20601068&refer=home&sid=aWssvqlta37Q.

Christman, J. 1994. *The Myth of Property: Toward an Egalitarian Theory of Ownership*. New York: Oxford University Press.

Collins, H. 1982. *Marxism and Law*. Oxford: Oxford University Press.

Constant, B. 1988. "The Liberty of the Ancients Compared with that of the Moderns", in Bianca Fontana ed., *Political Writings*. Cambridge: Cambridge University Press.

Cox, R.W. 1986. "Social Forces, States and World Orders: Beyond International Relations Theory", in R.O. Keohane ed., *Neo-realism and its Critics*. New York: Columbia University Press.

Critchley, J. 1978. *Feudalism*. London: George Allen & Unwin.

Crook, D.P. 1994. *Darwinism, War and History*. Cambridge: Cambridge University Press.

Darwin, C. 1964. *On the Origin of Species*. Cambridge: Harvard University Press.

Descartes, R. 1968. *Discourse on Method and the Meditations*. London: Penguin Books Ltd.

Devi, S.U. 1986. "Relevance of Malthus", in, J. Cunningham Wood ed., *Thomas Robert Malthus: Critical Assessments*. Kent: Croom Helm.

Dietz, F.C. 1927. *The Industrial Revolution*. New York: Henry Holt and Company.

Dugger, W. and Howard Sherman. 2000. *Reclaiming Evolution: A Dialogue between Marxism and Institutionalism on Social Change*. London: Routledge.

Dugger, W. 2003. *Evolutionary Theory in the Social Sciences, Vol. I*. London: Routledge.

Engels, F. 1953. "Darwinism: A Summary View", "Letter to Lavrov" in Meek, R.L. ed., *Marx and Engels on Malthus: Selections from the Writings of Marx and Engels Dealing with the Theories of Thomas Robert Malthus*. London: Lawrence and Wishart.

——. 1958. *The Condition of the Working Class in England*. London: Basil Blackwell.

——. 1977. "Outlines of a critique of Political Economy", in Marx, K. *Economic and Philosophic Manuscripts of 1844*. London: Lawrence and Wishart.

——. 1998. *Socialism: Utopian and Scientific*. New York: International Publishers.

Financial Post. 2009. US Consumer Confidence Tanks Again. 13 February 2009 (consulted 02 March 2009): http://www.financialpost.com/story.html?id=1286652.

Food Research Action Center. 2008. Hunger and Food Insecurity in the United States. 24 November 2008 (consulted 12 February 2009): http://www.frac.org/index.html.

Foucault, M. 1967. *Madness and Civilisation*. London: Routledge.

Friedman, M. 1982. *Capitalism and Freedom*. Chicago: University of Chicago Press.

Fukuyama, F. 1992. *The End of History and the Last Man*. London: Penguin Books.

Gamble, A. 1996. *Hayek: the iron cage of liberty*. Cambridge: Polity Press.

Global Property Guide. 2008. Irish Property Crash. 08 July 2008 (consulted 07 Mar 2009): http://www.globalpropertyguide.com/Europe/Ireland/Price-History.

Godwin, W. 1985. *Enquiry Concerning Political Justice*. London: Penguin.

Goodman, Peter, S. 2008. Too Big to Fail. *New York Times*, 20 July 2008 (consulted 17 February 2009): http://www.nytimes.com/2008/07/20/weekinreview/20goodman.html.

Gray, J. 1986. *Liberalism*. Buckingham: Open University Press.

Hadas, Edward. 2008. There is no Alternative to Bank Nationalization. *Telegraph.co.uk*, 09 October 2008 (consulted 07 March 2009): http://www.telegraph.co.uk/finance/breakingviewscom/3165709/There-is-no-alternative-to-bank-nationalisation.html.

Harvey, D. 2005. *A Brief History of Neoliberalism*. Oxford: Oxford University Press.

Hawkins, M. 1997. *Social Darwinism in European and American Thought*. Cambridge: Cambridge University Press.

Hayek, F.A. 1960. *The Constitution of Liberty*. London: Routledge.

——. 1978. "The Principles of a Liberal Social Order", in A. DeCrespigny and Jeremy Cronin eds., *Ideologies of Politics*. Oxford: Oxford University Press.

——. 1982a. *Law, Legislation and Liberty, Vol. I*. London: Routledge and Kegan Paul Ltd.

——. 1982b. *Law, Legislation and Liberty, Vol. II*. London: Routledge and Kegan Paul Ltd.

——. 1982c. *Law, Legislation and Liberty, Vol. III*. London: Routledge and Kegan Paul Ltd.

——. 1991. *The Road to Serfdom*. London: Routledge.

Hayes, P. 1998. Hobbes's Bourgeois Moderation. *Polity. 31*: 53–74.

Heffer, Simon. 2008. Financial Crisis: We're All Socialists Now, Comrade. *Telegraph .co.uk*, 19 December 2008 (consulted 02 March 2009): http://www.telegraph.co.uk/

comment/columnists/simonheffer/3562694/Financial-crisis-We're-all-socialists-now,-comrade.html.

Herman, E. 1997. *The Economics of the Rich. Z Magazine*, 01 July 1997 (consulted 25 February 2009): http://www.lbbs.org/zmag/articles/hermanjuly97.html.

Hilferding, R. 1981. *Finance Capital: A Study of the Latest Phase of Capitalist Development*. London: Routledge.

Hill, C. 1958. *Puritanism and Revolution*. Manchester: Panther Books.

Hobbes, T. 1968. *Leviathan*. Harmondsworth: Penguin.

——. 1998. *On the Citizen*. Cambridge: Cambridge University Press.

Hobhouse, L.T. 1911. *Liberalism*. New York: Henry Holt & Co.

Hobsbawm, E. 1995. *Age of Extremes: The Short Twentieth Century 1914–1991*. London: Abacus.

Hofstadter, R. 1944. *Social Darwinism in American Thought*. New York: George Braziller Inc.

Hunt, E.K. and Howard J. Sherman. 1978. *Economics: An Introduction to Traditional and Radical Views*. New York: Harper and Row.

Hunt, E.K. 1995. *Property and Profits: The Evolution of Economic Institutions and Ideologies*. New York: Harper Collins College Publishers.

Hunt, Terrence. 2008. Bush: Troubled Financial System is Basically Sound. *The Huffington Post*, 15 July 2008 (consulted 02 March 2009): http://www.huffingtonpost.com/2008/07/15/bush-calls-on-congress-to_n_112829.html.

Heritage Foundation. 2009. Index of Economic Freedom. (consulted 09 March 2009): http://www.heritage.org/Index/.

International Labour Organization. 2003. New ILO study highlights labour trends worldwide: US productivity up, Europe improves ability to create jobs. *World of Work Magazine. No. 48*, September 2003 (consulted retrieved 02 March 2009): http://www.ilo.org/wow/PrintEditions/lang--en/docName--DWCMS_080607/index.htm.

Kant, I. 1963. "What is Enlightenment", in Beck, L.W. ed. *On History*. Indianapolis: Bobbs-Merrill.

Keary, A. 1979. *Castle Daly: The Story of an Irish Home Thirty Years Ago*. New York: Garland.

Keynes, J.M. 1933. *Essays in Persuasion*. London: Macmillan.

Klein, N. 2007. *The Shock Doctrine*. London: Penguin Books Ltd.

Klein, P.G. 1992. *The Fortunes of Liberalism: Essays on Austrian Economics and the Ideal of Freedom*. London: Routledge.

Laski H.J. 1936. *The Rise of European Liberalism: An Essay in Interpretation*. London: George Allen and Unwin Ltd.

Laurent, J. and John Nightingale. eds., 2001. *Darwinism and Evolutionary Economics*. Cheltenham: Edward Elgar Publishing Ltd.

Lea, M. and Sam Fleming. 2009. Recession could be the worst since 1930s' warning as Brown admits: 'I never saw it coming'. *Mail Online*, 24 January 2009 (consulted 25 February 2009): http://www.dailymail.co.uk/home/index.html.

Lenin, V.I. 1996. *Imperialism: The Highest Stage of Capitalism*. London: Junius Publications.

——. 1996. *State and Revolution*. Beijing: Foreign Languages Press.

Livingstone, J. 2008. Their Great Depression and Ours. *Politics and Letters*, 06 October 2008 (consulted 01 March 2009): http://72.36.139.202/politicsandletters/showDiary.do?diaryId=159.

Locke, J. 1980. *Second Treatise of Government*. Cambridge: Hackett Publishing Company.

Lukacs, G. 1971. *History and Class Consciousness*. London: Merlin Press.

Lukes, S. 1973. *Individualism*. Oxford: Basil Blackwell.

Machan, T.R. 1990. *Capitalism and Individualism*. New York: St. Martin's Press.

MacPherson, C.B. 1962. *The Political Theory of Possessive Individualism*. London: Clarendon.

——. 1966. *The Real World of Democracy*. London: Oxford University Press.

——. 1977. *The Life and Times of Liberal Democracy*. Oxford: Oxford University Press.

——. 1980. "Introduction", in Locke, J. *Second Treatise of Government*. Cambridge: Hackett Publishing Company.

Macrae, D.G. 1969. "Introduction" in Spencer, H. *The Man Versus the State*. Harmondsworth: Penguin.

Malthus, T.R. 1951. *Principles of Political Economy: considered with a view to their practical application*. New York: Augustus M. Kelley.

——. 1973a. *An Essay on the Principle of Population. Books I &II*. London: J.M. Dent & sons Ltd.

——. 1973b. *An Essay on the Principle of Population. Book III*. London: J.M. Dent & sons Ltd.

Mandel, E. 1971. *Marxist Economic Theory*. London: Merlin Press.

——. 1993. Socialism or Neoliberalism? *Marxist Internet Archive*. (consulted 27 February 2009): http://www.marxists.org/archive/mandel/1993/02/neoliberal.htm.

Mannheim, K. 1950. *Freedom, Power & Democratic Planning*. London: Routledge and Kegan Paul.

——. 1960. *Ideology and Utopia*. London: Routledge and Kegan Paul.

Marcuse, H. 1972. *One Dimensional Man*. London: Abacus.

Marx, K. and Frederick Engels. 1974. *The German Ideology*. London: Lawrence & Wishart.

——. 1976. *Marx and Engels: Collected Works, Vol. 5*. London: Lawrence & Wishart.

——. 1992. *The Communist Manifesto*. Oxford: Oxford University Press.

Marx, K. 1953. "Relative Surplus Population", "Malthus as an Apologist", "Malthus on Over-Production and Over-Consumption", in Meek, R.L. ed., *Marx and Engels on Malthus: Selections from the Writings of Marx and Engels Dealing with the Theories of Thomas Robert Malthus*. London: Lawrence and Wishart.

——. 1971. *Capital: a Critique of Political Economy, Vol. III*. London: Lawrence and Wishart.

——. 1976. *Capital: a Critique of Political Economy, Vol. I*. Harmondsworth: Penguin.

——. 1977. *Economic and Philosophic Manuscripts of 1844*. London: Lawrence & Wishart.

McLellan, D. 1979. *Marxism After Marx*. London: The MacMillan Press Ltd.

——. 1986. *Ideology*. Milton Keynes: Open University Press.

McIntire, Mike. 2009. Bailout Is a Windfall to Banks, if Not to Borrowers. *New York Times*, 19 January 2009 (consulted 02 March 2009): http://www.nytimes.com/2009/01/18/business/18bank.html?hp.

Mendelson, K. 1976. *Science and Western Domination*. London: Thames and Hudson Ltd.

Merton, R.K. 1973. *The Sociology of Science: Theoretic and Empirical Investigations*. Chicago: The University of Chicago Press.

Meyer, A.G. 1963. *Marxism: The Unity of Theory*. Ann Arbour: Michigan Press.

Miliband, R. 1982. *Capitalist Democracy in Britain*. Oxford: Oxford University Press.

Mill, J.S. and Jeremy Bentham. 1987. *Utilitarianism and Other Essays*. Harmondsworth: Penguin.

Mill, J.S. 1992. *On Liberty; Representative Government; The Subjection of Women*. Oxford: Oxford University Press.

Mishel, L. and J. Bernstein. 2007. Economy's Gains Fail to Reach Most Workers' Paychecks. *Economic Policy Institute*, 03 September 2007 (consulted 01 March 2009): http://www.epi.org/publications/entry/bp195/.

Monbiot, G. 2001. *Captive State: The Corporate Takeover of Britain*. London: Pan Books.

Neal, D. 1822. *History of the Puritans Vol. I*. London: William Baynes and Son.

New York Times. 2008. Greenspan Concedes Error on Regulation. 24 October 2008 (consulted 17 February 2009): http://dealbook.blogs.nytimes.com/2008/10/24/greenspan-concedes-error-on-regulation.

Owen, R.A. 1991. *New View of Society*. Harmondsworth: Penguin.

Paine, T. 1993. *The Rights of Man*. London: J.M. Dent.

Parry, J.H. 1961. *The Establishment of the European Hegemony, 1415–1715: Trade and Exploration in the Age of the Renaissance*. New York: Harper & Row.

Patterson, A. 1997. *Early Modern Liberalism*. Cambridge: Cambridge University Press.

Perelman, M. 2002. *Steal This Idea: Intellectual Property Rights and the Corporate Confiscation of Creativity*. New York: Palgrave.

——. 2007. *The Confiscation of American Prosperity*. New York: Palgrave.

Peterson, W. 1986. "Malthus and the Intellectuals", in J. Cunningham Wood ed., *Thomas Robert Malthus: Critical Assessments*. Kent: Croom Helm.

Poor, Jeff. 2007. Ron Paul Says Federal Reserve 'Robbed' Americans of their Wealth. *Business and Media Institute*, 08 November 2007 (consulted 02 March 2009): http://www.businessandmedia.org/articles/2007/20071108180311.aspx

Popper, K.R. 1957. *The Poverty of Historicism*. London: Routledge and Kegan Paul, Ltd.

——. 1962. *Conjectures and Refutations: The Growth of Scientific Knowledge*. London: Routledge.

——. 1966. *The Open Society and Its Enemies*. London: Routledge and Kegan Paul, Ltd.

Porter, R. 1990. *Studies in European History: The Enlightenment*. London: MacMillan Education Ltd.

Prashad, J. and T. Ballve. eds., 2006. *Dispatches from Latin America: On the Frontlines Against Neoliberalism*. Cambridge: South End Press.

Rand, A. 1967. *Capitalism: The Unknown Ideal*. New York: New American Library.

Rasmus, J. 2008. The Deepening Global Financial Crisis: From Minsky to Marx and Beyond. *Critique: Journal of Socialist Theory*. 36(1):5–29.

Ridgeway, James. 2008. Is the Fannie/Freddie Bailout "Socialism". *Mother Jones*, 10 September 2008 (consulted 07 March 2009): http://www.motherjones.com/politics/2008/09/fanniefreddie-bailout-socialism.

Ross, E.B. 1998. *The Malthus Factor: population, poverty and politics in capitalist development*. London: Zed Books.

Rousseau, J.J. 1998. *The Social Contract*. Ware: Wordsworth.

Russell, B. 2001. *The Scientific Outlook*. London: Routledge.

Ryan, A. 1984. *Property and Political Theory*. Oxford: Basil Blackwell.

Schumpeter, J.A. 1943. *Capitalism, Socialism and Democracy*. London: Unwin University Books.

Schwrzkopf, J. 1991. *Women in the Chartist Movement*. London: MacMillan.

Screpanti, E. and Stefano Zamagnil. 1993. *An Outline of the History of Economic Thought*. Oxford: Clarendon.

Sherman, H. 1972. *Radical Political Economy: Capitalism and Socialism from a Marxist-Humanist Perspective*. New York: Basil Books, Inc.

——. 1995. *Reinventing Marxism*. Baltimore: The John Hopkins University Press.

Sklair, L. 1973. *Organised Knowledge: A Sociological View of Science and Technology*. London: Hart-Davis, Mac Gibbon Ltd.

Smith, A. 1976. *The Wealth of Nations*. Chicago: The University of Chicago Press.

Sohn-Rethel, A. 1987. *The Economy and Class Structure of German Fascism*. London: Free Association Books.

Soros, G. 2003. *The Alchemy of Finance*. Hoboken: John Wiley and Sons.

Spencer, H. 1851. *Social Statics*. London: Chapman.

——. 1896. *The Study of Sociology*. New York: D. Appleton and Co.

——. 1969. *The Man Versus the State*. Harmondsworth: Penguin.

——. 1975. *The Principles of Sociology*. Westport: Greenwood Press.

Struve, W. 1973. *Elites Against Democracy: Leadership Ideals in Bourgeois Political Thought*. Princeton: Princeton University Press.

Sumner, W.G. 1963. *Social Darwinism*. Engelwood Cliffs: Prentice-Hall.

Talbott, N. 2008. Where is the global economy heading? *Critique: Journal of Socialist Theory*. 36(1):31–44.

Tawney, R.H. 1948. *Religion and the Rise of Capitalism*. London: John Murray.

Taylor, M.W. 1992. *Men Versus the State: Herbert Spencer and Late Victorian Individualism*. Oxford: Clarendon.

The Economist. 2008. American Carmakers on the Edge. 13 November 2008 (consulted 09 March 2009): http://www.economist.com/business/displaystory.cfm?story_id=12601839.

——. 2009. Bailing Out the Banks: Still Seeking a Way Out. 10 February 2009 (consulted 09 March 2009): http://www.economist.com/world/unitedstates/displaystory.cfm?story_id=13095259.

Thomson, D. 1969. *Political Ideas*. Harmondsworth: Penguin.

Ticktin, H. 2006. Decline as a Concept and its Consequences. *Critique: Journal of Socialist Theory*. 34(2):145–162.

——. 2007. Critique Notes. *Critique: Journal of Socialist Theory*. 35(3):305–313.

Trotsky, L. 1963. "Their Morals and Ours", in Irving Howe ed., *The Basic Writings of Trotsky*. New York: Random House.

——. 1972. *Revolution Betrayed*. New York: Pathfinder Press.

Tuck, R. 1989. *Hobbes*. Oxford: Oxford University Press.

Tucker, D.F.B. 1980. *Marxism and Individualism*. Oxford: Basil Blackwell.

Vaughn, K.I. 1994. *Austrian Economics in America: The Migration of a Tradition*. Cambridge: Cambridge University Press.

Veblen, T. 1936. "Theory of the Leisure Class", in Wesley C. Mitchell ed., *What Veblen Taught: Selected Writings of Thorstein Veblen*. New York: Viking Press.

Viner, J. 1991. "Hayek on Freedom and Coercion", in J. Cunningham Wood and Ronald L. Woods eds., *Frederich A. Hayek: Critical Assessments*. London: Routledge.

Voltaire, M. de. 1818. "Locke", "Newton and Descartes", in Holmes, A. ed., *The Philosophical Dictionary of M. de Voltaire*. London: Sherwood, Neely and Jones.

——. 1947. *Candide*. London: Penguin Books.

Wallerstein, I. 1979. *The Capitalist World Economy: Essays by Immanuel Wallerstein*. Cambridge: Cambridge University Press.

Ward, L.F. 1970. *Psychic Factors of Civilization*. New York: Johnson Reprint Corporation.

Weber, M. 1976. *The Protestant Ethic and the Spirit of Capitalism*. London: George Allen & Unwin.

Wells, D. 1986. "Resurrecting the Dismal Parson: Malthus, Ecology, and Political Thought", in J. Cunningham Wood ed., *Thomas Robert Malthus: Critical Assessments*. Kent: Croom Helm.

Wolfe, D.M. 1941. *Milton in the Puritan Revolution*. New York: T. Nelson and Sons.

INDEX